IP 9445 —

$\frac{40-}{RS}$

SOVIET LITERATURE IN THE 1980s

N.N. SHNEIDMAN

Soviet literature in the 1980s:
decade of transition

UNIVERSITY OF TORONTO PRESS

Toronto Buffalo London

© University of Toronto Press 1989
Toronto Buffalo London
Printed in Canada

ISBN 0-8020-5812-4

Printed on acid-free paper

Canadian Cataloguing in Publication Data

Shneidman, N.N.
    Soviet literature in the 1980s

    Bibliography: p.
    Includes index.
    ISBN 0-8020-5812-4

    1. Russian fiction – 20th century – History and
    criticism. I. Title.

    PG3098.4.S54 1989   891.73'44'09   C89-093563-7

This book has been published with the help of a grant from the Canadian
Federation for the Humanities, using funds provided by the Social Sciences and
Humanities Research Council of Canada.

   The editors of *Canadian Slavonic Papers* and the *Slavic and East European
Journal* have kindly given permission to use material published in the 1985
volumes of those journals; sections of a chapter of this book appeared there in
slightly different form.

Contents

Preface

Soviet society and those who follow its development are currently under the spell of Mikhail Gorbachev's glasnost' and perestroika, which have influenced, in different degrees, all spheres of Soviet life. Soviet literature reflects the recent changes in different ways, but there is always a time lag between events and the artistic reflection and re-creation of these events in prose fiction.

I rely in this study mainly on original sources, and all translations from Russian, unless quoted from English sources, are my own. Any approach to transliteration is arbitrary; I have adopted here the widely used system of the Library of Congress. Titles are given first in Russian, with an English translation in parentheses, and later only in Russian.

I would like to acknowledge my debt and express my gratitude to all those who helped me in the course of my work on this book. I am indebted to Professor K.A. Lantz who read the manuscript and offered constructive criticism. A special note of thanks is due to the Soviet writers, scholars, and critics whom I had an opportunity to interview on my recent visits to the Soviet Union. Needless to say, my discussions with them helped me to gain a better understanding of the intricate forces that determine the evolution of Soviet literature.

I appreciate the support of the Centre for Russian and East European Studies and the Department of Slavic Languages and Literatures, University of Toronto, which made it possible for me to devote one term, free from teaching responsibilities, to the preparation of this manuscript.

I acknowledge with pleasure the assistance of many institutions and the help and advice of my colleagues and friends, but I accept sole responsibility for any inaccuracies and mistakes that may exist in this book.

Toronto, Canada   N.N.S.

SOVIET LITERATURE IN THE 1980s

Introduction

As a vehicle of education and ideology, Soviet literature has always reacted to political change, reflecting the life of Soviet people and society in the shifting conditions of the day. The same is true today. In official Soviet terms, Soviet literature is only as good as its ability to influence Soviet people in the necessary spirit. Its artistic relevance, which is determined by the standards of universal art, is always secondary to the impact it exerts on individual man and his social interaction. In the 1970s the term *Soviet literature* could have been regarded as ambiguous, because it could refer to authors whose works were published in official as well as clandestine publications. Today, most Russian 'dissident' writers reside in the West, and the term *Soviet*, as far as it relates to literary production, can be viewed as both a geographical and a socio-political notion.

Western critics and scholars are often slow in summarizing the changes occurring in the Soviet literary scene. Some do not adequately appreciate the social significance of Soviet literature as a means of creating public opinion and advancing the concerns of the state and the party and as one of the most important sources for the study of the social conditions, the attitudes, and the mentality of Soviet people. During the 1970s Western interest in Soviet literature was in the main generated by 'dissident' publications and by the few gifted writers, such as Iurii Trifonov and Valentin Rasputin, who expressed in their works contro-versial and nonconformist views. In the 1980s the number of talented writers has diminished, and the artistic level of literature has declined, but its thematic range has widened and the socio-political significance of literature has increased considerably. Alcoholism, narcotics, crime, and suicide, among others, have become the subjects of prose fiction. Issues such as the 1933 famine, the Stalinist purges of the late 1930s, the corruption of the Brezhnev regime, and Soviet political involvement around the globe are at present openly discussed in Soviet prose.

The emphasis in current Western Studies of Soviet affairs is on the Gorbachev era, beginning with 1985. It is necessary, however, to remember that Gorbachev and his contemporaries matured and joined the Soviet bureaucracy in the days of Brezhnev. Similarly, Soviet literature of the period of glasnost' is still rooted in the experiences of post–Second World War Russia. The purpose of this study is not to speculate about the future of the Soviet state but rather to assess the impact of the political and social changes of the last decade on the development of Soviet culture and literature.

This study endeavours to draw a broad picture of the Soviet literary scene between 1978 and 1988. It is intended as a general introductory survey and as a sequel to my *Soviet Literature in the 1970s: Artistic Diversity and Ideological Conformity* (Toronto 1979). I limit myself to the discussion of Russian prose officially published in the Soviet Union, thereby excluding both samizdat and tamizdat publications.* Works by non-Russian authors that transcend national confines in their thematic and artistic relevance, by writers such as Chingiz Aitmatov or Vasil' Bykov, are also included, but only if they are written in, or translated into, Russian. Current Soviet literature is a huge subject, and it would be futile to try to give a full picture of it in an investigation of limited scope. My selection of authors and works for discussion may not please everyone but is intended to be representative of contemporary Soviet literature and is determined by the artistic, thematic, and social relevance of these works. Similarly, for reasons of economy and convenience, authors have been grouped together according to theme, age, sex, or artistic inclination.

Chapter 1 gives a general overview of the intellectual, ideological, political, and social atmosphere that influences the process of artistic creation in the Soviet Union. Special emphasis is placed on the relationship between ideology, theory of literature, and literary practice. Chapter 2 gives a general survey of the literary evolution of the last decade. Special attention is accorded to important writers, themes, and problems to which no separate chapters are devoted. Valentin Kataev,

* 'Samizdat' refers to literature published unofficially and circulated clandestinely in the Soviet Union, usually reproduced by hand, typewriter, or mimeograph. 'Tamizdat' can be either works by Soviet authors unapproved for official publication and published abroad or, more restrictively, works by émigré authors. People using the latter meaning would expand 'samizdat' to include Soviet writers banned from official publication and published in the West.

Trifonov, and Vladimir Tendriakov are three important Soviet writers who died in the 1980s; their recent artistic output is examined in chapter 3. Chapters 4 to 9 discuss in greater detail countryside prose, war prose, the political novel, and women and family issues, including the works of the most prominent contemporary Soviet prose writers, such as Aitmatov, Viktor Astaf'ev, Iurii Bondarev, Bykov, I. Grekova, and Rasputin.

The study is expository in nature. It investigates artistic and social questions in an integrated manner, an approach that should enable the Western reader to appreciate the works of today's Soviet authors and the problems facing Soviet society in general. I hope that this study will be of interest to the student of Russian literature and Soviet society and that it will help the reader better to understand the intricate forces that guide the creative process of writers in the Soviet Union and the significance of contemporary literature as a social, political, and ideological tool and as a mirror of contemporary Soviet conditions.

1 Decade of Transition

GENERAL PERSPECTIVES

Cultural evolution and creative activity are closely linked in the Soviet Union with ideology and political development; hence, the objective of literature is not only to reflect the process of political and social change but also to influence it. But whereas political transition can occur overnight, social transformation is a slow process, and recording the artistic reflection of changes in social values and the mentality of people may take many years.

The second half of Brezhnev's rule is identified with the collapse of détente in international relations and economic stagnation, corruption, and moral decay in Soviet internal life. In literature the last years of Brezhnev's rule are identified with the increased emphasis on ideology and politics. New pressures were brought to bear on those who bypassed official Soviet editors and censors and published some of their works abroad. The famous case of the almanac *Metropol'* (1979) is perhaps the last open attempt by a number of leading Soviet writers, members of the Writers Union, to challenge the establishment and publish literature rejected by the literary bureaucrats.

Glasnost' and Perestroika

The death of Brezhnev in 1982 led to a number of rapid changes in Soviet leadership and culminated in the ascent to power of Mikhail Gorbachev. He is a representative of the younger generation, a man who matured in post–Second World War Russia. Gorbachev's new policies of so-called glasnost', or openness, in public life and so-called perestroika, which entails democratization, economic renewal, the reorientation in the thinking of Soviet people, and the reorganization and restructuring of the national economy, have influenced the cultural atmosphere in the country, opening for discussion a number of issues that until recently were taboo.

Many works, for years held back by editors and censors, began to appear in print. The novel *Novoe naznachenie* (New Appointment) by Aleksandr Bek, published in the West in 1971, appeared in the Soviet Union in 1986, twenty-two years after its completion. Andrei Bitov's *Pushkinskii dom* (Pushkin House), completed in 1971 and published in the United States in 1978, appeared in *Novyi mir* (New World) in 1987. *Deti Arbata* (Children of the Arbat; 1987) by Anatolii Rybakov was initially accepted for publicatiion in the 1960s but rejected by the censors. Vasilii Grossman's *Zhizn' i sud'ba* (Life and Fate) was completed in 1960 and submitted for consideration to *Znamia* (The Banner), only to be seized by the KGB. Smuggled out of the Soviet Union by Vladimir Voinovich,[1] the novel was published in the West in 1980 and appeared in *Oktiabr'* (October) in 1988, Boris Pasternak's *Dr Zhivago* (1958), which earned him a Nobel Prize as well as the scorn of the Soviet people and expulsion from the Writers Union, appeared in *Novyi mir* in 1988. Other previously banned works have appeared in print, including Evgenii Zamiatin's *My* (We; 1924), Andrei Platonov's 'Kotlovan' (The Foundation Pit), written in 1929–30 but first published posthumously in the West in 1968, as well as works by Vladimir Nabokov, Franz Kafka, and George Orwell.

Another positive sign is the readmission to the Writers Union of individuals previously expelled for ideological and political transgressions. The reinstated poet Vladimir Kornilov is one of those who have in the past expressed views officially repudiated by the government but now approved of and accepted by all.

Today's glasnost' has its parallels in the literary thaws of the immediate post-Stalin era. Then, glasnost' was connected with the legacy of a terrible past. Stimulated by Nikita Khrushchev's famous speech at the Twentieth Party Congress, the literature of this period denounced the personality cult of Stalin and uncovered the abuses and illegalities of his dictatorial rule. It soon developed into a spontaneous movement, led by the survivors of the Stalinist Gulag. Later it turned into open dissidence and the creation of samizdat and tamizdat literatures. Today's glasnost' has been stimulated by internal economic problems and by fear of the complete moral disintegration of Soviet society. Gorbachev's glasnost' has been instigated and is controlled by the new bureaucracy itself. It is viewed as a tool in the struggle against the survivors of the Brezhnev apparatus, as well as a means to fight corruption, the decline in the work ethic, and the moral decay in Soviet society.

While the glasnost' of the post-Stalin era was ultimately stifled by arrests, exiles, and expulsions, Gorbachev's glasnost' is kept in check by the bureaucracy itself, which constantly reminds the Soviet people that the call for criticism is not unrestricted permission to attack the system. To the question 'What are the limits of criticism and glasnost'?' Gorbachev has the following to say: 'We solve this problem within the framework of socialist pluralism of opinions. We are for the wide development of criticism and glasnost', but only if it is in the interests of society, socialism, and the people.'[2] In a speech delivered at a meeting of the Soviet Union's Supreme Soviet, the first secretary of the Writers Union, Vladimir Karpov, stated bluntly: 'It is necessary and possible to criticize those who have become distinguished, but businesslike analysis and argumentation should not be drenched in venom ... Previously unpublished works by Gumilev, Nabokov, and others appear in print ... But that does not mean in the least that these trends are to become most important in our literature ... One cannot agree with the tendency to write only about shortcomings, only about the negative aspects of our life. Today this is not the whole truth. It is only half-truth.'[3]

The immediate results of Gorbachev's glasnost' are evident and encouraging, but it is still too early to draw conclusions as to its long-range effectiveness. In the post-Stalinist era we can find earlier precedents in Soviet literature for the rehabilitation of writers. The publication of Dr Zhivago can be compared to the belated appearance of Mikhail Bulgakov's masterpiece *Master i Margarita* (The Master and Margarita; 1966–7). Close to thirty years have passed since the original publication of Pasternak's novel, and to young Soviet readers the new Soviet version of Dr Zhivago will be nothing more than another account of the turbulent years of transition in the history of twentieth-century Russia. Rumours have even been circulating about the possible publication of Aleksandr Solzhenitsyn's *Rakovyi korpus* (Cancer Ward) and *V kruge pervom* (The First Circle), only to be dismissed by a spokesman of the Ministry of Foreign Affairs, who evaded the issue by making reference to the author's ownership of the copyright to the novels. It is no secret that Solzhenitsyn's vision of a future Russia has many followers and supporters in the Soviet Union, particularly among the fringe elements in the neo-Russophile movement of Russian intellectual thought and in the Soviet cultural establishment. It is quite possible that in the current political climate these novels, initially submitted to *Novyi mir* in the 1960s, could be considered for official publication in the Soviet Union.

Much of the prose appearing in the leading literary journals in the mid-eighties is symptomatic of glasnost' and the relaxation connected with Gorbachev's ascent to power. But recently published works by Platonov, Zamiatin, Nikolai Gumilev, and Boris Pil'niak belong to a different era. Their appearance reflects recent political changes, but these works were written long ago, are set in a different reality, and say little about the creative process in contemporary conditions. Furthermore, since the notions of glasnost' and perestroika are ambiguous and mean different things to different people, their application in literature is not as simple as it may seem at first sight. One critic suggests that 'there is something uncertain, something feverish in the current atmosphere of glasnost'. As if we are in a hurry to say everything before it is too late.'[4] There are also those who question whether the excessive unmasking of past evils does not undermine the faith of the Soviet people in the system. In some opinions what is most dangerous in the current situation is the fact that no one comes out openly against perestroika, but many bureaucrats stifle progress and social change, promoting instead narrow personal interests. According to Evgenii Evtushenko, 'the first method of obstructing perestroika is sabotage under the guise of support. The other method resorts to smothering by hugging.'[5]

No wonder writers belonging to different extremes of thought accuse each other of abusing perestroika. Thus Viacheslav Gorbachev suggests in *Molodaia gvardiia* (Young Guard) that glasnost' makes it possible for the West to infiltrate Russia with reactionary ideas and that while there is already enough of Nabokov in the Soviet Union, there is certainly too much of "Nabokovshchina', or Nabokovism,[6] which can be compared to the negative phenomena of Dostoevshchina and Oblomovshchina.

In both the Khrushchev and Gorbachev cases, glasnost' can be viewed as a safety valve, as a means to quench the people's thirst for freedom of speech. But whereas in the 1960s dissidents were actively fighting for political freedom and new democratic institutions, the new glasnost' promotes limited democratization and economic renewal with the purpose of infusing the Soviet worker with a new spirit of dedication. It is obvious that as a tool of party policy glasnost' does not mean total freedom of expression, and its limitations are determined by the state. There are still forbidden themes in Soviet literature, and much is censored and removed from manuscripts.[7]

One of the main problems of perestroika is that it calls for new thinking that is essentially based on an old Weltanschauung. The conception of the party as the political vanguard of society remains in force.[8] In a planned socialist economy the influence of the market-place on the general production process is limited. In the 1970s NTR, or *nauchno-tekhnicheskaia revoliutsiia* (scientific-technological revolution), was the catch-word opening most literary discussions. It was to raise the living standard of the Soviet people by fostering industrialization and urbanization. NTR has apparently failed because there is little evidence that life in the Soviet Union has become today any better than it was in the seventies. Today the catch-word is perestroika. It emphasizes production incentives, new and more efficient methods of administration and planning, new pricing and foreign trade policies, as well as a gradual switch to market-oriented policies. The new Soviet leaders continue to stress the importance of technological progress, but they avoid the issue of raising living standards in the immediate future. NTR aimed at increasing industrial capacity, promising the Soviet worker a better life. The immediate objectives of perestroika are different. By combining socialist and capitalist methods of industrial management it aims at creating a healthier economy. It remains to be seen whether the new model, which includes many elements of the New Economic Policy (NEP) of the 1920s, is a viable alternative to the economic system in operation in the Soviet Union since the 1930s.

The Literary Bureaucracy

Gorbachev's perestroika has affected in various degrees all aspects of Soviet life. In the arts, calls to reorganize the administration of literary production and make changes in the publishing business have been heard time and again. The Writers Union is a rapidly growing institution, the membership of which increased by close to 15 per cent from 1981 to 1986, from 8,669 members to 9,584. This includes members of eighty-nine nationalities, writing in seventy-eight different languages.[9] But more than half of all Soviet writers, poets, playwrights, and critics write in Russian. The Writers Union publishes eighty-six journals and sixteen newspapers. The most important are those appearing in Moscow. The monthlies *Novyi mir, Znamia, Oktiabr', Nash sovremennik* (Our Contemporary), *Moskva* (Moscow), *Molodaia gvardiia*, and *Iunost'* (Youth) publish mainly works by Russian authors residing in Moscow and central Russia. *Druzhba narodov* (Friendship of the People) publishes, along with Russian titles, works by non-Russian writers translated into Russian. A number of Russian-language periodicals, including *Neva* (Neva), *Sever* (The North), *Don* (Don), *Baikal*

(Baikal), and *Volga* (Volga), are published in Leningrad and the provinces. Russian journals are also published in national republics, but a journal in a language other than Russian is seldom published outside the national region in question.

An attempt to modify the cumbersome edifice of the Writers Union was undertaken at the Eighth Congress of Soviet Writers, held in June 1986. But instead of reducing the bureaucracy, the congress elected 10 per cent more members to the board and to the secretariat. There is, however, a notable and positive change in the composition of the secretariat. It includes now a number of prominent writers, poets, and critics previously little connected with the literary bureaucracy. The prose writers G. Baklanov, V. Bykov, D. Granin, and S. Zalygin, as well as the poets E. Evtushenko and A. Voznesenskii and the critics I. Dedkov and E. Sidorov, were newly elected to the secretariat. The first secretary of the board, G. Markov, was elevated to the ceremonial post of chairman, and the former editor of *Novyi mir*, V. Karpov, was elected first secretary. A new body, called the bureau of the secretariat, was created. It is composed of eight secretaries and includes Ch. Aitmatov, Baklanov, Iu. Bondarev, Bykov, A. Gonchar, Karpov, Markov, and Zalygin. It is to supervise the work of the secretariat and to provide general guidance in the work of the Writers Union. In addition, Zalygin replaced Karpov as editor of *Novyi mir*, and Baklanov was appointed editor of *Znamia*.

The change in the leadership of the Writers Union is a positive step, but in practice it has so far little affected day-to-day operations of this institution, or of the publishing houses that it controls. Several years have passed since the bureau of the secretariat was elected, but not a single meeting of this body has yet taken place. The reasons for its inactivity are not discussed in public, but most insiders are aware that some bureau members do not speak to each other.

Signs of democratization are also evident in the Moscow writers' organization. For eleven years it was headed by Feliks Kuznetsov, recently appointed director of the Academy of Sciences' Institute of World Literature. In 1987 eight candidates were recommended by different creative groups for the position of secretary. Three, including the poet Evtushenko, the writer V. Shugaev, and the critic A. Mikhailov, were approved to stand for election. Every candidate had the opportunity to explain his platform. Evtushenko advocated collective leadership by lay secretaries. The board elected Mikhailov. It preferred a more structured approach to literary production than that suggested by Evtushenko.[10]

It is well known that the position of a creative writer evokes respect and admiration among ordinary Soviet people and that leading figures in Soviet culture belong to a prestigious élite whose earnings are much above average and who have ample opportunity to travel abroad. It may come as a surprise, therefore, to learn that the average income of a professional writer in the Soviet Union is much below the national average income. According to different sources, the average income of a writer is somewhere between 70 and 162 rubles a month, while the national average income is above 200 rubles.[11] At a time when *some* writers and literary bureaucrats earn enormous amounts of money, others can hardly exist on their meagre incomes from writing and have to resort to other employment in order to survive. Thus belonging to the Writers Union does not guarantee a good and easy life for all its members.

Nationality Problems

The Russian literary establishment, as well as the intellectual and artistic élite, is split into several antagonistic camps. The split that has been in evidence since the early 1970s has now come out into the open. Some Russian writers and critics support the unofficial society Pamiat' (Memory), which advocates chauvinistic views and displays lack of tolerance toward other nations; these attitudes are vehemently opposed by members of the liberal intelligentsia.

As Anatolii Anan'ev's novel *Gody bez voiny* (Years without War; 1975–84) shows, there is a constant and fierce struggle between the pochvenniki, who support the values advocated by the adherents of the nineteenth-century Russian native-soil movement and Slavophilism, and the zapadniki, or moderates, who support Western influences in Soviet life, culture, and thought. The former advance in their works the notions of Russian exclusiveness and spiritual superiority. They defend the Russian cultural and spiritual heritage from outside infiltration and blame foreigners, and Soviet people with foreign roots, for all Russia's troubles and suffering. The latter advocate internationalism, intellectualism, and the virtues of progress and Western civilization.

The acrimonious dialogue between these two groups is waged in the periodical and daily press. *Nash sovremennik, Molodaia gvardiia,* and *Moskva* render their pages to the adherents of Russian nationalist views, while *Znamia, Iunost',* and *Oktiabr'* serve as a forum for the moderates. *Novyi mir* continues its liberal middle-of-the-road position.

Although its new editor, Zalygin, sympathizes with many ideas propounded by the neo-Russophiles, he apparently does not support their extreme nationalistic views.

Those who are most sensitive to nationalistic pressures are bilingual writers, or members of national minorities who write in Russian. The nationalists suggest that works by such writers contaminate the purity of the Russian national spirit. Chingiz Aitmatov, who writes both in Russian and in his native Kirghiz, and Fazil' Iskander, who is the bard of Abkhazia, but writes in Russian, are obvious targets of neo-Russophile criticism. The prose produced by some writers of Jewish extraction is also attacked on similar grounds.

It thus seems clear that the relationship between the Russian intellectual élite and those representing the cultural intelligentsia in Soviet national regions is not as amicable as the Soviet authorities would have us believe. Some members of national minorities resent russification and the growth of Russian nationalism in a union of allegedly equal republics. An open clash between Russian and Georgian delegates at the Eighth Congress of Soviet Writers illustrates this antagonism convincingly. This skirmish was prompted by Viktor Astaf'-ev's story 'Lovlia peskarei v Gruzii' (Fishing for Gudgeons in Georgia; 1986), published in *Nash sovremennik*.[12] The story, about the author's visit to Georgia, contains some critical remarks about Georgian compulsive hospitality, the place of women in society, and the negative business practices of some Georgians. Astaf'ev was publicly denounced for his story by the Georgian writer Georgii Tsitsishvili, but Valentin Rasputin came out in Astaf'ev's defence, claiming that Russians are criticized more often by far in the works of non-Russian writers but take no offence. The confrontation at the congress is an expression of a hidden frustration and antagonism among representatives of different Soviet nationalities. It also reflects the attitude of different Russian personalities to the national question in general and to the new and changing demographic realities in Soviet society on the threshold of the twenty-first century.

The growth of Russian nationalism and the tensions between different Soviet nationalities are further exacerbated by intra-national frictions within national minorities. The intellectual élites of these minorities are divided among those who foster national values and traditions and those who see nothing wrong with the penetration of the Russian language and Russian values into native cultures. The danger of such intra-national strife is aggravated by its tendency to move easily from rational discussion to emotional expression, at which level reason gives way to instinct and passion. National disharmony is seldom the direct subject of Soviet prose, but the critical reaction to a work of art, regardless of its artistic merit, is often determined by its author's relation to Soviet internal, national, cultural, and political issues.

In the 1960s it was easier to publish controversial literature in a national republic than it was in Moscow. For example, Vasil' Bykov's 'Mertvym ne bol'no' (The Dead Feel No Pain; 1966) was critically acclaimed in his native Belorussia but severely criticized after its publication in *Novyi mir*. Today it is the other way around. Journals and publishing houses in national republics are more conservative and less sensitive to relaxation and change than the central bureaucracy, and many works by non-Russian authors appear in Russian translation before they are published in their native languages. A case in point is *Cherepakha Tarazi* (The Turtle Tarazi; 1985), by the Uzbek writer Timur Pulatov, published in Russian twelve years after it was written. Pulatov decries the fact that the rejection of a novel submitted for publication can hamper the future work of a writer and altogether change the path of his creative development. He tries to substantiate this argument by pointing to the experience of Andrei Bitov, who has published little in the last decade and was, in all probability, a victim of editorial policy.[13]

It is evident that, along with its positive effects on Soviet life, glasnost' has brought out into the open the simmering national strife that has been kept under the surface for years. According to V. Karpov, a number of recent publications devoted to national and international issues have deviated from Marxist-Leninist methodology. 'Society cannot let the development of national cultures drift without direction ... In current conditions nationalism becomes one of the main dangers of the practical implementation of *perestroika*.'[14]

Nonetheless extreme nationalist circles continue their activity with the undisguised support of some prominent Soviet writers. Thus, for example, it is suggested that the historic-patriotic society Pamiat' aims at becoming 'a new political organization that takes control over everything and all but bears no responsibility for anything.'[15] And Valentin Rasputin comes out against those who criticize Pamiat' and its objectives. According to him, blunders are possible, but the mistakes of Pamiat' are the result of sincere intentions.[16] Everybody is, of course, entitled to his or her own opinion, but Rasputin would certainly render better service to Russian literature by devoting his time to creative prose rather than to propagating subjective journalistic views.

Literary Criticism and Censorship

The new policy of glasnost' has expanded the confines of the freedom of expression and opened up new areas of Soviet life for critical inquiry. That does not mean, however, that there is absolute freedom of artistic expression in contemporary Soviet society. A writer is still at the mercy of editors and censors, whose demands verge sometimes on the absurd. Thus one writer reports a ludicrous incident when the editor of *Iunost'* requested him to move the action of his story from the open sea to a factory because the journal required a story about construction.[17]

Not less damaging to the quality of artistic production is self-censorship. Danilo Kiš, a Yugoslav writer and participant in the 1985 Literary Symposium in Budapest, summarizes it brilliantly: 'The self-appointed censor is the writer's double ... who leans over his shoulders and interferes with the text ... It is impossible to win out against this censor-double ... He comes out of your own brain, your own fears, your own nightmares ... In the final analysis, the writer's double succeeds in undermining and tainting even the most moral individual, one whom outside censorship had not succeeded in breaking. In refusing to admit self-censorship the author yields to lies and spiritual corruption ... Self-censorship is a dangerous manipulation of the mind, with grave consequences for literature and the human spirit.'[18] Self-censorship is an important component of artistic creation in the work of any Soviet writer. It is the result of education, upbringing, and mental conditioning, as well as of the subconscious instinct for self-preservation and survival of the fittest. By stating that Soviet literature 'lacks *genuine* freedom ... and is enmeshed in countless taboos, ... as if the writer is afraid of all he knows within himself, or sees in the life that surrounds him,'[19] the Soviet critic Vl. Gusev corroborates the views expressed by Kiš.

Along with censorship, editorial control, and the position of a writer in the Soviet political and cultural bureaucracy, official literary criticism often determines publication policy and the future fate of aspiring authors. Except for controversial works by leading writers, which challenge established criteria, most contemporary works of prose fail to attract the attention of reviewers, and only 10 to 12 per cent of all new books are mentioned in literary criticism.[20] Thus the selection of a novel for review is in itself a mark of acclaim. Moreover, most works receive laudatory reviews. In the years between 1981 and 1986 'the journal *Molodaia gvardiia* ... published over 300 reviews, all of them positive.'[21] The fact that much of the literature reviewed is the so-called sekretar'-

skaia proza (the prose of members of the Writers Union Secretariat) or is written by members of editorial boards of literary periodicals may explain the preponderance of positive criticism. Many such works, by writers such as Anatolii Anan'ev, Mikhail Alekseev, Aleksandr Chakovskii, and Vladimir Karpov, are ideologically correct but artistically deficient, lacking in depth and dramatic tension. Nonetheless, these works receive good reviews not only because subject-matter and social relevance are considered more important than artistic merit but also because it is safer not to criticize them. Negative criticism of contemporary works usually appears only in survey articles. It is directed at young or little-known authors and at works that emphasize negative aspects of Soviet life or have no positive heroes or social messages of educational value.

In the last decade, literary periodicals have begun to publish side by side the views of several critics, expressing divergent opinions about a single work of art. Similarly, controversial works of great social and artistic significance are often debated at 'round table discussions,' which may involve up to a dozen well-known writers, critics, and political figures. These forums are organized by editorial boards of literary journals. In both cases the editors of the periodical usually conclude the discussion by pointing out who is right and who is wrong and offering their own 'correct' interpretation of a work. At the Eighth Congress of Writers, works by Soviet literary bureaucrats were openly criticized for the first time in years. No wonder some bureaucrats are against giving literary critics blank permission to voice subjective views that allegedly run counter to the objectives of art and society. At a board meeting of the Writers Union, assembled to discuss the decisions of the Twenty-Seventh Party Congress, N. Gribachev came out strongly against the liberty to express different subjective opinions about a single work of art: 'We need criticism with exact criteria and with a knowledge of what to demand from literature today. We need criticism based on principle and not a collection of haphazard and unchecked opinions.'[22] By 1988 such views had become obsolete, and in some cases literary criticism has become an excuse for venting political, ideological, and nationalistic views with the purpose of influencing public opinion and the course of perestroika, as well as for securing an advantageous position in the newly realigned literary establishment.

The big literary debate is waged between different representatives of the 'liberal' and 'conservative' clans. The former view the publication of works by Platonov, Zamiatin, Pasternak, or Nabokov, and the unmasking of Stalinist terror, as great achievements of glasnost' and perestroika.

They claim that the conservatives, who were in control of literary institutions in the days of Brezhnev, are in the main mediocre writers who are afraid to lose their posts in the turmoil of perestroika. Hence, under the guise of defending their national positions, they are in fact trying to protect their own narrow interests. The conservatives, who oppose the publication of works by writers such as Nabokov, claim that these works 'degrade human and national dignity ... and cosmopolitanize consciousness.'[23] They assert further that the liberals, many of whom were repudiated in the days of Brezhnev, demand revenge, but in current conditions no new cultural purges are acceptable.

The literary debates of the mid-eighties bring to the fore the sensitive issue of the responsibility of those who collaborated with the regimes of Stalin and Brezhnev, the more so since Gorbachev himself was elevated to the politburo in the days of Brezhnev. In reply to demands for punishment of Stalin's accomplices, opinions are voiced today in the Soviet press that Stalinist henchmen were not only tyrants but victims as well and that in some cases compassion rather than revenge should be the order of the day.

As an example of the biting dialogue between Soviet writers and critics, which is conducted in the tone and spirit of the famous Russian satirical feuilletons, it is possible to cite the debate between Stanislav Rassadin and Vadim Kozhinov, on the relative merits of Rybakov's *Deti Arbata*,[24] or the dialogue between Benedikt Sarnov and Feliks Kuznetsov, on the place of Maiakovskii in Soviet literary history.[25] In the latter case, *Pravda* found it necessary to come out in defence of Maiakovskii as well as of Kuznetsov.[26] The dialogue between the two warring camps received further expression in the speeches of Iu. Bondarev, G. Baklanov, and V. Karpov at the Nineteenth Party Conference in June 1988.

The great paradox of the current situation is expressed in the fact that whereas glasnost' has given both groups the opportunity to come out in the open and express extreme views unacceptable to the previous administration, each does its best to silence the other and to become the dominant voice in Soviet thought. Soviet intellectuals, conditioned by their education and upbringing, in the shadows of Stalinism, have little experience of democratic tolerance of opposing views and of a social process in which a variety of divergent opinions is possible. They fail to realize that once a single ideology or view becomes dominant, relegating all other opinions to the realm of dissidence, the dialectical process ceases and the single 'truth' inevitably turns into a dogma that leads to stagnation. The Western student of Soviet literature must be cautious in his approach to contemporary Soviet literary criticism. Since Soviet critics and writers are today divided into several antagonistic camps, their critical opinions are often determined not by the artistic merit or social significance of a work of art but rather by the ideological, social, and national inclinations of its author.

Another important issue currently being discussed in Soviet literary criticism is related to the numerous distortions in Soviet literary history. The publication of previously forbidden works by Gumilev, Pil'niak, Zamiatin, Platonov, and others requires the rewriting of the history of Soviet literature in the 1920s. Bold demands to rectify the existing distortions are made by well-known personalities. Further, certain critics demand the reassessment of the prevailing attitude to Russian writers residing in the West. Thus, for example, A. Bocharov writes in *Voprosy literatury* (Problems of Literature) that 'literary historians know well about the gap created by the removal of V. Nekrasov's *V okopakh Stalingrada*'[27] (In the Trenches of Stalingrad; 1946) from Soviet histories of literature. Similarly, Bocharov suggests that works such as 'Odin den' Ivana Denisovicha' (One Day in the Life of Ivan Denisovich; 1962) by A. Solzhenitsyn, or 'Zvezdnyi bilet' (A Ticket to the Stars; 1961) by V. Aksenov, officially published before their authors went into exile, should again become part of Soviet literary history.

The issue of the relationship between Soviet writers and Russian writers, in the past Soviet citizens but currently residing in the West, is a sensitive one. But the little-publicized recent encounters between Russian émigré writers and official Soviet representatives indicate that a rapprochement is possible. One such meeting, organized by Danish Slavists, took place in the spring of 1988 in Denmark. The Soviet delegation, composed of the writers Grigorii Baklanov, Vladimir Dudintsev, and Fazil' Iskander, the playwright Mikhail Shatrov, the critics Natal'ia Ivanova and Galina Belaia, and others, met with a group of Russian émigré writers that included Vasilii Aksenov, Andrei Siniavskii, Anatolii Gladilin, Efim Etkind, and Lev Kopelev.[28]

Publitsistika and the Quality of Art

In the Soviet Union the limits of artistic freedom are always determined by political considerations, which at different times influence the form and content of a work of art in different ways. The literary output of the 1980s illustrates this proposition convincingly. In the early eighties cultural and economic stagnation stifled freedom of intellectual inquiry, and many writers often sought an outlet for their creative designs in the artistic innovation of form. In the post-Brezhnev era, social issues have been stressed with new vigour and many writers have turned to the exploration of controversial problems and the reassessment of Soviet life.

This new freedom exerts an unexpected effect on the artistic quality of current Soviet prose. Most contemporary works of literature concern themselves mainly with social and political issues, blurring the distinction between artistic fiction and journalism, or publitsistika. Most works published today can be labelled khudozhestvennaia publitsistika (artistic journalism). The events described are based on fact rather than on imagination, and the author, the narrator, and the main hero often speak in the same voice. The message delivered is usually unequivocal and explicit, and the author does not try to hide it. The distinction between the journalistic ocherk, or sketch, and prose fiction has almost disappeared in many works.

The recent penetration of journalism into artistic literature has generated heated discussion among Soviet writers and literary scholars. Those for whom creative prose is nothing more than a tool of political and ideological education see nothing wrong with it. Iurii Surovtsev, for example, suggests that 'publicism does not contradict artistry,' because it allegedly does not just transmit information but also concerns itself with the 'analysis of problems.'[29] But in his last article, published posthumously, Valentin Kataev disagrees strongly and refuses altogether to 'recognize the so-called publicistic prose.' He asserts that 'publitsistika usually follows on the hot scent of events and occurrences. Artistic prose, in contrast, permits impressions to settle, and only then submits them to artistic analysis.'[30] Kataev's opposition to the penetration of publitsistika into prose fiction is at the same time a call for artistry in literature, because paradoxically, in current Soviet circumstances, increased freedom of expression leads sometimes to a decline in artistic quality, as in the recent works of Valentin Rasputin, Viktor Astaf'ev, and Chingiz Aitmatov. The rush to uncover events until recently taboo to the Soviet reader, and the desire to deliver a new message, lead to stylistic and structural deficiencies, a dearth in artistic means, and the sacrifice of form for subject-matter.

The current situation in Soviet literature raises the important and provocative question of the relationship between liberalization and freedom, on the one hand, and talent and the artistic quality of the creative arts, on the other. The Hungarian writer Miklós Haraszti suggests that there is a myth 'that freedom is an essential condition of art; that anything which severs art from its anti-authoritarian essence will kill it; that the true artist is an individual who is independent, at least in his own creative process.'[31] But in essence, according to Haraszti, 'independent art is impossible because there is no independent audience.'[32] All this, of course, is relative. History provides us with many examples of art flourishing both in totalitarian regimes and in free democratic societies. The need to create under the surface and deliver a hidden message forces the oppressed writer to search for structural and stylistic innovation and to look for new symbolic devices and metaphors.

The death of Stalin and the thaw after the Twentieth Party Congress prompted the début of many gifted writers. That was the time when Chingiz Aitmatov, Iurii Trifonov, Vasil' Bykov, and many others appeared on the literary scene. It is possible only to surmise that during the Gorbachev thaw the situation could repeat itself. However, young writers today lack the life experience and may lack the mental and moral stamina of those who survived the Stalinist purges and the Second World War. In recent Soviet conditions liberalization does not necessarily guarantee any immediate rise in the level of artistic production, because most established writers sacrificed their ethical and social values and debased their talents in the service of a cause, and it may take years before a new generation of writers, free from the psychological shackles of the past, will appear.

The decline in the artistic quality of Soviet prose fiction has been further aggravated by a number of seemingly unrelated but closely intertwined factors. First, the death of a number of prominent writers has left a certain vacuum in Soviet literature. Iurii Kazakov (1927–1982), Iurii Trifonov (1927–1981), Vladimir Tendriakov (1923–1984), and Fedor Abramov (1920–1983) belonged to the most gifted representatives of the post–Second World War generation. Writers of the older generation such as Valentin Kataev (1897–1986), Mikhail Sholokhov (1905–1984), and Viktor Shklovskii (1893–1984) were closely connected with the literary traditions of the 1920s. The only surviving representatives of that generation who still continue to write are Leonid Leonov (born 1899) and Veniamin Kaverin (born 1902). In addition a number of less gifted writers who were active in post-war Russian literature have also died in the last decade. This long list includes Vladimir Chivilikhin (1928–1984), Vadim Kozhevnikov (1909–1984), Aleksandr Kron (1909–1983), Sergei Krutilin (1921–1985), Vil' Lipatov (1927–1979), and Konstantin Simonov (1915–1979).

In addition to the void created by the death of many important literary figures, there has been another drain on Soviet literature, namely, the departure from the Soviet Union of a number of talented writers previously connected with samizdat and tamizdat publications. By the beginning of the 1980s the polarization between the so-called dissident literature and the literature officially published by Soviet citizens in the Soviet Union had become almost complete. Vladimir Voinovich and Vasilii Aksenov were the last in a long list of important Soviet literary figures who were exiled, or left voluntarily for the West, during the Brezhnev years. In the early 1980s, except for writers such as Fazil' Iskander and Andrei Bitov, who were sporadically permitted by Soviet authorities to publish in the West works considered of dubious value to the Soviet reader and not approved for publication at home, samizdat and tamizdat literature dwindled to a trickle. Today this literature is no longer a political or cultural issue of great significance.

Some Soviet scholars decry the current state of Soviet literature by comparing it to a crisis. G.A. Belaia, for example, regards the low level of recent Soviet prose as the result of 'a drop in the level of artistic culture of the writer, reader, and critic.'[33] She states bluntly that 'the artist-creator has disappeared from the scene. He has been replaced by a worker, who is often a graphomaniac. Having dispensed with such notions as "inspiration," "intuition," "talent," and the appreciation that artistic gift is not given to everyone, we have created and continue to produce graphomania.'[34] These are harsh and sobering words from a critic who views literature first of all as a means of artistic expression.

The 'Young' Generation

The advent of a new generation of writers who do not measure up in talent, experience, or integrity to their departed mentors has failed to halt the decline of artistic quality in Soviet prose, caused by the penetration of journalism into prose fiction and the escape of artistic talent. But the average 'young' writer is not so young after all. He or she is well over forty. 'Young' writers are today better educated and more sophisticated than those belonging to the older generation, but they are also more pragmatic and opportunistic, and literature for many is not necessarily a calling but rather a profession that secures a good life and a position of prestige in society. As Vasil' Bykov suggests, some join the ranks of writers not because they have an inner urge for artistic creation but rather because they have made a rational decision to become writers.[35]

It appears that literature has never been a profession of the young in post-war Russia, but the current situation verges on the catastrophic. The Local Moscow Writers Union does not have a single member under the age of thirty, and among the 567 delegates to the Eighth Congress of Soviet Writers there were only three delegates younger than thirty-five.[36] Only 20 per cent of all those accepted into the Writers Union between 1981 and 1986 were under thirty-five.[37] No wonder some older and well-established writers despair. Viktor Astaf'ev asserts boldly that today's 'literature has been orphaned. Many feel unsure of themselves and confused ... while the young repeat and grind anew everything that has been grated already.'[38] Even more outspoken is Vladimir Krupin. He asserts that many works by young writers belong to the realm of service rather than creative activity, because they are written to order and in response to certain political, economic, or social needs.[39] Indeed, one of the major shortcomings of these works is the lack of sincerity and basic human honesty. Most young writers have a story to tell, but no message to deliver. Nonetheless, the situation of a young writer is indeed unenviable. When he submits for publication an ordinary story about the human predicament he is criticized for avoiding social issues, but when he deals with social problems he is censured for lack of psychological analysis. Grigorii Baklanov relates the experience of the young writer Iurii Stefanovich, who wrote a good story at the age of twenty-eight but published it only at forty-one.[40]

The current situation can be characterized by two opposing tendencies. The number of beginning authors and manuscripts submitted for publication grows ceaselessly, while the interest in the works of young writers drops continuously.[41] Strictly speaking, the situation of the young writer is indeed pathetic, because publishing affairs in the Soviet Union border sometimes on the absurd. The membership of the Writers Union has increased in the last decade by close to 15 per cent, but the productive capabilities of the printing and publishing industry have changed little. Over 3,000 manuscripts of prose, for example, were submitted for consideration to *Novyi mir* in 1985, but the journal can publish no more than twelve novels a year.[42] It is not difficult to see that for every manuscript accepted for publication more than sixty are rejected, and what should young writers do? They do precisely what they are criticized for. They write to order, listen to their own censor-double, acquiesce to the demands of editors, submit to the pressures of official censors, and wait, sometimes for years. It is no secret that such lengthy and complicated procedure can kill talent, inspiration, and sometimes the author himself.

THEORY AND IDEOLOGY

Regardless of recent changes in the Soviet leadership and despite the alleged relaxation in Soviet life, literature in the Soviet Union remains a vehicle of ideology and a tool that is used to change Soviet people into conscientious citizens and dedicated builders of a new social order. Soviet literary theory is founded on the philosophical premisses of Marxism-Leninism and reflects the current changes in the ideology of the Communist party.

In the West, literary theory concerns itself with the study of the basic principles of literature, its categories, and its criteria. Literature can be approached from a psychological, sociological, or philosophical angle, but in most cases theory investigates the poetics of artistic creativity in terms of genre, style, and the modes of narrative fiction. In Soviet theory of literature, the study of artistic form is always secondary to the examination of ideological and social relevance.

In the days of Stalin, socialist realism was the official 'method' of Soviet literature. It required 'from the artist a truthful, historically concrete representation of reality in its revolutionary development,' whereby 'truth and historical completeness of artistic representation must be combined with the task of ideological transformation and education of the working man in the spirit of socialism.'[43] In practice socialist realism limited the stylistic range of artistic prose and provided for a positive hero and a didactic message in any work of art. The situation changed after the death of Stalin. Liberated from the dangers of Stalinist repression, writers began to turn out works in which they presented a picture of reality contrary to the criteria established for the literature of socialist realism. This resulted in a disparity between the Soviet theory of literature and Soviet literary practice, in which the notions of socialist realism, socialist art, and Soviet art were no longer synonymous. Furthermore, literary theory could no longer prescribe how 'good' literature was to be written.

By the early 1970s socialist realism had lost much of its significance as a leading 'method' of Soviet art, yet Soviet literary theory was still slow in generalizing the experience of literary practice.[44] Attempts to adapt the theory to the new literary realitites were unsuccessful because the original rigid confines of socialist realism were no longer applicable, yet there were few who could agree on the new theoretical essence of the 'method,' or on a clear definition of its meaning. The situation has changed little since.

In the 1970s D. Markov, a leading Soviet literary theoretician and director of the Institute for Slavic and Balkan Studies of the Soviet Academy of Sciences, set the tone in the debate on the essence of socialist realism. He defined it as a 'historically open system of artistic forms.' Somewhat later Markov was forced to adjust his formulation of socialist realism by asserting that it is a 'historically open system of the truthful portrayal of life.'[45] According to Markov, socialist realism 'is not an immanent system, locked up in itself. It is open to the truth of life, and it finds itself in the process of continuous development which is connected with its Marxist-Leninist philosophical foundations.'[46] Markov's definition of socialist realism is supported with minor reservations by many scholars. One of them, N. Anastas'ev, postulates the view that 'the superiority of socialist realism over all other artistic methods is expressed first of all in the fact that it is completely free from any limitations.'[47]

By offering his flexible interpretation of socialist realism, Markov comes out against the two extreme tendencies in contemporary Soviet theoretical thought. One is dogmatic and adheres to a number of old and inflexible rules contained in the original formulation of socialist realism of 1934. The other is dubbed 'subjective-revisionist,'[48] because it allegedly leads to the penetration of modernist tendencies into Soviet art, thus undermining its ideological foundations.

But Markov's notion about the 'openness' of socialist realism has many vigorous opponents. One of them, Iurii Andreev, claims that 'it is impossible to use the term "open system" with any degree of scientific exactitude, because there is simply no such term at all. Instead, there is a conglomeration of unstable, continuously changing ... formulations which include different phenomena every time.'[49] According to Andreev, the analysis of poetic form is always secondary to the investigation of subject-matter: 'The ruling principle of literature is contained in its content. The theoretical or practical investigation of poetics is interesting only in so far as it can lead to the understanding of something essential in the literature of socialist realism.'[50] Similarly, S.M. Petrov refuses to accept the premiss that socialist realism is an 'open aesthetic system.' According to Petrov, such a formulation denies the fact that 'as an aesthetic system socialist realism has never been, and could never be, open to all winds and influences.'[51] Furthermore, in an open system 'the object of portrayal, as the criterion of truth, is inadvertently replaced by the subject or the artistic will of the writer.'[52] Petrov suggests that socialist realism as an open system of artistic forms would 'lead not to the truthful portrayal of life, but to a purely subjectivist play of forms which diverts one from realism in general and serves, at the same time, as ... a guarantee against criticism, and as a kind of indulgence, forgiving all future "sins." '[53]

Markov's definition of socialist realism as an 'open system' also introduced confusion in accepted Soviet literary terminology. Until recently socialist realism was regarded as a 'method,' but since Markov's concept of aesthetic systems includes also the notion of artistic method, it appears that socialist realism is no longer *the* method, but one of many included in the suggested 'open system' of socialist realism.[54] The supporters of Andreev emphasize that 'method' is a mode of perception that refers to content, while Markov's notion of 'system,' instead of combining, as it intends to, the discussion of content and form, degenerates into a 'system of artistic forms.'[55]

By the mid-1980s the debate about the 'openness' of socialist realism became quite acrimonious, with the adherents of Markov dubbed 'poetisty' and those supporting Andreev 'soderzhanisty.' These designations could lead one to the erroneous assumption that the main argument is about the relationship of form and content in a work of art. In fact, no one questions the primacy of content over form. Andreev asserts that 'scientifically perceived historical content'[56] is one of the main peculiarities of socialist realism, and P. Nikolaev, a supporter of Markov, seconds him by saying that 'all works, the content of which expresses socialist ideology, belong to the literature of socialist realism.'[57] But whereas Markov and his followers suggest that literary theory in general, and socialist realism in particular, be open to change in conformity with new developments in Marxist-Leninist philosophy, and in response to new political and ideological realities, Andreev and his supporters demand definite criteria for the evaluation of a work of art, because they do not consider the author's Weltanschauung as adequate 'confines' for the proper assessment of creative literature.[58]

If one is to compare the relationship between literary scholarship and literary criticism in the days of Stalin and today, the apprehensions of Andreev, Petrov, and Baskevich may appear justified. Then there was no rift between theory and practical criticism. The former set the guidelines, and the latter followed them consistently. Today the gap between theory and practice is obvious. Literary scholars are concerned with the theoretical substantiation of literary notions, while critics try to interpret and explain works of literature in relation not to theory but rather to contemporary circumstances of life. One seldom encounters today a review in which the author's compliance with the requirements of socialist realism is discussed. In fact the term *socialist realism* has almost completely disappeared from the vocabulary of practical literary criticism.

One can hardly blame the critics for avoiding the use of the term *socialist realism*. Its meaning has become so vague, and its relevance to the literature of the day so trivial, that it is safer to eschew discussing it altogether. In any event, there are few in the Soviet Union today who could agree on whether a given work complies with the requirements of socialist realism or not. A case in point is Chingiz Aitmatov's novel *I dol'she veka dlitsia den'* (The Day Lasts More Than a Hundred Years; 1980).[59] Aitmatov himself considers it a work of socialist realism, but the Soviet scholar N. Fed', appearing at the Ninth International Congress of Slavists, refused to place it among the works of socialist realism, because it does not conform to the criteria of the method to which Fed' adheres.[60] The situation is indeed paradoxical. Everyone talks about socialist realism as the leading method of Soviet literature. The program of the Communist Party of the Soviet Union (CPSU), adopted at the Twenty-Seventh Party Congress, in February–March 1986, states unequivocally that 'the art of socialist realism is based on the principles of partiinost' and narodnost'. It combines bold innovation with the truthful re-creation of life, which adopts and develops further all progressive traditions of our culture and that of world cultures.'[61] And yet no one knows exactly what it means.

On recent visits to the Soviet Union I had an opportunity to interview many writers, scholars, and critics with the purpose of clarifying the meaning of socialist realism.[62] Unfortunately I received no two identical replies. Creative writers display a general disregard for literary theory, while literary critics claim that socialist realism has little practical relevance to their daily work. Literary scholars expressed a number of divergent opinions, echoing the views aired in discussions in the Soviet periodical press.

D. Markov reasserted his view that socialist realism encompasses everything positive and progressive in socialist cultures and that it should be regarded as an 'open aesthetic system.' Markov's associate, Iu. Bogdanov, claimed that the old formulation of socialist realism has outlived its usefulness and that a qualitatively new approach, which would conform to the current political and ideological situation, is required. According to Bogdanov, Markov's contribution to literary theory paved the way for this new approach.

D. Urnov, from the Institute of World Literature of the USSR Academy of Sciences, asserted that although the old notion of socialist realism is no longer relevant to current literary production, because there are no longer heroes such as Pavel Korchagin, socialist realism is to continue the historical optimism connected with a definite conception of a social environment and contained in the classical works of socialist realism.

A. Ushakov, a scholar at the same institute, defines socialist realism more succinctly: it is the literature that expresses an optimistic view of life, faith in mankind and in positive human qualities, as well as the ability to withstand difficulties within the context of Soviet social significance. Another scholar from the same institute, N. Fed', advocates definite confines for socialist realism and claims that only art that contains deep social analysis can conform with the requirements of the 'method.' According to Fed', Aitmatov's works cannot be placed within the realm of socialist realism because they lack a clearly defined aesthetic ideal and are written in poor Russian. Fed' expresses here the view of the extreme fringe of Russian nationalists who regard the Russian language as the domain of ethnic Russian writers only.

The boundaries of socialist realism are more clearly defined in literature textbooks for schools and institutions of higher learning. But even there ambiguity persists. A textbook on Soviet literature for grade 10 students, approved for the 1987–8 academic year, and edited by V.A. Kovalev, of the Leningrad Institute of Russian Literature of the USSR Academy of Sciences, states clearly that the basic formulation of socialist realism was adopted by the First Congress of Soviet Writers in 1934: 'The new, more precise, wording adopted at the Fifth Congress of Soviet Writers defines socialist realism as "a method of truthful, historically concrete portrayal" which can be characterized by artistic diversity, "a wealth of artistic means and styles" which "make possible innovation in various genres of literary creativity and the expression of individual peculiarities of one's talent." ... The formulations adopted at these two congresses are the most laconic and concise definitions of socialist realism. They retain their significance today.'[63]

The textbook explains further that socialist realism provides for the portrayal of social reality in the best traditions of realism, narodnost', ideinost', truthfulness, and concrete historicism; that the analysis and interpretation of reality should be based on the principle of partiinost' and should be approached from social, class, and Marxist-Leninist positions; and that literature should educate in the spirit of socialist humanism, Soviet patriotism, and internationalism. Having defined the current requirements of socialist realism, the authors conclude by saying that 'the enumerated peculiarities of socialist realism are not compulsory norms. These are just generalized traits which could manifest themselves, at different times and in different genres, not in full measure ... The art of socialist realism can be characterized by artistic and stylistic variety, freedom to express one's peculiarities of individual talent, artistic imagination, as well as creative initiative and innovation.'[64] It is obvious that the last paragraph confuses the issue more than

it clarifies, because the demand to comply with the stringent requirements of socialist realism as outlined above contradicts the very essence
of artistic freedom.

The more glasnost' takes hold of Soviet society, the greater becomes
the disarray in Soviet theory of literature. In the second half of the 1980s
most Soviet scholars agree that Soviet literary theory is in a state of
crisis.[65] Some question even the very notion of Marxist theory of
literature and admit that few understand its essence.[66] The view that
socialist realism 'is neither an aesthetic nor ethical term, but rather a
political and ideological notion,'[67] is now openly broached. The history
of socialist realism is well summarized by Natal'ia Ivanova. She writes
that 'the literary term "socialist realism" ... did not spur development
but became a barrier to creative freedom. Hundreds of monographs
have been published and dissertations defended, but today, when the
literary façade has crashed to the ground before our eyes, it has to be
admitted that the volumes on the history of our literature are inconse-
quential and do not reflect the reality.'[68] Voices are even heard today
saying that the term *socialist realism* should be dispensed with
altogether. And yet many leading scholars, including academician D.
Markov and Professor I. Volkov of Moscow University, continue to
assert that socialist realism is an important aesthetic notion and an
indispensable component of Soviet theory of literature.[69]

Early in 1988 the board of the Writers Union discussed at its plenary
meeting the new edition of its constitution. Many writers suggested that
the term *socialist realism* be removed from the books altogether. But the
secretary of the Writers Union, Iu. N. Verchenko, came out strongly
against such suggestions and asserted that Soviet literary scholarship,
rather than the notion of socialist realism, was behind the times.[70]

The theoretical dialogue in the Soviet periodical press makes it clear
that glasnost' has done little to do away with the existing confusion in the
interpretation of socialist realism. Most writers and critics fail to
understand its meaning or its relevance to their work. Many scholars,
theoreticians, and bureaucrats, however, cling to this antiquated
notion, because they have invested much effort in keeping this artificial
creation alive.

Literary theory is called upon to explain literature, but not to regulate
it. Creative talent is always original, and each artist has his or her own
vision of the world. Any attempt to regulate talent is tantamount to the
corruption of art.

No wonder the opinions of Western observers of Soviet literature are
just as divided. Max Hayward suggested in 1972 'that the development

of Soviet literature over the last 18 years has led to the slow dissolution of Soviet literary theory.'[71] Katerina Clark continues her study of socialist realism by attempting to fit contemporary works within the framework of the original doctrine and by doing so to investigate the changes occurring in post-Stalin Soviet literature.[72] According to Edward J. Brown, 'literature published in the Soviet Union roughly since the emergence of Solzhenitsyn in 1962 seldom fitted the precepts of socialist realism laid down in the Stalinist period ... Socialist realism by the late seventies and even earlier was a concept irrelevant to the facts of Russian literature.'[73] Maurice Friedberg 'would like to record that vintage socialist realism is very much alive, if not always well ... The news of its death has been greatly exaggerated.'[74] It appears that, in their own ways, both Brown and Friedberg are correct. Although socialist realism has lost much of its previous impact on the work of many Soviet writers, there are still many authors who produce novels in the old traditions of Stalinist socialist realism.

The title of Geoffrey Hosking's book *Beyond Socialist Realism* (1980) is in itself an indication that to him socialist realism is a thing of the past. He suggests that 'the doctrine of socialist realism, though imposed by the party, was generated from the literary practice of writers them-selves, and therefore the practical development of the doctrine, and its ultimate transmutation into new and ever less recognizable forms, also lies in the hands of writers.'[75] Hosking's proposition applies only to circumstances in which the notions of socialist realism and Soviet art are synonymous. That is of course true of Stalin's era. Today, however, there is a clear distinction between socialist realism and Soviet art in general. In fact, some Soviet writers, including Iurii Trifonov and Sergei Zalygin, have turned out officially published works, some of which are regarded as works of socialist realism, and some not. The relationship between socialist realism and Soviet art is today tenuous at best and is determined more by ideological considerations and the political situa-tion than by the theoretical deliberations of literary scholars and critics. In any event, in order to avoid confusion, it is advisable to define terms before embarking on a discussion of socialist realism.

It seems clear that because theory has lost control over literary production, the party has been obliged to step in and reassert its ideological dominance over all spheres of cultural activity. In recent decades, the CPSU Central Committee has adopted a number of resolutions aimed at improving ideological and educational work among writers and critics,[76] and political and literary bureaucrats have continued to stress the ideological importance of literature. In fact, literaturovedenie, or the study of literature, has now been included among the social sciences.[77] The importance of literature as a tool of ideology has been well summarized recently in an editorial of *Literaturnaia gazeta* (Literary Gazette): 'The wisdom of party leadership in literature is expressed in the fact that it gives the artist the widest possibilities for creative inquiry. But that does not mean, in the least, that the development of literature is a spontaneous process, not controlled or directed by anyone ... The party cannot remain indifferent to the ideological content of the arts. It justifiably considers that the social value of an artist's labour is determined, first of all, by his Weltanschauung and the ideological and political position that he asserts and actively promotes in his work.'[78]

In practical terms many voices are raised against the 'deheroization' of the Soviet character and for the creation of a new positive hero who would embody all the positive qualities of contemporary Soviet people. Fedor Abramov's Priaslin (in *Brat'ia i sestry* – Brothers and Sisters; 1958–78), Vasil' Bykov's Sotnikov ('Sotnikov' – Sotnikov; 1970), Iurii Bondarev's Kniazhko (*Bereg* – The Shore; 1975), and Chingiz Aitmatov's Edigei (*I dol'she veka dlitsia den'*; 1980) are cited as worthy models.[79] In theoretical terms a Soviet character should embody and express the essence of the 'collective, social and international, as well as the unity of the national and individual in the make-up of the hero.'[80]

The ascent of Gorbachev to power and the calls for glasnost' and perestroika, which are accompanied by a certain relaxation in Soviet life, are linked with recurring demands for the strengthening of ideological work among the Soviet people. According to Gorbachev, 'Social corrosion negatively affected the spiritual state of Soviet society and undermined its high ethical values ... This resulted in a drop of interest in social affairs, in a lack of spirituality, in scepticism, and in the lowering of moral stimuli for work ... The ideology and psychology of stagnation affected also the spheres of culture, literature, and the arts. The criteria for the evaluation of artistic activity have been lowered.'[81] Gorbachev's enumeration of current social ills is usually coupled with denunciation of the Brezhnev past, and Soviet writers have reacted to this new situation by producing works in which they emphasize the negative aspects of Soviet life. Valentin Rasputin's 'Pozhar' (The Fire; 1985), Viktor Astaf'ev's *Pechal'nyi detektiv* (The Sad Detective Story; 1986), and Chingiz Aitmatov's *Plakha* (The Execution Block; 1986) are among the better-known works that uncover the moral decay of Soviet people and the ethical disintegration of society.

According to the current Soviet leadership, it is necessary to expose the evils of the past in order to clear the way for new and positive achievements. So far Gorbachev's policies have produced little in terms of economic accomplishments, and the emphasis in his rhetoric remains on improving the state administration and the quality of Soviet man. He seems to call for the development of an ethical, morally stable, and selfless citizen, who does not drink, who places social needs above personal interests, who is also a good family person, and who is, most important, a good and productive worker. Thus the immediate objective of party ideology is to change the mentality of the Soviet people, with literature assigned a major role.

Since perestroika refers to economic reconstruction as well as to re-orientation in thinking, 'writers have an important role to play in bringing about a psychological, ethical, and socio-economic change ... The climate in Soviet society ... demands a new and active hero – a leader.'[82] No wonder, therefore, that Gorbachev places new emphasis on the primacy of theory over any practical endeavour,[83] and his politburo associate, E.K. Ligachev, reasserts the 'close links between ideology and life.'[84] It seems that ideology, adapted to current political needs, is one of the few areas of Soviet life where no perestroika is called for. It remains the backbone of the system and a practical guide for action.

The new emphasis on literature as a vehicle of ideology, the immediate task of which is to help modify the people's mentality, is reminiscent of the Stalinist notion that regards writers as 'engineers of human souls.' But experience has shown that laws, regulations, and even governments can change overnight. Changes in human nature, however, are usually slow to come about, because people are both rational and irrational, logical and intuitive, and good and evil; at bottom, people resist change.

Despite recurring official declarations about the primacy of theory and the unity of ideology and life, there is a glaring disparity between the ideological premises of the Communist party and the practical aspects of daily life in the Soviet Union. In literature, this is illustrated by the purely academic discussions on the essence of socialist realism which are detached from the realities of Soviet literature. Furthermore, some critics question even long-accepted Soviet interpretations of human phenomena. Thus Igor' Zolotusskii asserts: 'Everyone wants to know whether there is a god in this world and in man, or whether man himself is god. And what is then nature, destiny, or the sun? What is one's relation to nature?'[85] And L. Anninskii declares: 'Now it is clear that there is nothing, and there will never be anything final; that the continuing history of manking is just as dramatic as its "prehistory,"'[86]

Such ideas challenge the very foundations of Marxist-Leninist philosophy, according to which the world is knowable and human cognition unlimited. They also express the frustrations of a generation that is tired of hearing each new leader blame his predecessors for all social and personal ills.

It seems clear that in the Soviet Union today literary theory is developing with little relation to literary practice. In other words, theory is in no position to guide the literary process. Moreover, it has also lost the ability to explain literature, because there is no uniformity in the interpretation of literary notions or in the understanding of human phenomena. It is claimed in the Soviet Union today that socialist realism continues to be the leading method of Soviet literature, but no clear formulation of what it actually means is provided. In present circumstances there is only one common denominator allegedly uniting all socialist realist writers: it is their world outlook. One critic suggests that socialist realism is 'realism plus Weltanschauung.'[87] But even that is not satisfying, because there is a new uncertainty and vagueness in the interpretation of certain philosophical notions. Thus the only recourse left to the government is direct interference in the creative process, through the issuing of party directives and censorship regulations which should work to stimulate artistic production in support of government and party policy.

In the mid-1980s Soviet writers are able to make use of a wide range of artistic means, including fantasy, hyperbole, the grotesque, myth, and parable. They can turn out literature that criticizes the recent Soviet past or different aspects of contemporary Soviet life. But they are encouraged and expected to affirm in their works the internal changes introduced by the new leadership of Mikhail Gorbachev and to support the foreign policy of the Soviet government.

2 The Literary Scene

The bulk of contemporary Russian prose deals with several major time spans in the development of Russia and the Soviet state: the tsarist past, the early post-revolutionary period, the Second World War, and the Stalin era. Most extensively, however, it depicts current Soviet reality. It covers a wide range of topics, and it is set in the city and in the countryside, as well as in remote foreign countries. Soviet literature of the 1980s defies classification. Its thematic range is so diverse, and works appear in such a variety of genres, styles, and narrative modes, that it is not easy to categorize them. In truth, a good work of art is always original and resists generalization.

Today writers are classified in the Soviet Union according to age, place of residence, thematic interest, or artistic inclination. Works of prose are grouped together according to theme, genre, artistic means, or the level of publitsistika in a particular work. Most works of prose are classified according to theme, rarely according to artistic quality or popularity. In fact the popularity of a novel is seldom determined by its artistic level and is often in reverse proportion to its ideological reliability. Some popular works by writers such as Valentin Pikul' and Iulian Semenov belong to the so-called mass or pulp fiction. Their popularity is stimulated by the publication policies of the literary establishment, which often foster the development of poor taste in the Soviet mass readership.

The thematic approach to contemporary Soviet prose is accepted by many Soviet scholars and critics, but the thematic confines are in the process of constant change, and the boundaries between different themes are not always clearly defined. Thus 'village prose' of the 1960s and 1970s addresses itself to the issues of urbanization, technological progress, and the forceful intrusion of 'civilization' into the remote

Russian countryside. It deals with these problems in ethical and spiritual terms. Today most works about the countryside emphasize practical issues of everyday life, describing them in ecological, agricultural, and economic terms. Countryside prose of the 1980s can be subdivided into three distinct streams: ecological, Russophile national, and new settlement, or economic. Ethical issues reflect the changes that have occurred in rural Russia in the last few decades. The works of Fedor Abramov, Valentin Rasputin, and Viktor Astaf'ev suggest that a way of life has been destroyed. The damage has been done, and now society reaps the consequences.[1]

There is also a certain evolution in the development of the war theme. There is new emphasis on documentary evidence and personal experience by the few surviving writers who still remember the war, but there is also a gradual transformation of works about the Second World War into historical fiction. In most works about the war the historical past is juxtaposed with present-day reality, and the war generation is contrasted with contemporary Soviet youth. There is also a new emphasis on current political issues, on the struggle for peace, and on the suffering of the civilian population under Nazi occupation.[2]

The political prose of the 1980s is also different. In the past the political novel concerned itself with major political issues, diplomacy, and foreign affairs – its main characters were usually important political figures. Today the new political novel, exemplified by Aleksandr Prokhanov, is set in a foreign country, such as Afghanistan, Nicaragua, or Mozambique. Its main characters are ordinary Soviet citizens, who are there allegedly to help the native population in their struggle for freedom. Contemporary political prose reflects the changing realities of international relations and promotes Soviet military and political interests around the globe.[3]

The city prose of the 1970s emphasizes the study of human relationships, concentrating on the investigation of people's behaviour in family and personal life. Works by well-known writers such as Iurii Trifonov, Daniil Granin, Sergei Zalygin, and Sergei Krutilin study the intricacy of human nature by placing intimate life under a magnifying glass. Much of this prose belongs to the so-called byt literature, which stresses the negative aspects of daily city life in the Soviet Union. Faithlessness, broken homes, infidelity, and permissiveness are the rule rather than the exception in such works. Most of the characters are unethical and concerned with momentary pleasures and personal well-being. The term byt has been often contrasted in Soviet literary criticism with the notion of bytie. As opposed to byt, which refers to personal and family existence only, bytie refers to the life of an individual in general, including all social, economic, ideological, personal, and other concerns. In the mid-1970s byt literature was criticized as advancing hedonism and a lack of moral principles over true ethical values.

In the 1980s many continue to write in the tradition of the byt prose of the 1970s. The subjects of marriage, love, divorce, abortion, and illegitimacy are as popular today as ever before. The theme of pure and youthful love has almost disappeared from Soviet fiction. What is described in most cases today is not love in the tradition of Pushkin, Turgenev, or Chekhov, but rather love affairs between married, or previously married, mature individuals. This literature points clearly to the growing ramifications of family instability. It also questions the viability of the contemporary institution of marriage. Except for I. Grekova[4] and several others, who deal with these problems in a mature and artistically refined manner, most contemporary works about love and marriage do not measure up to the prose of the 1970s. They are superficial, mediocre, and similar to each other in tone and substance. No wonder serious Soviet critics ignore most of these works completely.

Iurii Nagibin's 'Terpenie' (Patience; 1982),[5] for example, is a story close in spirit to the byt theme, in which the moral decay and ethical corruption of the city intelligentsia are vividly portrayed. Aleksei and Anna Skvortsov are respected scholars and highly placed Leningrad academics. Together with their children, both students, they go by boat to a nearby island for a day of rest and sightseeing. What is intended as a day of recreation turns into a tragedy that exposes the essence of a family in which there is no love, honour, or respect. It is also an example illustrating that old mistakes are difficult to rectify and that lies 'have short legs.' On the island Anna meets the invalid Pasha, her husband's friend from before the war, and a man she has loved all her life. Anna offers herself to him; she implores him to come back with her, but he refuses. Returning with the family to the city, already far from shore, Anna makes a desperate, suicidal attempt to swim back to the island, but dies from heart failure instead. The title 'Terpenie' refers to Anna's patience. She has been married for thirty years to a man who loved her, but whom she never loved. Her husband had lied to her about the fate of his best friend and had wished him dead. The consequences of such a marriage are dreadful. The parents are indifferent, and the children are depraved.

'Terpenie' is a story with an engaging plot and high dramatic tension. Much of the story is revealed through flashbacks, digressions, and internal monologue. But Anna's actions lack psychological motivation and are not very convincing. Thirty years is a long time, and her suicide can be explained only by the fact that she hates her husband more than she longs for her old love. In the final analysis, Pasha is superior to all of them. He drives away Anna out of consideration for her. He understands that after all those years there is little in common between them and that Anna's offer to look after him is just another attempt to perpetuate an old dream.

The story uncovers the terrible lot of the war invalids. These people sacrificed their well-being for their motherland, but their country did not repay them in kind. Mutilated by war and by fate, neglected and abandoned, they are unable to return with dignity to a normal life. Many go into self-exile in order to spare themselves humiliation. On the island there is an old monastery where the invalids gather to spend the rest of their days. The proud nature of Pasha could not bear pity and degradation. He goes into seclusion among his equals, who accept and respect him. Anna's personal suffering and her frantic hysteria seem trivial in comparison with the tribulations of these people. Nagibin's story reveals a little-known corner of Soviet life. Society is more comfortable when the war veterans are isolated on a remote island, out of sight.

City prose does not limit itself to the subject of love and marriage. Some experienced writers try to place family problems in a broader perspective, while some make family issues secondary to economic and social questions. For example, Liliia Beliaeva and Maiia Ganina present family problems from a feminine perspective in their novels,[6] and Vladimir Tendriakov examines the Soviet system of secondary education.[7] Il'ia Shtemler depicts the Soviet business world and underground economy, while Anatolii Anan'ev attempts to draw a broad picture of the Soviet intelligentsia.

The urbanization of the Soviet countryside and the migration of millions of rural inhabitants into big cities have blurred somewhat the previously marked distinction between the average dwellers of a major city and the inhabitants of the provinces. Besides, recent migration has created a new stratum of city dwellers, people who are physically located in the city but who remain emotionally attached to the village, its ways, and its traditions. This situation has resulted in the appearance of a number of thematically marginal works in which city and countryside affairs are dealt with in a combined manner.

Georgii Semenov deals with problems that affect equally city and countryside dwellers. In his povest' 'Loshad' v tumane' (A Horse in the Fog; 1980),[8] city and countryside themes merge into a narrative in which the setting becomes secondary to the general discussion of man's nature and the human predicament. The external framework of the story is reminiscent of old 'village prose': it is set in the countryside; but the action is put into motion by the arrival of a city family for the summer. The Lukovnikovs rent a house from Boris Bredikhin who works in town but prefers to live in the countryside. The family history of the Lukovnikovs is at the centre of the plot. Their daughter, Zhenia, has borne a son of a man who refuses to accept responsibility for the child. The Lukovnikovs decide to give the child up for adoption, thus making it possible for Zhenia to study and defend her candidate of science dissertation. Now they all feel so guilt-ridden for abandoning their own blood and kin that they are ready to do anything to get the boy back. Common tragedy can bring a family closer together; in this instance it sets them further apart. Mother and daughter compete for the affection of the same man – Boris. Mrs Lukovnikov is unfaithful to her husband: Sergei Lukovnikov is jealous. He hates Boris because he suspects him of having an affair with his wife. In the background there is the juxtaposition of two ways of life. Boris, who lives apart from his family, accepts his past and looks with confidence to his future. Unable to reconcile themselves to their past, the Lukovnikovs torment each other in the present and destroy all prospects for a satisfying future. Semenov gives only a sketchy picture of his characters; we know little about their past. But the narrative flows smoothly; the language is unobtrusive, and the message is clear. People often strive toward illusory goals, thinking that the ultimate objective in life is the satisfaction of material needs. Zhenia attains her academic degree, but she loses her inner peace, and the Lukovnikov family disintegrates.

Delovaia proza

So-called delovaia proza, or prose that investigates and portrays Soviet trade and the service industries, is an important variation in the mainstream of city prose. The prolific Leningrad writer Il'ia Shtemler concentrates almost exclusively on this subject. In the last decade he has published four novels, each dealing with a different aspect of city business life. *Taksopark* (Taxi Fleet; 1980)[9] looks at the internal life of the taxi-cab industry. *Univermag* (Department Store; 1982)[10] examines the official and unofficial sides of Soviet retail trade. *Utrenee shosse* (The Morning Highway; 1983)[11] explores the workings of the underground economy and its Mafia-style criminal activities. *Poezd* (The Train; 1986)[12] studies the Soviet railway system. All his novels are based on first-hand experience. Shtemler worked for a year as a cab driver and repair man in a taxi fleet, he served as a train conductor on the Leningrad–Baku and Leningrad–Murmansk routes, and he was employed as an inspector of the organizational department of a large department store. In all instances only the chief executive officer knew that Shtemler was a writer and had joined the organization with the purpose of describing it later in his novels.

In *Univermag* Shtemler takes the reader behind the closed doors of a department store and exposes the shortcomings of the highly centralized and bureaucratic system of Soviet retail trade and commerce. The director of the store, Firtich, and his accountant, Lisovskii, appear to be honest, but they are so overwhelmed by prevailing corruption that both are helpless and go down to defeat. Theft, bribes, blackmail, and speculation are daily occurrences in a retail system ridden with inefficiency, incompetence, and criminal negligence. The notion that one cannot remain honest and continue working in the Soviet retail trade permeates the novel. If one refuses to co-operate, one is abused, blackmailed, and forced to submit. Lisovskii does not give in; refusing to take a bribe, he resigns his position instead, but his health breaks down and he dies of a heart attack. Most characters are driven by insatiable greed for material things. Lisovskii is the only protagonist opposed to the all-pervading spirit of veshchizm. Firtich does not benefit directly from the criminal activity of others, but he is a passive tool, unable to withstand the spontaneous wave of crime and corruption.

Soviet critics have attacked Shtemler for his picture of the Soviet retail trade. F. Chapchakhov criticizes him for his failure to provide a prescription for how to fight evil. He claims that in *Univermag* 'honest and decent people look like victims, or at best like passive observers. Moreover, they often express opinions that run counter to the elementary notions of common honesty and decency.'[13] It seems fruitless to demand from a writer answers to questions that the government, in all its wisdom, cannot solve. There is no strong positive hero in the novel, able to fight evil and overcome all shortcomings, because the novel is based on fact, rather than imagination, and the author has simply not come across such a hero in his experience. The above notwithstanding, the criticism of *Univermag* has some effect on its author. The 1984 book edition of the novel[14] includes an 'Afterword' in which the author asserts that he views Firtich as an active and positive character of the type that, with the help of the young, will be able to turn around the Soviet retail trade. It is worthwhile noting that the debate between the writer and his critics has little to do with artistic criticism. They argue about the truth of the novel not as a work of art but rather as a factual report that should also reflect a particular social bent. The novel should be typical in a generalizing positive sense, otherwise it could misguide the reader and fail to serve the current objectives of Soviet literature.

The two main heroes of Shtemler's next novel, *Utrenee shosse*, live double lives. Serafim Odintsov is in charge of the merchant navy technical supply warehouses in the city of Iuzhnomorsk, but he is also the godfather of a Mafia-style clandestine criminal organization, involved in stealing government property, smuggling goods from abroad, and producing merchandise that is in great demand and selling it for exorbitant prices on the black market. Anton Kliamin is an ordinary cab driver, but he also works for Odintsov, helping him transport his stolen property. Kliamin is introduced to Odintsov by another driver who allegedly commits suicide. In truth, he is murdered by Odintsov's henchmen. Now, the same fate awaits Kliamin. The police are on the scent of the gang, and Kliamin is told to accept full responsibility for all the crimes. He knows that if he refuses, his fate is sealed: he will be murdered. But on his way to meet Odintsov, Kliamin makes a sudden decision; he increases the speed of his vehicle and collides head on with Odintsov's Lincoln Continental. Both are apparently killed. In another plot line Kliamin's daughter Natal'ia, an offspring from an old affair, comes to see her father. She learns about her father's criminal activities and tries to save him from their possible repercussions. She is murdered in the process by Odintsov's people in what appears to be a car accident.

Kliamin is a complex character. Good and evil are closely interlaced in his nature. He is bold and daring, yet he has a guilty conscience when he mistreats people. He values his freedom and thinks that he will be young forever, yet in essence he is alone and lonely and fears for his future and old age. Crime helps Kliamin accumulate things that mean nothing to him and that he does not need. Corruption and hoarding are also Odintsov's way of life. Odintsov has no children, nor does he love his wife, yet he enjoys the excitement of taking risks and the power he wields over others. The structure of *Utrenee shosse* reminds one of a detective novel. There are many melodramatic scenes and there is much suspense and surprise, but there is no competition between cops and criminals. The police are in the far background, and their activities are not described. Instead the novel emphasizes the relationships among the different levels of the criminal world. There are intimations that the gang has connections with people of consequence in the local government, but no one is identified, nor is anyone arrested.

There is little of a positive nature to be found in Shtemler's novels.

Most thieves and speculators in *Univermag* are petty criminals; *Utrenee shosse* is about big stakes and violent crime. The plots of these novels are absorbing but the author does not adequately motivate the actions of his heroes. The final act that Kliamin plays out, of suicide and murder, is not very convincing. It has not been rooted in his psychological make-up, nor does it seem to flow from his previous experience. But the importance of Shtemler's novels lies in their social significance rather than in their artistic merit. They reveal a fragment of Soviet life until recently seldom discussed in fiction or journalism. The reader is introduced to little-known realities of Soviet daily existence.

The Labour Theme

The labour theme is yet another variation of city prose. In the heyday of socialist realism the image of the worker or production foreman was usually at the centre of a work of art. Today, despite constant prodding by critics and literary bureaucrats, few gifted authors set their novels at the workplace, and the so-called labour theme or production prose is the domain of writers who have little to offer to the refined reader of the eighties. In fact, writers such as Garii Nemchenko, Anatolii Krivonosov, Arnol'd Kashtanov, and Iurii Skop, who deal with production problems in their works, concentrate mainly on the portrayal of the intermediate level of the labour force. They depict the industrial manager rather than the simple worker. The Central Council of Soviet Trade Unions and the Writers Union regularly conduct a competition for the best work of prose fiction about the contemporary working class. The first prize for 1982–3 was awarded to the little-known writer N. Gorbachev for his novel *Belye vody* (White Waters).[15] In 1984–5 over three hundred manuscripts were submitted, but not a single one was considered worthy of the first prize.[16]

In most works of 'labour prose', the conflicts bear a mark of artificiality. Production issues are detached from, or poorly integrated with, the characters' private lives. Moreover, this prose lacks the universality and concern with general human problems that are the hallmarks of great literature. Works in which production issues are discussed within the context of a worker's general psychological and emotional make-up are more interesting. Aleksandr Pletnev's novel *Shakhta* (The Mine; 1979)[17] deals with the connection between population migration and problems of industrialization. After his army service the main hero, Mikhail Sveshnev, does not return to his native village in Siberia. Instead he joins the labour force and becomes a coal miner in the Far East. But Sveshnev, a good worker and family man, is not happy in his new position. A gnawing longing for the countryside, augmented by fear and the danger of working in a mine, drives him back to his native Chumalovka – but not for long. The old village has changed beyond recognition. Most people have joined the new sovkhoz. Sveshnev realizes that there is no return to the past. He goes back to the mine.

Pletnev, who worked as a miner for twenty years, and his hero accept reality; they do not challenge fate. Sveshnev's old father tells him: 'Go back. It is good for me when you are better off. And Chumalovka is like a man: it is dead. You can feel sorry for it as long as you want, but you can never bring it back.'[18] Pletnev promotes the official government view of the relationship between the so-called NTR, or scientific-technological revolution, and the natural environment. Nature has to be protected, but industrialization and economic development are the first priority. Pletnev depicts in his novel a number of conflicts in the workplace, as well as the relationships among the members of a coal-miners' brigade, but the most important element is his attempt to study the mentality of an individual transplanted from one social environment into another. Unfortunately, Pletnev neither adequately analyses the psychology of Sveshnev's emotional experiences nor motivates his deeds sufficiently. Thus some of Sveshnev's actions come as a surprise to the unsuspecting reader.

Post-Revolutionary Russia

The re-examination of the Soviet historical past is another important subject in contemporary Soviet prose. Sergei Zalygin devotes most of his time to this topic. In *Solenaia pad'* (Salt Valley; 1967) he studies the internal contradictions plaguing the revolutionary forces in the civil war; in *Komissiia* (Commission; 1975) he explores the fate of the Russian peasant in a remote Siberian village in the period of civil war; and in 'Na Irtyshe' (By the Irtysh; 1964) he offers new insights into the process of collectivization in Russia.

In his last novel, *Posle buri* (After the Storm; 1980–5),[19] Zalygin sketches a broad picture of Siberian Russia between 1921 and 1929. He investigates the problems that beset the local population in the period of the NEP (New Economic Policy), which is identified with a certain political relaxation and a temporary revival of economic activity and private initiative. But as opposed to Zalygin's earlier works, where most characters are simple peasants, in his recent novel the main hero, Kornilov, is a member of the White intelligentsia and a former tsarist officer.

The novel has seven parts, each with an independent story, and each set in a different time. The character of Kornilov thematically unites all the subplots and gives meaning to the narrative. Zalygin uses a number of narrative techniques and melodramatic devices in the novel. By withholding information he attempts to keep the reader in suspense. He complicates the plot by giving his main protagonist a double identity. The plot is constructed around an inventive scheme: the White officer, Petr Vasil'evich Kornilov, who is a captive of the Bolsheviks, assumes the name of his neighbour in the camp, Petr Nikolaevich Kornilov, who is due to be released but is dying from typhoid fever.

The novel begins with Kornilov's arrival in the city of Aul in 1921. He goes to the other Kornilov's wife, Evgeniia Kovalevskaia – an enigmatic woman and a nurse – and forces himself upon her. At first she rejects him, but later she falls in love with him. Saving people is her passion, and she loves Kornilov even more than her husband because she saves him. Kornilov takes over the inheritance of her husband. He prospers for a while, but the Cheka finally gets on his tracks. Kornilov tries hard to conceal his real identity. He moves to a remote village in Siberia and simulates death, but to no avail. One cannot run away from oneself.

In book 1 Zalygin portrays the general upheaval in Russian society caused by the revolution. The blizzard swept through, devastating the social fabric and the lives of people. In book 2, which covers 1928–9, transition leads to transformation and some semblance of order is in sight. But the fate of man and his present social position are still determined by his past, which follows as a dark shadow from cradle to grave. Zalygin addresses in the novel the problem of the surviving tsarist intelligentsia, the so-called 'byvshie', the 'have-beens,' and tries to vindicate some of them. To him they are all Russians who represent a link in the endless chain of the Russian cultural heritage. Zalygin intimates that people are often helpless in the face of historical events of great magnitude. The majority are passive victims of blind destiny, who want simply to survive. The few who refuse to become tools of blind fate and make a conscious decision to take a stand usually pay for this daring with their lives.

Most of Zalygin's characters are thinking people. Even his simple peasants are inclined to philosophize and often express original thoughts. Some characters are remembered only by what they say, rather than by their actions. No wonder Zalygin's novels do not always make easy reading. His prose is intellectual, polemical, and philosophical. It requires interpretation and thought. In fact, *Posle buri* is a novel about ideas, some of which go back to Dostoevskii. Thus one of the minor characters, Ivan Ippolitovich, writes a *Book of Horrors*. He is preoccupied with the notion of fear. According to him people are terrified by horror, which is their God. Positive thinking is the only saving grace of man. The old Kornilov reiterates the same thoughts. He claims that the world can be saved only by living wisely, which is impossible without the new energy of thought. Zalygin tries to connect Kornilov's obsession with the end of the world with the danger of a nuclear holocaust in the 1980s.

Zalygin began his novel in the mid-1970s but finished it in 1985. In the mean time much had changed in Soviet life and in international relations. It is evident from the ending of the novel that the author has departed from his original plan and has written a conclusion that reflects more the spirit of the mid-1980s than the atmosphere of the 1920s.[20] Surprisingly, the novel ends with a letter from Kornilov who is still alive and claims to have read the novel. He adds some new facts about his life, argues with some interpretations offered by the author, and contemplates the human predicament. Most of his ideas are obviously not those of a former tsarist officer, an old man of close to ninety, but rather those of the author himself. Kornilov comments on the current international political situation; he ridicules the president of the United States; he comes out against Star Wars – the (us) strategic defence initiative – and he advocates nuclear disarmament. Kornilov draws a parallel between the 1920s and the 1980s. He comes to the conclusion that the danger of foreign intervention is always there and that vigilance is required at all times. Kornilov fails, however, to note the differences between the period of NEP and the 1980s. In the 1920s individual vitality, imagination, and initiative were evident on both sides of the political spectrum. Young revolutionaries were still idealistic and ready to make sacrifices for their cause. Today the idealism of the 1920s has been replaced by complacency and cynicism. The contemporary bureaucrat has inherited the worse traits of the NEP-man. He makes no sacrifices for society but exploits the system for personal benefit.

One may wonder why an author of Zalygin's stature should append to his novel a conclusion that is artistically little connected with the main plot and written in flat, journalistic prose. It is apparent that the political atmosphere in the country exerts indirect pressure on the artist and intrudes on his creative process. The Soviet critic Arsenii Gulyga makes a preposterous suggestion that concluding *Posle buri* 'with political journalism is just as logical as the philosophical conclusion of *War and Peace*.'[21] Gulyga fails to see that the appendix to *War and Peace* does not destroy the artistic unity of the plot. It elucidates instead Tolstoi's ideas expressed in artistic form in his fiction. In *Posle buri* the main character comes back to life, intrudes into the natural creative process, and destroys the artistic unity of the plot. But then political relevance is apparently more important today than artistic unity. *Posle buri* lacks the narrative unity of 'Na Irtyshe' and *Komissiia*, but the sketchy and sometimes impressionistic portrayal of fast-moving characters and scenes renders well the spirit of the times, the atmosphere of confusion and social discord, and the instability of human fate.

Mikhail Alekseev's *Drachuny* (Pugnacious Fellows; 1982),[22] which was nominated for the 1984 Lenin prize in Literature, is another novel that contrasts the historical past of the young Soviet state with contemporary reality. It is an autobiographical story, told in the first person, in which the author describes his childhood village life in the 1920s and 1930s. His youthful experiences are later commented upon by the mature author-narrator, who returns in the 1980s to his native village to view the past from contemporary perspectives. In part I the narrator relates the story of a great friendship between two village boys which turns into a quarrel and a feud between two families. In part II he describes the process of collectivization and the great famine of 1933. The population of his native village, Monastyrskoe, in the Saratov region, has dwindled in those years from six hundred to just over a hundred families. Alekseev points out that the famine was not a natural calamity, but rather the result of mismanagement. But by putting the blame on the eagerness and callousness of local officials, he absolves higher Soviet authorities from all responsibility for this great disaster. He also asserts that despite the tribulations and temporary difficulties, the Soviet people did not turn against their motherland and supported it selflessly in war and peace. Alekseev's novel has a number of structural and compositional deficiencies. The author does not investigate the psychological implications of collectivization and of the famine on the mentality of the Soviet people, nor does he probe into the hearts and minds of the victims of Stalin's abuse of power. Nonetheless, the appearance of *Drachuny* is an important social occurrence. It is not often that young Soviet readers get a first-hand, graphic account of the suffering of their parents in the first two decades of Soviet rule.

In 1987 two important new novels dealing with the period of collectivization appeared. Vasilii Belov published the third part of his *Kanuny. Khronika kontsa 20-kh godov* (On the Eve: A Chronicle of the Late 1920s; 1976),[23] and Boris Mozhaev published *Muzhiki i baby* (Countryfolk),[24] completed in 1980, but rejected by several journals. The first two parts of *Kanuny* are set in 1928; part III in 1929. *Muzhiki i baby* is set in 1929–30 in the villages of the Riazan' region. In Mikhail Sholokhov's *Podniataia tselina* (Virgin Soil Upturned; 1931, 1960) the process of collectivization is portrayed through the eyes of those who have come to the village to remove the kulaks and establish collective farms. In *Muzhiki i baby* the picture is given through the eyes of those who are victimized by this process. *Podniataia tselina* ends on a positive note; a kolkhoz is established, and several peasants join the party. In *Muzhiki i baby* a peasant rebellion is put down by force and the kolkhoz disintegrates. Mozhaev's novel is a strong critique of Stalinist collectivization policies. It is also a veiled call for the reintroduction of an NEP-like economy and the rehabilitation of the Russian church.

Stalinism Reconsidered

Glasnost' made possible the appearance of a number of works written at different times before the ascent of Gorbachev to power but officially published only after 1985. These works include the already mentioned *Deti Arbata* by Rybakov,[25] *Novoe naznachenie* by Bek,[26] and *Zhizn' i sud'ba* by Grossman,[27] as well as Iurii Trifonov's *Ischeznovenie* (Disappearance; 1987)[28] and Vladimir Dudintsev's *Belye odezhdy* (Robed in White; 1987).[29] These works differ in scope, size, and quality, but all have one thing in common: they denounce Stalin and his rule of terror.

Works criticizing the role of Stalin in post-revolutionary Soviet history began to appear in the Soviet Union soon after the leader's death. Thus, Konstantin Simonov makes an attempt in his trilogy *Zhivye i mertvye* (The Living and the Dead; 1959, 1964, 1971) to examine and analyse the role of Stalin in the pre-war purges. But Stalin's personal shortcomings and his leadership are not the main subject of these earlier works. In the recent novels Stalin and Stalinism are at the centre. The personality of Stalin hovers over all, creating an atmosphere in which ardent faith and dedication to the communist cause and to the personality of Stalin are intricately intertwined with fear, doubt, and blind submission. In *Deti Arbata* and *Novoe naznachenie* Stalin is an active character, while in *Ischeznovenie* he is in the distant background, but in all three the invisible spectre of Stalinism poisons the atmosphere and reigns supreme.

The action in *Deti Arbata*, the most popular novel to appear in the Soviet Union in 1987,[30] takes place in 1933–4 and is set mainly in the Moscow district of Arbat. One plot line deals with the fate of the children of Arbat – in the past classmates, and currently young Soviet adults.

One of the them, Sasha Pankratov, a student and a dedicated party member, is arrested, convicted, and exiled to Siberia for alleged anti-Soviet propaganda. Another plot line concentrates on the personality of Stalin and those around him. Some relatives and parents, who are important Soviet bureaucrats, as well as Sasha's friend Iurii Sharok, a mean hypocrite and opportunist who joins the security service, connect the main plot lines. The novel is narrated in the third person. Chapters about Stalin alternate with chapters about the young people. Stalin's internal monologues are often interlaced with authorial digressions which make it difficult, at times, to separate the views of the author from those of the protagonist.

The novel is no great work of art. Many characters are poorly delineated, and their actions often lack psychological motivation. But the novel is an important social phenomenon. It exposes Stalin's cruel, power-hungry character and his fear and suspicion of everyone around him. Fear and submission are expected from his associates: a man can easily change his ideas and attitude, but fear is there to stay. According to Stalin, those removed from power can return, but those destroyed, never. The novel concludes with the assassination of Kirov, which is the prelude to the great purges of the late 1930s. Although not stated clearly, there are strong hints in the novel that Stalin himself arranged the murder.

The chapters dealing with the young people of Arbat are much weaker than those depicting Stalin. But Rybakov avoids the issue of the relationship between the dictator and the system which made it possible for him to take total control and subjugate the whole nation. Nor does he address the question of whether Stalin had anything to fear before resorting to terror. The appearance of *Deti Arbata* has generated a heated and mixed critical reaction. Most critics give the novel positive reviews,[31] but some defend Stalin from what they consider groundless accusations and accuse Rybakov of falsifying history.[32]

Bek's *Novoe naznachenie* is a documentary novel-chronicle based on real facts from Soviet life. The action in the novel ends in the days of Khrushchev, in 1957, but it covers over twenty years in the life of the highly placed Soviet official Aleksandr Onisimov. Onisimov is a survivor of Stalin's terror. Work in the Stalinist apparatus turns him into a blind follower, and a man who executes directives but has little initiative of his own. Onisimov saves himself by acquiescence, blind worship, and total submission to his leader, which are nurtured by overwhelming fear.

The novel was written in the days of Khrushchev, and its author has died long since,[33] but it has many important parallels with contemporary life. Onisimov, the Stalinist bureaucrat, is an enemy of innovation and change; he is set in his ways; he is afraid of perestroika. Aleksandr Bek, who coined the term perestroika, reminds his readers that changes in people's mentality are not accomplished overnight and that perestroika is not so much a political or economic issue as a psychological one. Bek's novel explains, in a way, one of the difficulties of Gorbachev's perestroika, which is hampered by the silent passivity of the survivors of the Brezhnev apparatus.

Novoe naznachenie centres on the fate of one man. In *Zhizn' i sud'ba*, Grossman, in contrast, charts a broad canvas of Soviet life. His main interest is in the general social process and the political atmosphere in the country rather than in the fate of individual characters. The central event in the novel is the struggle for Stalingrad, during the Second World War. Paradoxically, according to Grossman, the people fighting for freedom and against Nazi occupation are at the same time fighting for their subjugation to Stalinist tyranny. The first part of the novel opens with a scene in a German camp; later we are introduced to life in Soviet camps. At the beginning of the novel we read that 'National Socialism has created a new type of political criminal: criminals who had not committed a crime.'[34] By the end of the novel we realize that the same is true of Stalinist Russia. Grossman draws thus a parallel between the atrocities of Hitler and those of Stalin – between fascist and communist rule. No wonder the novel was seized by the KGB, and Grossman was warned by the police not to disclose the real truth about the manuscript to anybody.[35]

Trifonov's uncompleted novel *Ischeznovenie*, published six years after his death, is different from most other works discussed here. It is dedicated to the study of the psychology of fear and its intricate relationship with the dedication of the people to a cause they have served selflessly all their lives. The story covers alternately two years: 1937 and 1942. The events are described as perceived by the youthful hero, Igor' Baiukov. In 1937 his father is still a high Soviet official; in 1942 the father is a purged man. The arrest of Igor's father is not shown, but Trifonov renders well the atmosphere of terror and senseless cruelty which breeds fear and uncertainty among the Soviet people. Stalin himself is in the background, but the spirit of Stalinism makes everybody vulnerable. People arrested are forced to admit to crimes they have never committed. Later they recant, but they are never trusted again. In *Ischeznovenie*, which has many parallels with 'Dom na naberezhnoi' (The House on the Embankment; 1976) and *Vremia i mesto* (Time and Place; 1981), Trifonov makes a number of subtle observations about family relations in conditions of great political, social, and emotional strain. He explores the futile attempts of honest people to understand and to come to terms with criminal injustices of such magnitude that no human reason can fathom them. *Ischeznovenie* is a tribute to Trifonov's family – to their love, comradeship, and dedication. It is also a memorial to his parents, victimized in the Stalinist purges.

The Historical Past

Russian history is another subject that receives much attention in the prose of the 1980s. The Soviet historical novel has always reflected more accurately the times in which it has been written than the period that it describes. Although the same is true today, some contemporary writers of historical fiction, such as Bulat Okudzhava[36] and Iurii Davydov, are skilful writers, possessing a sense of measure and tact, while others, like Valentin Pikul', are poor craftsmen and, what is worse, tendentious students of Russian history.

Paradoxically, precisely for that reason Pikul' is perhaps more important than his skilled compatriots, if not as an artist, then at least as a social phenomenon and a writer of pulp literature. His works appeal mainly to the mass readership which seeks in a book nothing more than an engaging plot and an easy-to-read story that requires no concentration. The same reader is attracted by Pikul' 's strident nationalism and anti-semitism, his glorification of strong Russian leaders, and his exaltation of Russian military power. Pikul' 's prose is popular with Soviet readers because it reveals the seamy sides in the life of Russian rulers. It is promoted because it introduces the reader to the past glory of Russian arms and portrays Russian diplomacy as less corrupt and more skilful than that of Western powers. Furthermore, it presents Russian occupation and the conquest of foreign lands as a historically progressive act that has its parallels in contemporary Soviet history.

In 1979 Pikul' published the novel *U poslednei cherty. Roman khronika* (At the Last Mark: A Novel-Chronicle),[37] which was greeted enthusiastically in narrow-minded Russian nationalistic circles but denounced as poor art and an expression of growing Russian xenophobia by sober minds. *U poslednei cherty* is a novel about the last years of the Romanovs' rule. At the centre of the novel is the famous character of Rasputin, who allegedly exerts enormous influence over Tsar Nicholas's wife, Alexandra. By cleverly manipulating facts and randomly selecting detail, Pikul' advances the notion that Rasputin is an accomplice of international masonry and Zionism bent on destroying the

Russian empire. The tone of the novel is sarcastic and self-assured. The author tries to create the impression that he knows all the facts and that there can be no doubt as to the truthfulness of the picture he paints. But since the relationships of Alexandra with her husband and Rasputin are not described, the reader may wonder about the psychological justification for Rasputin's emotional hold over the tsarina. Furthermore, it appears from the novel that the Russian empire crumbles and disintegrates from within because its strength is undermined by internal enemies of foreign origin.

In his next novel, *Favorit. Roman-khronika vremeni Ekateriny II* (Favourite: Novel-Chronicle of the Times of Catherine II; 1984),[38] Pikul' gives a sketchy and tendentious account of eighteenth-century Russian history. The political role of Catherine II in building a strong Russian empire is stressed. Her deeds are perceived as a continuation of the task that Peter the Great failed to complete. Catherine's private life, her shortcomings and her behaviour as a woman of low morals, are described in restrained terms. But the real hero of the novel is Potemkin. He is Russian, while Catherine, although Russianized, is still foreign. Potemkin is hailed for defeating the Turks and the Crimean Tartars and for expanding the boundaries of Russia to the Black Sea. The structure of *Favorit* is similar to a kaleidoscopic cinema montage in which the action moves rapidly from one place to another, each time with a new set of characters. In fact, there are altogether too many characters in the novel, and unless one is familiar with eighteenth-century Russian history, one has a hard time following the course of events.

Pikul''s novels are inferior as art and inadequate as history. The author does not create artistic images but corrupts the images of historical figures. By skilfully selecting and manipulating historical facts, he creates a false picture of reality which appeals to the nationalistic emotions of the unsophisticated reader. The well-known Soviet writer V. Kaverin decries the fact that 'not a single literary scholar wants to consider why, for example, the novels by Pikul' which ... are a negative phenomenon, meet with such success? That surely speaks for the loss of taste! Of course his novels are entertaining, but they are commonplace. It is entertainment that has no connection with depth of conception. It is recreation and not a quest for knowledge ... It is precisely the mass culture that is worth so little.'[39]

The answer to Kaverin's question is provided by G. Belaia. She states bluntly that 'the success of Pikul' is a natural phenomenon: when there is a crisis in cultural development – pseudo-culture blossoms. It has always been that way, and in itself, it poses little danger. It becomes, however, dangerous when pseudo-culture is raised by critics to the level of a norm, of a canon.'[40] But that does not deter Pikul's official supporters, because for them the quality of his art is secondary to the social and political influence it exerts on the reader. They share with the author the same vision of Russia's past, because it serves well as a guide for its future.

The New Soviet Epic

In the 1960s and 1970s the predominant genre of Soviet narrative prose fiction was the story, novella, or povest'. With few minor exceptions the evolution of the novel lagged far behind. One Soviet critic has suggested that 'contemporary Russian prose lacks the necessary wide-reaching artistic and philosophic view of reality ... The writer and thinker in a [current] work of art are usually detached from each other. [This] situation prevents the attainment of major artistic objectives and hinders the process of passing on unchangeable and important spiritual values to future generations.'[41] Little has changed since. In 1987 another critic asserted that the Soviet 'novel cannot become the leading literary genre because it acutely lacks a developed and philosophically well grounded artistic conception, and its authors lack the mature skill required.'[42] Most contemporary Soviet literature seems deficient in the basic artistic qualities that characterize great novels: it is very topical; its relevance is limited in time and scope; most important, it lacks refinement and depth. The above notwithstanding, and despite a further decline in artistic quality, the 1980s have seen a revival of the novel.

Along with many established writers such as Iurii Bondarev, Daniil Granin, and Sergei Zalygin, who continue to work in this genre, Chingiz Aitmatov[43] and I. Grekova, as well as the poet Evgenii Evtushenko,[44] published their first novels in the 1980s. The traditional Russian multi-volume novel, which attempts to cover a slice of contemporary life in its totality, also reappeared. Anatolii Anan'ev's *Gody bez voiny* (Years without war; 1975–84)[45] is a good example. Its size and title are reminiscent of Leo Tolstoi's *War and Peace*, but Anan'ev lacks the insight, sophistication, and artistic talent of his great predecessor.

Gody bez voiny covers approximately one decade between the mid-1960s and the mid-1970s. Most of the action takes place in Moscow, but many scenes are set in provincial and rural Russia. Though the novel is of epic proportions, paradoxically it is difficult to identify its main protagonists. Some characters appear in the early parts of the novel only to re-emerge much later when they are almost forgotten. Others, including historical figures, such as Aleksei Kosygin and General

Charles de Gaulle, make a short appearance in order to move the plot along. The situation is further complicated by family relations so entangled that it is difficult to follow who is related to whom. For example, Natasha, the daughter of Colonel Korostylev, lives with Arsenii, an academic and former husband of Galina, who is in turn the adopted daughter of the retired rural party official Sukhogrudov. Galina's first husband, Lukin, a former protégé of Sukhogrudov, is the father of their teenaged son, Iurii, who has been adopted by Arsenii. Iurii comes in the night to rob his adopted father, who accidentally kills him. Arsenii is arrested but dies mysteriously in jail before his trial, and the plot can move on.

The intricate family relationships illustrate vividly the instability and disintegration of the Soviet family. There is not a single example of a strong, tight-knit family unit. The family abode is no longer a home, in the traditional sense, a source of spiritual and emotional strength. People are constantly in continuous motion, which is both fruitless and destructive. Even more distressing, the relationship between most unrelated characters is also far from amicable. The title of the novel indicates that the author intends to investigate a generation that matured in times of peace and lives in a society without antagonistic contradictions. The novel however, shows clearly that antagonism between classes has been replaced by conflict between individuals, which is just as dangerous and pernicious.

The complex family ties are used as a means of bringing together a number of diverse characters who deliberate on a variety of issues that concern Soviet people. Scholars, diplomats, party officials, journalists, painters, and construction, mining, and agricultural workers move through the pages of the novel, discussing culture, the arts, politics, and family problems. The question of agricultural production and of the peasants' attachment to the land receives much attention, and Anan'-ev's characters draw extensively on Tolstoi's experience in *Resurrection*. Similarly, the intellectual dialogue between the pochvenniki and zapadniki is widely discussed. Anan'ev satirizes both extremes, but his distaste for the neo-Russophile fringe of the Moscow intelligentsia is unmistakable. He ridicules those who write with fervour about the countryside but have never seen a Russian village; he derides those whose Russianness is limited to a visit to a restaurant that serves Russian national dishes.

Despite Anan'ev's attempts to introduce some positive notes, the novel's general picture of Soviet society is not very encouraging. Although the economy appears to function, the bureaucracy seems to work, and the government is in full control, individuals appear morally unstable and emotionally insecure. They are in constant pursuit of the momentary and the illusory, moved by jealousy, greed, and egotism. That is true of the Moscow intelligentsia, as well as of those from the countryside who move to the city in order to get an education. Boris Luk'ianov, a young diplomat and the son of a front-ranking collective farmer, is ashamed of his peasant background, and his brother Roman decides to desert his wife and two children in order to arrange for himself, in the big city, a marriage of convenience.

Anan'ev is often hailed in the Soviet Union for his attempt to create a synthetic picture of society. Indeed, the narrative is useful as a social document and a picture of Soviet reality, but as a work of art it has little to offer. The novel is a compilation of different topics, styles, and narrative techniques indiscriminately mixed together. It contains elements of byt, political, village, intellectual, and documentary prose, interspersed with a heavy dose of journalism. Its structure is baggy, the chronology is handled poorly, and the composition lacks compactness. *Gody bez voiny* is a descriptive rather than an analytical study. Anan'ev tells us a lot but shows us little. There is a lot of discussion, but little action in the novel, and the philosophizing is repetitious and superficial. Since the novel is set in today's reality and is based on actual events, it is not difficult to see the sympathies of the third-person omniscient narrator, who speaks for the author. Moreover, most characters are one-dimensional and are perceived by the reader the way the author himself sees them.

Anan'ev's attempt to create a modern epic of Soviet life is no great success. He neither places at the centre strong, well-developed, and memorable characters, who represent their generation and reflect their age, nor provides an important conflict. Rather, he presents a grey mass of indistinct characters who act little but talk a lot about issues that are of little relevance to ordinary people. No wonder such discussions excite no one, and such heroes are soon forgotten.

Sorokaletnie

Another new development in the last decade is the appearance of the so-called sorokaletnie, or forty-year-old, whose works are also dubbed 'Moscow school prose.' Both designations are misnomers, because most of these writers are closer to fifty than to forty, and many began publishing in the early 1960s. To the outside observer, the only thing they have in common is that, at present, all reside in the capital. In fact many are not Moscow natives, and their past reflects their thematic and artistic interests. Thus the works of Vladimir Lichutin and Vladimir Krupin are in the tradition of village prose. The writings of Vladimir Makanin and Ruslan Kireev are closer to city, or byt literature. Aleksandr Prokhanov deals with a variety of topics, most recently issues of international politics. The prose of Anatolii Kim is grotesque and surrealistic.[46] Anatolii Kurchatkin, Georgii Bazhenov, Anatolii Afanas'-ev, and others belong to the same generation.

One of the more interesting writers of this group is Vladimir Krupin. He was born in 1941 in the Viatka region in northern Russia. His works are close in spirit and subject-matter to those of Vasilii Belov, Astaf'ev, and Rasputin. The main hero of his 'Zhivaia voda' (Living Waters; 1980)[47] is the old man Kirpikov, who decides one day to stop smoking and drinking and begins, in his own simple peasant way, to search for the meaning of life. His evolution from a drunkard into a man concerned with goodness and common decency is at the centre of the plot. In the background is the juxtaposition of city and countryside and the contrast between the spirituality of the old and the materialistic practicality of the young. 'Zhivaia voda' is a refreshing piece of prose in which a realistic setting is combined with fantasy and hyperbole. Its language is colourful and close to the simple peasant's vernacular. It is a satire full of irony and comic intonations.

Until the appearance of 'Zhivaia voda,' Krupin's works were accorded little critical attention. 'Zhivaia voda' received in the main positive reviews, but Krupin was not that lucky with his next stories. 'Kolokol'-chik' (Handbell; 1981)[48] is a sketch in which Krupin describes a visit to his native village, for the celebration of the six hundredth anniversary of the nearby city of Viatka. He is asked to recite on the radio some of his stories, but when he wants to listen to his own reading, there is no spare radio and he is told to go outside to listen to the public address system. The handbell is a metaphor for radio: it makes much noise, but few listen to it. Krupin idealizes the old ways of the Russian village and takes pride in the fact that the Viatka is the only river in sight without a dam for a hydroelectric station. According to him, the intrusion of civilization destroys village life. He also makes derogatory remarks about other nationalities whose languages are allegedly inferior to Russian, and he blames foreign influence for the bad habits of smoking and drinking.

Krupin's next work, 'Sorokovoi den'' (The Fortieth Day; 1981),[49] is a narrative in epistolary form, composed of fourteen letters by a nameless journalist to his wife in Moscow. He uses his letters as a confession and form of escape and as a possibility to express himself fully, because he knows well that anything he writes for official publication is 'castrated' anyway.[50] He claims that 'one thinks one thing, says something else, and writes something completely different.'[51] He suggests that officially a journalist is supposed to occupy himself with the education of the reader's soul, but he asks: 'How can one educate others, when one is one-self shallow and base?'[52]

Krupin's reflections expose him to sharp criticism, because some of his statements question his ideological reliability. At one point he suggests that 'all culture originates from language, and language from nature, and nature from the cosmos. The rapprochement of nations will come about not through Esperanto, but first of all through national identification, later through religion, later through race, and later ... who knows how.'[53] Krupin forgets, of course, that according to Marxism people are identified, first of all, by their membership in a class, which overrides all other ethnic, national, and racial considerations. Krupin readily agrees with his critics. He is ever ready to admit his mistakes and recant his erroneous views.[54] But after having read 'Sorokovoi den',' one wonders whether one should take him seriously. After all, his narrator tells us unequivocally that he thinks one thing and tells us something completely different.

Georgii Bazhenov is another original writer of the same generation. His conflicts are close in spirit to those of city byt literature, but his plots are set in the Ural region and northern Russia. His characters are refreshingly different from those appearing in the stories set in the big cities of central Russia. They are bold, decisive, and ready to take risks. One of Bazhenov's best stories, 'Dasha' (Dasha; 1982),[55] is set in a northern logging camp. One of its main heroes, Fedor, is a gloomy, taciturn, and mysterious loner. He keeps to himself most of the time. Believing that man is evil, he trusts no one. The only woman in camp, Dasha, has a tender heart. She is sorry for Fedor and identifies with his suffering. Their relationship has for a while a humanizing effect on him, and they become intimate.

While on a visit to his native town, Fedor delivers a letter to the girl-friend of his fellow logger Dmitrii. Fedor deceives her by telling her that Dmitrii is unfaithful to her, and he seduces her – not because he desires her but mainly because he wants to prove to himself that all women are base and cannot be trusted. Upon his return, Fedor learns that Dasha is pregnant. He is ecstatic because he has feared that he will never be able to father a child. In the mean time Dmitrii finds out the truth about Fedor's behaviour and tells Dasha. She induces an abortion and dies shortly thereafter. The novella ends in tragedy. Dasha, the only positive character, suffers through no fault of her own. The good is destroyed by evil forces. Fedor, who has gained most from Dasha's tenderness and understanding, is punished as well. His wicked deeds are avenged by fate. Evil is repaid with evil. People cannot go through life committing evil without receiving retribution.

Bazhenov's plots have much potential. His stories are truthful to life, but his prose lacks psychological insight. We do not learn what his characters look like or what they think; all we know is what they do. To make up for his inadequate narrative skills, Bazhenov complicates his plots, places his heroes in extreme situations, and applies many melodramatic devices. His stories abound in scenes of violence, murder, alcoholism, and infidelity. In his short novella 'Vozvrashchenie liubvi' (The Return of Love; 1982),[56] two different women attempt to commit suicide for inadequately explained reasons. Bazhenov's prose reflects the life of the middle class in provincial Russia. People face daily problems similar to those encountered by members of the Moscow intelligentsia, but they handle them differently. They are less manipulative and hypocritical, more honest with themselves, and straightforward with their adversaries.

The prose of Ruslan Kireev, another member of the 'sorokaletnie,' is more intellectual than that of Bazhenov, and it aims at sophistication. His novel *Podgotovitel'naia tetrad'* (The Rough Note-book; 1981)[57] is a first-person narrative with many philosophical digressions and references to Western writers and thinkers. The main hero, Viktor Karmanov, is a journalist and a fiction writer. He has been twice divorced and married again to the same woman. He is a man who strives for nothing and asks little from life. He appears always to be getting ready for something new and important, but inadvertently he accomplishes nothing. In other words, he is a notorius failure. Karmanov is contrasted with Svechkin, a man without much education, but one who is promoted from a lowly job in the administration to the position of manager of all the clothing factories in twon. Svechkin is a go-getter who knows how the system works and is able to make good use of it to his own advantage. Both the weak Karmanov and the strong Svechkin are abused by their unfaithful wives. Svechkin's fortitude and determination do not extend within the walls of his apartment, where his wife, El'vira, rules completely.

One of the most noted members of the 'sorokaletnie' is Vladimir Makanin. His first novel, *Priamaia liniia* (Straight Line), was published in 1967. His plots are original and full of dramatic tension, and many of his characters are in transition from one mode of life to another. One of his best-known novellas is 'Gde skhodilos' nebo s kholmami' (Where the

Sky Met the Hills; 1984).[58] Its main hero, Georgii Bashilov, is a well-known composer and musician of well over fifty. He is a native of a remote workers' settlement in the Ural, which is rich in musical traditions and famous for its good singers.

The young Bashilov, an orphaned child with great musical ability, has been taken to Moscow to study. The mature Bashilov becomes famous for his compositions, which take root in the folklore of his native settlement and in the songs of its inhabitants. Paradoxically, the development of Bashilov's skill is accompanied by the disintegration of the singing traditions of the native villagers. Some of them, as well as Bashilov himself, regard this decline as a result of the departure of those who are most gifted, who have allegedly stolen and carried off something that belongs to the people. The old Bashilov is overwhelmed by a gnawing sense of personal guilt and fear of retribution. He goes to his native settlement with the intention of reviving old traditions by starting a children's choir. But one cannot return to the past, and Bashilov is ridiculed by the young inhabitants of the village. The story ends on a symbolic, perhaps optimistic note. The only one to join Bashilov in his song is the village idiot. But their voices are joined by a third, that of an unnamed and unseen boy soprano.

Makanin addresses in his novella a number of significant issues. Most important, perhaps, is the question of the intricate peculiarities of the creative process as they relate to the artist's skill, talent, personal background, and experience. It is accepted today that most artists draw inspiration from their roots and return to the people a new art that is more refined and sophisticated, but different from the original. This transformation of the individual artist is usually the result of mass migration, which causes the dispersal and cultural disintegration of generations who have given rise to and perpetuated the people's artistic lore. The personal tragedy of Bashilov reflects this complex relationship which is part of the general predicament of people and society in an age of industrialization.

The prose of the 'sorokaletnie' has lately received much attention in Soviet literary criticism. After all, this is the generation expected to replace the recently departed Kataev, Sholokhov, Abramov, and Trifonov. Some critics hail their works as the great new achievement of Soviet literature, but others warn that it is still too early to view their prose as great art. Most of their works, which portray people unable to cope with the complicated social conditions of life today, are criticized for a 'laxity in the authorial position, the predominance of "ambivalent" heroes ... and the prevalence of self-contained byt.'[59] It is suggested that the 'sorokaletnie' have created a new kind of 'superfluous man,' who is a 'vacillating' hero. He is a passive man without commitment, who refuses to make a choice between good and evil. Vadim Sokolov designates such works 'the prose of "group egotism"' and suggests that these characters 'vacillate' because their creators also do so. They observe reality from the outside, refusing to take a stand.[60]

Among the writers under forty whose works appeared in print for the first time in the 1980s, Tat'iana Tolstaia, Sergei Kaledin, and Viacheslav P'etsukh are mentioned most often. Tolstaia made her literary début in 1983, P'etsukh his in 1986, and Kaledin his in 1987. Tolstaia and Kaledin are in their late thirties; P'etsukh is somewhat younger. Kaledin's first story, 'Smirennoe kladbishche' (Humble Graveyard; 1987),[61] appeared nine years after his graduation from the literary institute. It is a 'physiological' sketch with some psychological insights, set in one of the Moscow cemeteries. To the uninitiated reader a cemetery may appear a peaceful place of eternal rest. To bury the dead is a social service, but it is also a job, and a means of making a living for those who work at the graveyard. Kaledin introduces the reader to an array of interesting characters. Many of those who inhabit this murky world are social outcasts, alcoholics, and derelicts, in conflict with society and with the law. Others are there with the sheer purpose of making money. Kaledin is a good observer. He knows his characters well; they may be alienated and corrupt, but they are all human, each with his own nature and character traits.

The cemetery in 'Smirennoe kladbishche' is a microcosm of Soviet society. It functions according to the same rules and morals that govern other segments of life, but the characters portrayed there are new social types in Soviet literature. They may be alienated outcasts, and people residing on the fringes of society, but they are still part of the system that makes their existence possible, perhaps even necessary.

Viacheslav P'etsukh is a young writer of some promise whose prose is often surrealistic and who is concerned with the eternal questions of goodness, freedom, and happiness. His recent stories, published in *Novyi mir*,[62] are parables, set in the realities of Soviet daily life, but their meaning transcends the confines of time and space. In 'Bilet' (Lottery Ticket), P'etsukh develops the Dostoevskian notion that there is no real happiness without unhappiness. And in 'Novyi zavod' (The New Plant), he suggests that true freedom is possible only if one avoids becoming a slave to job, family, or social convention. Only work that is independent in spirit and does not stifle the aspirations of the individual is an expression of real freedom. Both stories criticize the rigid social framework of contemporary society, which deprives people of their individuality. The plots of P'etsukh's stories are original, but his images are not as vivid as one could wish, and his style lacks polish.

There are a number of established Soviet writers who cannot be identified with one particular theme or genre, but whose prose is topical and timely. One such writer is Daniil Granin. His novel *Kartina* (Picture; 1980)[63] is set in the provincial town of Lykov. Its main hero is Losev, the local district executive committee chairman. According to the city plan, a new industrial project is to be constructed in an area that is connected with the historical and cultural past of the town. At first Losev is in favour of industrialization, but then, under the influence of a beautiful painting of the site marked for destruction, he changes his mind and leads the fight for the preservation of historical monuments and the environment. The subject of the novel is not new. The clash between encroaching technological progress and the desire to protect nature and the past is one of the main topics of 'village prose'. Here Granin assumes a centrist position in this conflict. Losev acts not because he is emotionally attached to a cause but because he believes in justice and wants to live according to his conscience. That is not easy, however, because, as one of his superiors tells him, conscience cannot be translated into production quotas or the fulfilment of plans.

Under the surface there are two issues that concern Granin. One is the overpowering force of artistic beauty which inspires Losev and leads to a change in his attitudes, and the other is the search for a meaning to life. The novel implies that most people are so caught up in their daily struggle for survival that real life passes them by. Losev's refusal to follow the easy and well-worn path is also an attempt to find meaning in life. Granin's greatest talent lies in describing the daily workings of the local Soviet bureaucracy. His criticism is always low-key. He does not attack the establishment directly. Instead he shows that one has to know whom and when to please and to be ready to sacrifice personal opinion for the sake of promotion.

Granin's most recent povest', or novella, 'Zubr' (Bison; 1987),[64] was greeted by the Soviet intelligentsia with great interest. It relates the life of the biologist N.V. Timofeev, a victim of Stalin's terror, who was sent in 1925 to work in the West, in Germany, but was arrested and sent to Siberia on his return home after the war. In 1956 he was finally permitted to return to Moscow. Granin somewhat idealizes Timofeev, apparently with the purpose of uncovering the true nature of Trofim Lysenko and his followers, who, by advancing their pseudo-scientific theories in biology

and genetics, set back the development of Soviet science. In 'Zubr'
Granin takes us back to the 1920s and 1930s. He attempts to restore to
favour members of the White intelligentsia. He renders well the
atmosphere in Moscow and in Berlin between 1937 and 1942, when the
Soviets were purging their greatest minds, including academician N.I.
Vavilov, while supporting Nazi Germany in its war against the West.
Granin sketches only a vague, impressionistic picture of that period, but
it is not often that Soviet foreign policy is described in a tone of sarcasm
and derision.

Another writer who diversifies his creative output is Boris Mozhaev,
previously identified with 'village prose'. His story 'Poltora kvadratnykh
metra, povest' – shutka v chetyrnadtsati chastiakh s eiplogom i
snovideniem' (One and a Half Square Metres: A Tale-Joke in Fourteen
Parts with an Epilogue and Dream; 1982)[65] is a satire of the provincial
bureaucracy. The plot is set in motion by a ludicrous incident connected
with the installation of a door in the main hero's apartment, which is
used by the author as an excuse to expose most city officials as lazy and
corrupt thieves and drunkards. Most of the bureaucrats speak in
elevated language but act in a destructive manner. They abuse the law
and the power of their office; they destroy nature and the environment.
Symbolically the town is called Rozhnov, from the Russian 'rozhon,' to
ask for trouble. The name of the police superintendent, Zhulikov, evokes
the Russian 'zhulik,' swindler or rogue. The main hero, Poluboiarnikov,
is regarded as a trouble-maker and is finally driven out of town. Indeed,
Poluboiarnikov is a habitual writer of complaints, yet most of his ideas
and recommendations are logical and make sense. The narrator
caricatures and ridicules the local officials, but the realistic detail
presented is true to life. The povest', narrated in the first person, is
dubbed a joke, and a special note 'From the Author' is appended, in which
Mozhaev tries to soften the message and inject some optimism. The
serious reader will not be misled by such an ending. It is clear that
Mozhaev had difficulty with the publication of his narrative and was
forced to append the conclusion in order to mollify the editors and
censors.

Andrei Bitov is another important writer who is outside the mainstream of official Soviet prose.[66] His stories are well constructed and
balanced, his style has a peculiar lyrical quality, and his prose is
autobiographical and intellectual. The main subject of Bitov's prose is
the intricate relationship between people and nature, which he usually
discusses within the context of cultural evolution, intellectual thought,
and the creative potentialities of individuals. Most of Bitov's narratives

are almost plotless and provide no answer to the questions posed. The problems discussed belong usually to the 'eternal' or 'cursed' issues, which have beset mankind from time immemorial and have no readily available solutions.

Bitov's most recent povest', 'Chelovek v peizazhe' (Man in the Landscape; 1987),[67] is stylistically and thematically similar to his earlier works but with a more clearly defined plot and narrative structure and some intriguing detail. The intellectual essence of the story is expressed in the dialogue between the first-person narrator – the lyrical 'I' – who obviously speaks for the author, and the landscape painter Pavel Petrovich, a notorious alcoholic, who is, however, little affected by his addiction and remains lucid at all times. Bitov has probably invented the landscape painter in order to reveal his own internal dialogue and facilitate the transmission of his own views.

Bitov muses in the story about the essential duality of people and about the relationship of the process of natural creation and the creative genius of the individual. True genius is rare, and its suffering is great. But most important to Pavel Petrovich is the idea. The complexity of the artistic process, according to him, is expressed in the fact that 'to embody the image or the word means not only to recreate it, but to *falsify* it as well, making it thus conform with the initial intentions'[68] of the artist. Bitov addresses here the issue of the relationship between idea, perception, reflection, and the record of reality. The artist's imagination transforms reality, but there is always a disparity between the artist's perception and his record of reality – between the artist's initial intention and his final creation.

This recent povest' is precise, stimulating, and infused with irony. But it is also challenging. It gives food for thought. No wonder Bitov's controversial prose has been shunned for years by Soviet editors and publishers. Even today some well-known Soviet writers, including Georgii Semenov, admit that Bitov's prose is beyond them.[69] It is complex and requires careful reading and interpretation.

This brief survey of the Soviet literary scene has sketched only a general picture of contemporary Soviet prose, which is vibrant, dynamic, and challenging. Soviet writers investigate human nature and human relationships in the shifting social and political conditions of the 1980s. Until recently the main problems discussed in Soviet literature centred on the conflict between the individual and society. Now a new subject has been added: the individual's own internal conflict.

61 The literary scene

Writers today work in a variety of genres and styles and apply diverse narrative techniques, but social issues are their main subject, and most works of prose fiction are replete with journalism. This is true of the writers discussed here, as well as of the most gifted Soviet authors such as Chingiz Aitmatov, Valentin Rasputin, Vasil' Bykov, and Viktor Astaf'ev. Most of the works discussed in this introductory survey fall short of the requirements for good art, but even the recent works of Aitmatov and Rasputin, which are discussed in the following chapters, show how social pressures intrude into the creative process and lead to the sacrifice of artistry for the sake of social and ideological relevance.

3 The Passing Generation

End of an Era: Valentin Kataev (1897–1986)

Valentin Kataev, one of the few surviving first-generation Soviet writers, was in his ninth decade as prolific as ever and active till the very last days of his life. He celebrated his eightieth birthday in January 1977. After that, he published in *Novyi mir* a number of important narratives of different length and significance. Of these, the most important is the controversial *Almaznyi moi venets* (My Diamond Crown; 1978),[1] which generated lively but far from unanimous critical reaction. It was followed by 'Uzhe napisan Verter' (Werther Has Already Been Written; 1980),[2] *Iunosheskii roman moego starogo druga Sashi Pchelkina rasskazannyi im samim* (The Youthful Novel of My Old Friend Sasha Pchelkin, Told by Himself; 1982),[3] 'Spiashchii' (The Sleeping Man; 1985),[4] and 'Sukhoi liman' (The Dry Estuary; 1986).[5]

The recent works of Kataev, in particular *Almaznyi moi venets*, are similar to his narratives of the mid-1960s and early 1970s, especially *Sviatoi kolodets* (The Holy Well; 1966)[6] and *Trava zabveniia* (The Grass of Oblivion; 1967),[7] which are regarded as a turning-point in his creative activity and heralded the appearance of a 'new Kataev.' These works are identified with the writer's innovative and experimental development of style and methods of narration, as well as with a new approach to plot construction and subject-matter. In addition, beginning with the mid-1960s, Kataev's personal life and past experiences become the main focus of his fiction. Although Kataev's recent works appear to deal with the past of his contemporaries, he himself is always at the centre of events, and everything that happens gravitates around his personality. Instead of acting as an impartial and objective observer of people and events, Kataev assumes the roles of judge, prosecutor, and advocate.

He manipulates past events and records them in a manner that seems to suit his interests best. No wonder Kataev's subjective portrayal of the 1920s often generates severe criticism from friends, well-wishers, and adversaries alike.

In *Trava zabveniia*, Kataev juxtaposes the poets Bunin and Maiakovskii, the two mutually exclusive great influences on his life. In *Almaznyi moi venets*, Kataev paints, in the form of fictionalized memoirs, a picture of the literary byt of the 1920s. The narrative is composed of impressionistic and subjective portraits of the most important literary personalities of the decade. Most of them appear under pseudonyms, but the true identities of Maiakovskii, Esenin, Bagritskii, Pasternak, Babel', Zoshchenko, Aseev, Bulgakov, Olesha, Il'f, and Petrov, among others, are easily recognizable.

The genre of memoirs is at present quite popular in the Soviet Union. Writers and actors, generals and bureaucrats, including the late Leonid Brezhnev, reminisce about their past and leave to posterity what seems to them to be – or what they would like us to believe is – a realistic picture of their past. Kataev does not pretend. He rejects the notion that *Almaznyi moi venets* contains his memoirs, but he refuses to identify its genre, leaving the reader puzzled and guessing. Kataev begs his readers not to perceive his work as reminiscences. He claims that he cannot stand memoirs and that his work is the result of his soaring fantasy, based on and rooted in real events, 'which his memory could probably not retain correctly.'[8] According to the writer, the narrative is 'not a novel, not a story, not a novella, not a poem, not reminiscences, not memoirs, not a lyrical diary ... So what is it? I do not know!' He explains: 'An idea uttered is a lie ... but a lie that is more truthful than the real truth. The truth that is born in the secret convolutions of my mechanism of imagination ... In any event, I guarantee that everything written here is undeniable truth, and, at the same time, the most obvious fantasy.'[9]

One cannot blame Kataev for his refusal to vouch for the authenticity of the events described. Only a perfect photographic memory could preserve the original substance of occurrences and facts that took place many years ago. Imperfect human memory is affected by constant erosion. Time changes our perception of the past; the memories of events of half a century ago are filtered through the prism of the author's life experience and influenced by the conscious objectives of his art. Nonetheless, since the work of any writer is at least partially conscious and since the prototypes for Kataev's heroes are well-known literary figures, the author's ethical responsibility to those he claims to have been his friends and to posterity should lead him to attempt to give a full, balanced, and objective picture of his contemporaries – friends and adversaries alike. There is much doubt as to whether Kataev discharges this responsibility to the best of his ability. Most of the poets discussed died or perished young; several committed suicide; others were purged and disappeared behind the barbed wire of labour camps. But the author devotes many pages to unimportant events and trivial details from their daily lives without mentioning, even in passing, what is most important: the reasons for the tragic end of these talented individuals. What are the causes of the destruction and the premature departure of the flower of twentieth-century Russian poetry?

The Soviet critic V. Kardin is correct in questioning Kataev's sincerity when Kataev detaches discussion of the poets' daily lives from the literary and political problems that shape their tragic destinies. Kardin decries the fact that one may deduce from Kataev's prose that in those days 'there were no reasons for personal dramas, "self-destruction," or all kind of complications.'[10] Kataev posthumously attaches funny pseudonyms to his closest friends and often shows, not necessarily in the best light, only one side of their personalities. 'The hero narrator seems to continue his old biting attacks, his conceited competitiveness. This process, however, is unfortunately one-sided,'[11] since the people described cannot defend themselves; they are long since dead.

Kardin's well-founded criticism notwithstanding, *Almaznyi moi venets* has some merit. Kataev comments here on matters that literary histories fail to write about. He shows the hard labour of artistic creation; he illustrates the total dedication of the poet to his craft, failing to point, however, to the social pressures that demand the poets' submission. Of those discussed in the narrative, Kataev was the only one still alive. He survived the purges because he could respond to the needs of the times, because his talent showed enough agility and flexibility to adapt, because he was able to compromise, and most of all because he was lucky.

On the surface, *Almaznyi moi venets* is also an example of the author's adaptation to current circumstances. But it is more than that. It could also be read as an expression of Kataev's guilty conscience; hence, his desire to immortalize those who were for years downgraded and repudiated for no reason other than their total dedication to their craft. It is said that writing poetry is not a job, but a destiny. Kataev's friends lived out their destinies to the fullest; they accepted fate, but did not compromise. The expression of their innermost feelings and sensations became their duty, and they perished. In Kataev's case, reason and duty to the state overshadowed his impulsive and irrational talent, and he survived to pay guarded and careful homage to comrades and intimate friends from the days of his youth. It is not much, but apparently not much more is possible yet. The time is not yet ripe for the whole truth to be told and, besides, the old and mature Kataev is no longer the Kataev of the 1920s.

Artistically, *Almaznyi moi venets* is a combination of biography, autobiography, literary history, reminiscences, literary byt of the 1920s, and contemplations on literary theory and artistic creativity – all of them fictionalized and indiscriminately intertwined. There is no consistency or chronology. The plot is held together by the association of many unrelated events, places, people, and experiences. All of these merge in the author's mind, which in turn is influenced by his creative imagination. The narration resembles a sequence of internal monologues in which the stream-of-consciousness technique prevails. There is constant transition from one place to another, from one time period to another. Scenes, images, events, and people, as in a cinematic montage, glide in space and time, time indefinable, eternal, static, and at the same time moving. First-person narration gives a semblance of authenticity, but 'imperfect memory' is at the root of this manifold story.

Structurally, this free and disorderly outpouring of a seeming mixture of fact and fantasy is framed between the narrator's two visits to Paris, some fifty years apart. On his first visit, the narrator meets a French sculptor searching for a special material worthy of rendering the leading luminaries of Russian culture. In the concluding pages the narrator is back in Paris. He meets again the sculptor, who happily reports that he has found a substance worthy of the people to be immortalized in his art. It is the same material that forms the physical foundation of the universe. The narrator goes into the park and sees – or, rather, has a vision of – the sculpture-images of his dead friends portrayed, discussed, and imagined in the preceding pages. He encounters there kliuchik (The Key) Olesha, sineglazyi (Blue-Eyes) Bulgakov, konarmeets (Cavalryman) Babel', and many others. They are all dead, but they are immortal. Their silence passes judgment on all who try to justify their own survival. Paradoxically, Kataev's long discourse about his dead, yet immortal friends and contemporaries sounds shallow in comparison with their silence. From the abyss of death they rise to the glory of immortality and eternity, while Kataev, by virtue of his very existence, continues to be fallible.

However, Kataev is not only fallible; he is also accountable. He has to satisfy his own conscience in relation to the past and to account for his present actions to ever-watching mentors. His next narrative, his first to appear in the 1980s, 'Uzhe napisan Verter,' could not be published without an editorial introduction, which attempts to set the tone and to clarify the author's intentions, possibly different from what appears on the surface. The first passage of the introduction is basically correct: 'At the root of this prose are not definite reminiscences, but memories of a whole epoch. It unites in an odd way things that have been seen, lived through, felt, and read, as well as things that have been thought out, guessed, and are the product of imagination.'[12] These words summarize the essence of the 'new Kataev's' style.

The second part of the introduction is quite different. It emphasizes the timeliness of the narrative and tries to explain its political and ideological significance. The editors find such an explanation indispensable, because the author deals here with a very sensitive issue: the atrocities of the Cheka in the immediate post-revolutionary period. Despite the facts that all evil in the story is identified with the name of Trotskii and that the majority of culprits are not 'honest Communists,' but Socialist Revolutionaries with Jewish names who try to gain control of and pervert the revolution, further explanation is required because the activity of the Soviet secret police is usually taboo and not a subject for fiction. The Soviet reader cannot be trusted with the important task of separating the heroes from the villains; therefore, an editorial introduction is needed to make clear who is a good murderer and who is a bad one.

The uninitiated reader may indeed wonder about the reasons for Kataev's sudden interest in political issues and the description of the criminal wickedness of the secret police. One may only suspect that this is a device to distract the attention of some suspicious readers from the central drama played out in the shadow of the 'revolutionary' struggle.

'Uzhe napisan Verter' is the story of a young cadet, Dima, the son of a lawyer who abandons his wife to join the Whites. The young man, an aspiring painter, at one time toys with the idea of joining an anti-revolutionary group, but he never becomes involved in its activities. He marries instead an attractive woman, without realizing that she works for the Cheka and that her only purpose is to spy on him. Betrayed by her, he is condemned to die in a Cheka garage together with other counter-revolutionaries. His desperate mother wants to save him at any price. She persuades an old acquaintance, a writer and former Socialist Revolutionary who spent time in exile together with the present head of the Cheka, to entreat the latter to spare her son. The young cadet is saved, but his name appears on the list of those executed, posted the next day in town. The frantic woman commits suicide, and Dima returns home to find her dead. When it is discovered that a traitor has been set free, all those involved in the case, including Dima's wife, are put to death. Years later the executioner is also killed for his role in assisting the cause of Trotskii.

The tragic story of a loving mother who attempts to save her only son but who destroys herself in the process has all the ingredients of human drama. She is old, helpless, and deceived by her husband. Her young and inexperienced son is her only succour and hope for the future. Her ingenuity and sheer determination help save his life, but a strange twist of fate destroys her hopes, and life becomes meaningless for her.

The predicament of the executioners is not much better. Most are idealistic and dedicated to the cause they serve, but they are used as passive tools in a game they cannot control and the rules of which they do not understand. They commit evil while thinking that they are doing good, without realizing that evil breeds evil and that murder leads to further killings.

The whole story appears to be the author's dream, his nightmare. He wakes up and is relieved that he is alive and well in a peaceful world. There is little consistency in the narrative, and no clear distinction is made between the real and the imagined. Narrators change; scenes and images replace each other indiscriminately. Scenes of crime and violent murder alternate with pictures of dedication and tender love, creating a general atmosphere of instability and insecurity, of a sensation of helplessness and lack of direction. The conclusion of the story is not very optimistic, and, from the point of view of the editors of *Novyi mir*, it justifies in a way the introduction. The narrator wakes up in severe pain, but he is relieved of the universal pain of human suffering caused by 'wars, revolutions, political murder and executions, counter-revolutions, dictatorships, Auschwitzes, Hiroshimas, Nagasakis.'[13] The narrator decries the useless suffering of man victimized for no guilt of his own, but he is careful to condemn those who kill for an idea. He tells them in his conclusion: 'You will not waver when killing a human being, but you, the martyrs of a dogma, are also victims of the age.'[14]

Kataev tries hard to vilify the Trotskyites and the Socialist Revolutionaries and portrays them as enemies of the people. But the reader cannot help but be moved by the personal tragedies of Dima and his mother. Besides, under the surface lurks the idea that the crimes committed during the revolution started a chain reaction, leading to constant abuse of power and many more executions and murders. The removal of the Trotskyites and the Socialist Revolutionaries from positions of power in the young Soviet state did not stop further atrocities and purges, which lasted till the final days of Stalin's rule. Kataev is well aware of this situation, and his attempt to justify those who kill for an idea by calling them blind 'victims of the age' is not very applicable to Soviet conditions. Most purges and murders in the Soviet Union have been committed precisely because those in control of the party and the state relinquished their faith in the dogma, holding on instead to power at any cost.

Kataev's next novel, *Iunosheskii roman moego starogo druga Sashi Pchelkina, rasskazannyi im samim*, is stylistically similar to his other mature works. Still, it exhibits some notable differences. First, it has a difinite narrative structure, and the plot is set, with minor exceptions, in a precise chronological framework. Next, unlike the other works discussed here, in which the narrator plays a central but often inconspicuous role, its autobiographical main protagonist, Pchelkin, is also narrator. The relationship between fantasy and reality, and between creative imagination and fact, is also different. Many events and experiences related in the novel are well known from the author's biography, but the narrator, gives, in the form of fiction, a new assessment of these events and sheds new light on Kataev's youth.

The novel begins with the description of a meeting between two old acquaintances – the narrator Aleksandr Sergeevich Pchelkin,[15] and an elderly woman, Min'ona. She returns to him letters he wrote her many years earlier, in 1916, when he served in an army detachment commanded by her father. The letters are reproduced in the novel and form the structural framework of the plot.

The story is narrated on many different levels. First, there are the letters. In them, the narrator relates his experiences in the army, which he joined as a volunteer after having failed in his studies at school. Then there are reminiscences of the old narrator, who gives additional details and qualifies and interprets the events described in the letters. In addition, using a sub-plot that weaves through the whole novel, the narrator tells us about his deep, irrational love for a certain girl who does not even know of his great passion. Finally, perhaps most important, there is the author's psychological investigation of man at war and his re-evaluation of past political and historical events.

In the context of apparently innocent reminiscences about his youth, the narrator probes people's fear of death and investigates their lives in conditions of constant danger. Contemporary Soviet war prose contains only one character whose emotions and feelings are reminiscent of Pchelkin's: the protagonist of Bulat Okudzhava's 'Bud' zdorov, shkoliar!' (Good Luck, Schoolboy!; 1961). Both are scared to death and want to live; both are sorry for themselves and are not ashamed to admit that they would rather be anywhere else than fighting a useless war.

If we accept that the narrator's views are similar to those of the author, the Kataev who emerges from the pages of the novels is a convinced pacifist and fatalist. War, according to Pchelkin, is 'a complete fraud,'[16] which causes him 'to lose his faith.'[17] It does not spare anyone. The victors and the defeated are equally affected by it. It destroys not only man's body but also his soul.[18] Thus Pchelkin the pacifist preaches peace at any price, while Pchelkin the fatalist admits that he is helpless in his efforts to attain it. He recognizes that he is a blind tool of destiny and that he can do little to change the course of history.[19] Kataev advocates here the Tolstoian notion that chance determines everything, that free will is an illusion, and that one false step in life can change its course in an unexpected direction, from which there is no return.[20]

Kataev's last novel is, in a sense, an afterthought. In his previous works he tried to rethink his past, redefine his position in life, and come to terms with himself and with his deceased friends. Now he admits that it has been a futile task, because whatever one does it is impossible to run away from oneself: life inevitably catches up and takes its course.

Deming Brown suggests that Kataev's recent prose is 'a subjective attempt to recapture and understand past time.'[21] But Kataev himself tells us that there is no time, and he supports this allegation by quoting Dostoevskii, who claims that 'time does not exist, time is a figure, time is the relationship of being to non-being.'[22] Indeed, as an abstract notion, time is an intangible entity: it is infinite in its duration and it has an indefinitely continued existence. But, as Kataev showed convincingly in his 1932 novel Vremia, vpered! (Time, Forward!), there is also definite time. This is time with limits, time that is related to events, actions, and experiences, time that determines the mode of human interaction in a definite social environment. This is the time that Kataev wants to recapture and re-evaluate, and the instrument of this recovery is memory. Leo Tolstoi once suggested that memory destroys time – hence memory is an expression of man's victory over time. But it appears that this victory is illusory, because time is indefinite and infinite, while human memory is of limited duration and fallible.

Commenting on his letters of many years earlier, Pchelkin says: 'Memory removes the misty cover from events and discloses some artificiality in them; some empty spots which, despite an obvious and determined desire to be honest to the end, were then consciously or unconsciously concealed and only now filled in.'[23] In essence, time removes the bias from one's perception of the past. That may be so. However, Kataev tells us that the old bias is replaced by a new and different one, influenced and formed by new experiences and events and by the constant process of maturing and ageing. This new bias, the view of the past from present positions, is ever present in all of Kataev's recent works. It is as if the 'new' and old Kataev would place himself within the environment of his youth and judge his past life with his present-day values.

Kataev does not always judge harshly the contemporaries of his youth. He has many warm words for Olesha, Bagritskii, and others. In this respect his memory is a memorial to those who did not survive to reap the rewards their talents certainly deserved. They have 'all left for the country of eternal spring, from which there is no return.'[24] The motif of 'eternal spring' recurs time and again in Kataev's recent works. It is a symbol of the continuous motion and renewal that lead to inevitable death, and it signifies immortality for those who have earned it. The writer's continuous search for this 'eternal spring' is also a search for his own immortality and for a place in the pantheon of Russian letters, next to his famous friends.

Kataev's prose of the last two decades has a gliding quality. It flows smoothly, moving effortlessly from place to place, from one era to another. Kataev claims that he has lived always in two dimensions, the real and the imagined. 'Only the blending of the two elements can create an art that is truly beautiful.'[25] This, according to Kataev, is the essence of his new literary school, called mauvisme, which on the surface advocates one's right to write badly. Much has been written about mauvisme,[26] and Kataev himself made a number of contradictory statements about it to pacify annoying interviewers, but much remains unclear. On one occasion Kataev terms mauvisme 'nothing else than a polemical joke ... an expression of his desire for new forms.' He suggests even that 'in relation to Derzhavin, Pushkin was also to some degree a mauviste.'[27] In another place Kataev advocates the need for a new innovative prose and asserts that 'it is impossible to write any longer in our old ways. We continue to follow slavishly classic examples; we repeat ourselves much too often ... As far as possible, in my recent works, which some call the "New Kataev" ... I search for new paths in literature, and this, I think, does not contradict the principles of socialist realism, but rather enriches it.'[28]

Consequently mauvisme, according to Kataev, is connected with the rejection of all 'conventions devised by literary scholars and critics, who have no sense of beauty. And what can be more beautiful than artistic freedom? ... It is a shift from a search for beauty to a search for authenticity, even if it is very bad.'[29] It is obvious that these different explanations of the essence of mauvisme confuse the issue more than they clarify it; here, one has to agree with the Soviet critic N. Krymova, who suggests that 'if it is true that style is the form of behaviour in literature, then "mauvisme" is the form of evasion and elusion.'[30]

Kataev's experimental and innovative approach to prose begins to manifest itself clearly after his departure from *Iunost'*, where he spent seven years as chief editor (from 1955 to 1962). His contact with representatives of the 'young prose' of the early 1960s, who published most of their early works in *Iunost'*, may have influenced the transformation of Kataev's style. And if mauvisme means writing badly, then, according to Kataev himself, 'there is only one person in the whole world who can write worse than me, and that's my friend the great Anatolii Gladilin, mauviste number 1'[31] (a steady contributor to *Iunost'* who was expelled from the Soviet Union for his literary nonconformism). By Western, and even Russian pre-revolutionary, standards there is little new in Kataev's rhythmic, subjective, and very intimate prose or in his narratives without plot or chronology. But in Soviet conditions, Kataev's recent works break new ground and challenge established literary criteria, giving the writer an elusive means of self-expression not available to the conventional Soviet realist. Hence the signs of a certain duality in Kataev's recent works, of a split between duty and feeling, between reason and sensation. Much is said in his subjective narratives, but much more is left untold. Kataev is often criticized both for what he writes and for what he omits, and his works are open to different critical interpretations.

Overtly, there is no intended anti-Soviet message in Kataev's recent works, and there is no reason to question the sincerity of his convictions. Kataev was a member of the Communist party from 1958. He was over sixty when he joined it, and he tried to serve the party well. He criticized the West, Soviet dissidents, and exiles from the Soviet Union. Speaking about the Russian writer Kuprin, who returned from exile to die in Russia, Kataev said: 'Even the most talented people who by misfortune lose contact with their motherland and its people become soon degraded and turn into philistines.'[32] But Kataev was born long before the revolution and was educated in the old Russian cultural traditions, and these influences lingered. As Violetta Iverni writes in *Kontinent*: "Kataev is entirely a Soviet man ... His world outlook has been developed by a state that is based on violence. But his attitudes were born before the state he loves so much came into existence, and they remain attitudes of a free man. Mauvisme is an attempt to reconcile these two mutually exclusive categories. In a sense, as a method of reflecting Soviet reality, Kataev's mauvisme is quite successful. It is not a direct reflection, but rather an oblique one; not a projection but a reflecting prism.'[33]

The case of Kataev exemplifies vividly the Marxist notion that being determines thinking: that practical reality influences and shapes one's ideas. Indeed, experience and circumstances of life condition one's reasoning. But man is both rational and irrational, both conscious and subconscious, and no element of the past can be wiped out entirely from his intellectual faculties. It appears that, as in the case of many contemporary Soviet writers, Kataev the man is a conscientious Soviet citizen, dedicated to the cause of the party, while Kataev the artist seeks freedom and independence for his artistic endeavours. Therefore, he turns to an art in which form becomes the message, an art in which there is a subtle balance between the real and the imagined, and between what is stated and what is alluded to. Mauvisme thus is an attempt to gain freedom for complete self-exploration and total self-expression. It is a desire to voice both the obvious and the hidden, the permitted and the forbidden.

No wonder mauvisme and Kataev's stylistic innovations meet with little sympathy from the Soviet literary establishment. The 'new Kataev' not only rejects old artistic forms but also questions many facts, values, and ideas accepted in contemporary Soviet society. Hence the editorial introduction to 'Uzhe napisan Verter' and the departure from the essential artistic premises of mauvisme in his most recent novel. Even an old and respected writer such as Valentin Kataev is not totally free from official constraints and has to acquiesce to the demands of official literary policy.

Kataev's last two stories, 'Spiashchii' and 'Sukhoi liman,' are close in spirit and subject-matter to his earlier works. Both are set in Odessa, the city of Kataev's childhood and youth. 'Spiashchii' is similar in its dramatic irony, plot construction, and style to 'Uzhe napisan Verter.' It is a story told intermittently in the first and third persons by a narrator who is asleep and sees a dream in a dream. The narrator is nameless; hence the possible conclusion that all life is a dream, an illusion. But the world that the sleeper perceives in his dream is very real. Odessa is under Austrian rule during the First World War. The atmosphere of instability and confusion creates a feeling of complete freedom which degenerates into chaos. The rich try to enjoy life for as long as they can. Vasia, the owner of a yacht, is in love with Nelly. She, in turn, is courted by Manfred, who loves her passionately and promises to take her away to Italy, where she will be able to become a great singer. Nelly agrees, but Manfred is killed while robbing a jewellery store in order to get the money required for their escape. Nelly never finds out about Manfred's fate. To her he is one of the braggarts who cheat and deceive and can never be trusted. She does not even suspect that she is the cause of his death.

The tragic conclusion of this little episode makes the reader aware that in this general chaos there is still room for love and duty, and for life and death. An individual disappears, but life goes on, and, as if nothing happened, the dream continues. 'Spiashchii' is rich in metaphoric language and symbols. The storm at sea can be compared to the storm in life where nothing is stable and everything is fluid. The revolution is also a storm which is to stifle the violent social chaos and introduce order and tranquillity.

According to Kataev, his last story, 'Sukhoi liman,' is 'a free variation on the theme of a family chronicle,'[34] which is based on someone else's rather than his own life. The story, which is told in the third person, covers over half a century of narrated time. The two protagonists meet after a long separation. Aleksandr Sinaiskii, a scholar from Moscow, goes to visit his older cousin, Mikhail, a retired general-physician, in a hospital where the latter is recovering from a heart attack. The cousins walk and reminisce about their large family, of which they are the only survivors. We learn from their impressionistic stories that most relatives died young, in unexplained and poorly understood circumstances. The kaleidoscopic portrayal of the disappearing Sinaiskiis creates an impression that generations pass, governments change, but death always rules. Mikhail, the materialist, does not believe in premonitions, as his cousin does. He is realistic about life. He asks his cousin: 'Is it possible that you still do not understand that death chases all of us,'[35] including myself?

The atmosphere of 'Sukhoi liman' is permeated by the languor of a man expecting to die soon. Mikhail Sinaiskii does not fool himself. He is a physician who knows that he cannot survive another heart attack. The eighty-eight-year-old Kataev tells a story that is, perhaps, the fiction of his imagination, but he identifies closely with its main protagonist. Kataev is a realist in life, but his last story could also be read as a premonition of his own impending death. Kataev follows here in the steps of his hero: he does not want to delude himself; he knows that death chases all.

Valentin Kataev died on 12 April 1986. His official obituary was signed by all the members of the politburo and the secretaries of the Central Party Committee. It attests to the important place assigned to him in Soviet culture, tradition, and society. But only time will tell whether he will secure for himself the place he so much desired in the pantheon of Russian letters, next to his long-departed, immortal friends.

Art Foreshadows Life: Iurii Trifonov (1927–1981)

The sudden death of Iurii Trifonov on 28 March 1981 cut short the life of one of the few contemporary Soviet writers whose works are well known in both the Soviet Union and the West.[36] The widespread interest in his work is generated in different countries by diverse motives, but the universal appeal of his art is based probably on recognition of the difficult position of a Russian writer who chooses to remain a Soviet citizen, while telling the truth about himself and his country.

In the 1970s Trifonov had concerned himself with three major problems of Soviet society. The first is sociological and is illustrated in his portrayal of the everyday life of the Soviet middle class and the new urban intelligentsia. The second is ethical, and it manifests itself in Trifonov's moral judgment on contemporary Soviet byt. The third is historical and is concerned primarily with the re-evaluation of the Soviet past, which in turn is linked closely with Trifonov's own family background and experience.

In his prose of the 1980s Trifonov reaches a new level of maturity. He continues to develop the same themes, but he also strikes a new note. He abandons his earlier detachment and places his own life and feelings at the centre of his prose. Trifonov's recent works are complex; they have an intricate narrative structure; they reflect the author's endeavour at self-analysis and self-examination and an attempt to come to terms with his life and with his past. In addition, Trifonov's prose of the 1980s is charged with a new emphasis on metaphysical questions. The recurring discourses on problems of life and death, happiness and suffering, destiny and chance, as well as on the elusive relationship between time and place, indicate a change in Trifonov's world outlook and a certain uneasiness, connected apparently with the process of ageing and his experience of mature life.

Trifonov's last works were published posthumously. Six stories under the title *Oprokinutyi dom* (The Overturned House; 1981)[37] appeared in the July 1981 issue of *Novyi mir*, and the novel *Vremia i mesto* (Time and Place; 1981)[38] in the September and October volumes of *Druzhba narodov* the same year. The date at the end of the former indicates that it was completed on 19 November 1980. The date at the end of the novel is December 1980; but an editorial note states that the text and publication of the novel had been prepared by Trifonov's widow, Ol'ga Miroshnichenko-Trifonova. It is unclear if any changes were introduced in the novel after the author's death, but there is reason to believe that it was the first to be written and that it was finished before December 1980.[39]

Trifonov began writing *Vremia i mesto* during the summer of 1978. In a letter of 11 August 1978 he wrote: 'I returned yesterday from a long trip to the Baltic republics at the time of which I began writing a new thing. It is a povest' about the beginning of a writer's path ... The action takes place in 1947–1948, but it will not be a book of reminiscences, not something documental, but a novel, fiction.'[40] On 3 July 1980 Trifonov wrote from France: 'I finished the novel before departure. I submitted it [to a journal] but I do not know what its fate will be. In the mean time its title is *Vremia i mesto*, but it is possible that I will change it.' In a conversation with the East German journalist R. Schroeder, he stated that after completing *Vremia i mesto* he had begun work on a cycle of short stories about his travels in foreign countries.[41] It is clear then that *Vremia i mesto* was completed long before December 1980.

Trifonov's first major novel, *Studenty* (Students; 1950), is a classic of socialist realism. It deals with the life of Russian literature students and the workings of a Soviet institution of higher learning in the days of Stalin. 'Dom na naberezhnoi' (The House on the Embankment; 1976) deals with similar problems, but Trifonov takes us there a step further. He investigates the mechanics and the ethics of the creation of a Soviet literary scholar. 'Dom na naberezhnoi' is not only artistically vastly superior to *Studenty*; it also debunks everything for which *Studenty* stands. Here Trifonov goes from one extreme to the other. He attempts to cleanse himself of his past sins and of his acquiescence with a regime the evils of which he was perhaps too young to understand.

At first *Vremia i mesto* seems to continue the theme begun in *Studenty* and followed up in 'Dom na naberezhnoi,' but in fact it soon takes a new turn. Trifonov examines here not only the intricate process of becoming a Soviet writer, but also the laws and values that determine the operation of the bureaucracy and the institutions connected with Soviet literary production. The novel can be read as an artistic confession and self-assessment. By comparison with the earlier works, it is more autobiographical and personal, more introspective and philosophical.

Vremia i mesto is a novel in thirteen chapters. It covers a time span of close to forty years. Each chapter is set in a different period and has its own characters, plot, and conflict. Major characters in one chapter become secondary in another, or disappear altogether. Only the main hero, the writer Sasha Antipov, is fully developed and appears in most chapters. The others, including the 'I' narrator, whose name is mentioned only twice in passing, are drawn sketchily and impressionistically. The titles of ten chapters refer to specific locations in Moscow, where the action takes place; two others relate to the seasons of the year, and one chapter, the twelfth, is symbolically entitled 'Vremia i mesto.'

The novel is narrated on several different planes. The life story of the main character, Antipov, is told in the third person, or in quasi-direct discourse in which the subjective voice of the hero can be discerned through the voice of the narrator. Four chapters and the introduction to another are told in the first person by the 'I' narrator. In addition, a number of lyrical digressions, such as the thoughts and reminiscences of the writer Kiianov, or the internal monologues of the paralysed old Bolshevik woman Elizaveta Gavrilovna, are also told in the first person.

Basically the story unfolds in chronological order, but there are two distinct levels of narration with different characters in each of them, and there is a certain overlapping in time sequences. This makes it sometimes difficult to follow the exact course of events, especially as there are many parallels between the life stories of Antipov and of the first-person narrator. They are both of the same age, they work during the war in the same plant, and they have common acquaintances. Both aspire in their youth to become writers, and both live without parents. After the war, fate separates them for many years. We encounter the narrator again, some thirty years later, in the last chapter of the novel, when he visits his daughter in a hospital that has been built in the place where he spent his childhood. The narrator is now in his fifties. He is a scholar mathematician and a widower. His mentally unstable daughter is treated by Dr Stepan Antipov, the son of the writer Antipov. Before long an encounter between the narrator and the protagonist Antipov is arranged. They return to their old places, but they can never return to the old times.

Trifonov's narrative technique, in particular his use of the first person in what seems to be a third-person narrative, has often been criticized.[42] Trifonov, however, considered that this device permitted him to penetrate deeper into the souls of his characters.[43] The critic Valerii Golovskoi has complained that the first-person narrator in *Vremia i mesto* 'is a cold and indifferent commentator on Antipov's fate who interferes with the action in the novel.'[44] Golovskoi has failed to see that the voice of the author is not always that of the narrator and that the narrator is there not just to comment on the life of Antipov but also to live his own life, which is just as complex and unpredictable as Antipov's. *Vremia i mesto* is a polyphonic novel in which the author's voice blends with the voices of different characters, including those of the narrator and Antipov. According to Mikhail Bakhtin, 'from every contradiction in one man, Dostoevskii attempts to create two people.'[45] Trifonov follows here in the path of Dostoevskii, and he assigns different aspects of his past and present dilemmas to different characters in the novel.

Vremia i mesto is a compact novel, charged with dramatic tension. Its structure is complex, and its mood subdued. It is a montage of reminiscences, contemplations, impressionistic detail, and fiction, all indiscriminately intertwined and united by the highly symbolic notions of a common place and time.

The notion of a house or a 'place,' somewhere to live, zhilaia ploshchad', lies at the root of most of Trifonov's prose. It is something akin to the concept 'mother earth' in village prose of the 1960s and 1970s. The dramatic collision in 'Obmen' (The Exchange) (1969) is centred over a struggle for a larger apartment, in 'Dolgoe proshchanie' (The Long Goodbye; 1971) over a room and a garden plot, and in *Starik* (The Old Man; 1978) over a summer cottage. In 'Dom na naberezhnoi' the house symbolizes a station in life and the social and historical upheavals in the lives of the heroes. In *Vremia i mesto* the action moves from house to house, from one Moscow district to another. The city grows and expands, but the shortage of living space, which makes Antipov's life at times unbearable, seems paradoxically only to grow worse. The feeling of claustrophobia symbolizes the general social atmosphere and the quality of life.

So too with time, which can influence and determine human destiny. Most of Trifonov's Moscow novellas contain a sense that time is running out, that it changes mercilessly people's internal essence and external appearance, and that it drags people along its path of infinity, allotting to each individual only a tiny fraction of its eternal existence. In *Vremia i mesto* the theme of time is worked out on several different levels: personal, biological, internal.[46] Trifonov's emphasis is now less on the general flow of social and historical time than on the moments when a man is forced to take crucial decisions or is confronted with loneliness, illness, suffering, and the possibility of death.

The chapter, 'Vremia i mesto,' that gives its name to the novel is the most pessimistic one. Antipov is fifty-two. He is lonely, depressed, and tired of life, a situation that can be rectified only by social contact and a close relationship with supportive people. But at the same time Antipov wants to become free of everything; he wants to run away from life. 'The idea of becoming free occupies him constantly. He wants to get free from the worries about this grown-up children, from unnecessary furniture, from the pains of vanity, from the power of women, from the egoism of friends, from the terror of books.'[47] And yet subconsciously Antipov clings to life and fears death. When he learns that Viktor Kotov, a friend from his student days, has died unexpectedly, he realizes that 'Kotov was a part of his life and that with his disappearance ... his own, Antipov's, life died and became shorter. It says in the obituary: bezvremenno (untimely). An absurd word! It implies: unexpectedly, without cause, without illness, without a prepared and determined date, i.e. *not at the right time* (bez vremeni).'[48]

The mother of Markusha, one of Antipov's remaining friends, would say that 'everything has its time and place,'[49] and Antipov realizes all of a sudden that Viktor Kotov 'did not understand his place or the time allotted to him. People are in a frenzy because they do not understand. That is why these deaths occur bez vremeni (untimely).'[50] Reflecting on the possibility of absolute knowledge, however, Trifonov shudders. There is 'nothing more terrible than to find out one's *place and time*,'[51] he says.

Trifonov often compares the passage of time to the flow of water. It is impossible to stop the flow of a river, just as it is impossible to stop the passage of time. Time is a gust of the wind, volcanic lava. It is a blind force over which people have no control. But time and place find themselves in a complex relationship. People can change the face of the earth; they can move from one place to another but have no power over time. Time moves mercilessly on, leaving behind the place but taking along its inhabitants. The title of the book, then, is particularly significant. In Trifonov's earlier works, *mesto* had usually referred to physical space and *vremia* to chronological time in its personal, social, or historical context. In *Vremia i mesto* these considerations are secondary to the author's overriding concern with man's destiny. The emphasis is not on when and where one lives but rather on when, where, and how one dies.

Despite differences in genre and scope, there is much in common between *Vremia i mesto* and *Oprokinutyi dom*. Both are autobiographical and introspective; both dwell on problems of life and death, emphasizing the elusiveness of true happiness and the futility of life. Both are permeated by the same spirit of dejection and pessimism, reflecting the author's own deep anxiety and his premonition of impending death.

Oprokinutyi dom consists of six separate stories, united by a common theme and mood. Each story is triggered by a recent experience in a foreign country, leading in turn to thoughts of events long past and reflections on the human predicament. The stories should not be read as mere travel impressions. As a rule Trifonov refused to write reports about his visits abroad. Most travel impressions, he claimed, were fleeting anyway. One of the stories, 'Smert' v Sitsilii' (Death in Sicily), begins with the question: 'What can one understand in a few days in a foreign country? Can one guess how people live, or how they die?'[52] In another story, set in Las Vegas, Trifonov observes that there is much in common between people all over the world. They are united by an invisible thread that 'consists of death, hope, disappointment, and despair, as well as of moments of happiness that are as short as the gust of a wind.'[53] But Trifonov also recognizes that, despite these similarities, the American will never understand what moves the Russian, nor will the Russian ever understand what induces the American to act. This pessimistic observation alludes to the deep chasm dividing people living in different social systems, and in different parts of the world, and it points to Trifonov's own predicament as a man and a writer torn between East and West.

A spirit of despondency pervades Trifonov's recent prose. A. Bocharov points out that the number of chapters in *Vremia i mesto* is ominous in itself.[54] So is the imagery: most things are painted in dark colours and happen in the winter or late fall. Nature is dead. A similar mood permeates *Oprokinutyi dom*. The image of the overturned house recurs always when the writer travels far from home.[55] Logically, home should be a place of stability and serenity, but for Trifonov there is no peace or security anywhere. Danger and death lurk in the dark, ready to strike anywhere and any time. The unexpected death of Viktor Kotov drives Antipov into a fit of anxiety and depression. The premature death of Trifonov's friend Boria in 'Oprokinutyi dom' forewarns him of his own imminent death. Years ago Trifonov and Boria had paid their last respects to a departed common friend. Boria's words then – 'Surely one day death will strike us in a similar way' – had dumbfounded Trifonov, 'not because it was not true, but precisely because it was a sudden cruel truth ... Death is a whirlwind that acts with the speed of lightning.'[56]

Illness and death pervade many of Trifonov's earlier works. The main conflict in 'Obmen' is triggered by the illness and impending death of Kseniia Fedorovna. Genadii Sergeevich, the main protagonist of 'Predvaritel'nye itogi' (Preliminary Results; 1970), is a sick man who is spared only at the last moment.[57] Sergei Troitskii, the main character in

'Drugaia zhizn' (Another Life; 1975), is driven to death at the young age of forty-two. There are many other such instances. In fact, every work by the mature Trifonov alludes to the fact that people are always in the process of motion and transition from one state into another; from birth, through life, and on to death. But, if in his works of the 1970s Trifonov had dealt with these problems unemotionally, in the 1980s he rejects this pose and becomes both the subject and the object of his art.

Trifonov imparts to the reader his own pessimism and his realization that life is transitory and futile. Furthermore, he appears to share with his protagonists a certain weariness of life and a feeling that death is inevitable and not too far distant. This state leads characters such as the writer Kiianov, in *Vremia i mesto*, or the editor in 'Vechnye temy' (Eternal Themes)[58] to a strong premonition of death. An intimate friend of Trifonov's had written in one of his letters: 'The works by Trifonov published posthumously in *Novyi mir* bear the imprint of a consciousness that the life of the author and of his contemporaries is drawing to an end ... These works are imbued with the spirit of languor characteristic of a dying man. This condition has been brought on by the death of his close friends as well as by his own poor health.'[59] Trifonov himself said of *Vremia i mesto* in one of his letters: 'Perhaps I will finish it in the spring of next year – e.b.zh., as Tolstoi used to write, i.e. esli budu zhiv (if I will be alive).'[60] Trifonov's condition is similar to Antipov's. When he finds out about the death of Kotov he is smitten emotionally, but physical punishment follows soon.

The novel that Antipov tries unsuccessfully to complete is about a writer who writes a novel he cannot complete, about a writer who writes a novel ... Its title is *The Nikiforov Syndrome*. The novel is a 'system of mirrors' and an analysis of an unfulfilled life (nesochinivsheisia zhizni).[61] But it is more than that. Nikiforov is sick. His illness is expressed in his fear of life. Nikiforov is the alter ego of Antipov, just as Antipov is the alter ego of Trifonov. At one time they had all hoped and dared, but now they are tired and dejected; they fear life, because it inevitably ends in death.

In Trifonov's earlier fiction the motifs of 'great possibilities' (velikie vozmozhnosti), 'changing one's fate' (peremenit' sud'bu), and 'another life' (drugaia zhizn') recur time and again. Most characters delude themselves that a new flat, a new job, or a new wife will change the course of their lives and give them true happiness. The characters in *Vremia i mesto* and *Oprokinutyi dom* have no such delusions. Their great possibilities never materialize. The change of fate, as in the case of Boria, is sudden, unexpected, and spells death. Many characters in

Trifonov's recent prose have no desires, they strive for nothing. Life for them is meaningless. Some even commit suicide. Stanislav Semenovich, the stepfather of the narrator's friend in *Vremia i mesto*, is a sick man: 'He lies all day in a dark room and wants nothing. He does not eat, read, write, or speak ... This is the essence of his illness – to want nothing.'[62] If their fate 'changes,' it is only for the worse, bringing illness and death.

In the last chapter of *Vremia i mesto* Trifonov contemplates his own predicament. Antipov appears to have weathered the storm, for the time being, and he makes a new beginning. He recovers from a heart attack and his state of depression, and he manages even to marry a young woman who bears him a child. But there is a strong feeling that the reprieve is only temporary, that after the short honeymoon real life will dispel his fleeting state of bliss and intoxication. Similarly, the life of the narrator is also not happy. He too has a friend, a young woman. She is beautiful, but capricious and unreliable. Of little help when needed most, she refuses to move in with him. He is burdened with a multitude of problems and is haunted by recurring nightmares. In his sleepless nights he is frequented by the image of an ugly, witch-like woman. He is terrified. Every time she appears from the dark, he sees in her the face of destiny. Fate laughs at him.[63]

It is evident that neither Antipov nor the narrator can solve the dilemma of approaching old age. Neither can come to terms with it because they avoid the main issue: one's youth and time past can never be recovered, while the future holds in store only loneliness, suffering, and ultimate death. Trifonov himself is just as far from a satisfactory solution to his predicament. But at this point one may wonder: why such dejection and preoccupation with death at a relatively young age? Why such anxiety at a time when Trifonov seems to have reached the peak of his creative maturity? Three distinct sources of pressure have most affected the life and creative work of the mature Trifonov: his attempt to come to terms with his past, his personal and family life, and those pressures to which every Soviet writer is exposed, particularly one who wants to retain integrity and professional honesty.

Born of mixed parentage and orphaned at the age of eleven, his parents arrested and victimized in the Stalinist purges, the young Trifonov grew up under much stress. In the days of Stalin, the young writer, constantly aware of his dubious political background, did his best to acquiesce and co-operate with the system, this being the only path to physical survival. In the post-Stalin period the process of self-examination began. It led to a search for his roots and an attempt to find new strength in a better understanding of his past. At this stage Trifonov still believed that only the past could supply the necessary inspiration for the future, for the present, as illustrated in his byt fiction, is vacuous and shallow and cannot serve as a guide for the future.

According to Trifonov, the past and the future are fused together in daily reality. Present existence is influenced by the past as well as by concern for the future. However, as the novel *Starik* illustrates, the re-examination of the past and its juxtaposition with the present leads the main hero, the old man and former revolutionary Letunov, nowhere. He realizes, along with his creator, that people are blind tools of circumstances. He participates in historical events, deluding himself that he is in possession of the truth, while in reality he is only emotionally attached to a cause without being able to make a rational decision about the real course of events. Thus reassessment of the past fails to supply Trifonov with a new meaning for life, and in the end there remains only nostalgia for a lost youth that did not prepare him adequately for a fulfilling life.

Trifonov's prose of the 1970s suggests an inherent instability in most families. Genadii Sergeevich, the main hero of 'Predvaritel'nye itogi,' intimates: 'The contemporary marriage is a most tender institution. The idea of an easy parting and an attempt to start everything from the beginning, before it is too late, is constantly in the air.'[64] But it is one thing to write about someone else's troubles – and a completely different thing to face similar problems in one's own family. After having worked on *Vremia i mesto* for close to half a year, Trifonov wrote in one of his letters: 'I spent much time in travel, having written only a third of the novel. In addition, there was also a change in my life. I parted with my former wife and married again ... It is good to write about all these perturbations in books, but in life they demand much strength and nervous tension, precisely the things that are so necessary for literature.'[65]

Trifonov's family life was no less complicated than that of the main protagonists in *Vremia i mesto*. His first wife, Nina Nelina, died unexpectedly in the mid-1960s at Druskeninkai, a health resort in Lithuania. Several years later he married the well-known Moscow personality Alla Pastukhova, but she refused to move into the apartment where Trifonov's first wife had lived; her own flat was too small for the two of them. Thus, although married, they lived apart, creating complications that interfered with Trifonov's life and his creative work. Trifonov's third marriage, to Ol'ga Romanovna Miroshnichenko, appeared happy, but she was much younger than her husband, and their child was born prematurely, causing much anguish and stress to the father.

There are many other parallels between the fate of Trifonov and that of the protagonists in his recent works. Thus the internal pressures affecting Trifonov's life are linked closely to the predicaments of writers in contemporary Soviet society. There are many examples in *Vremia i mesto* attesting to the difficulties faced by a writer in the Soviet Union. The young Antipov lives in poverty, but he refuses to compromise his conscience by agreeing to write a false review. His wife is forced to have an abortion, 'only because *a manuscript, eighteen pages long, has been rejected in the editorial offices of one journal.*'[66] A writer's connections are shown to be more important than the quality of his writing. Thus Antipov is supported by the middle-aged secretary of the faculty because he reluctantly becomes intimate with her. His first novel is published quickly because his teacher Kiianov takes it to a journal and writes an introduction. Trifonov had been just as lucky with his first novel, *Studenty*, which Konstantin Fedin, his teacher at the Literary Institute, had recommended to Aleksandr Tvardovskii, the editor of *Novyi mir*, without even having read it.[67] The mature Trifonov is not that lucky. He is criticized on numerous occasions for failing to create a positive hero, for the lack of a direct message, and for his insistence on retaining autonomy in the selection of his characters and conflicts.

Trifonov managed to publish his works in official Soviet journals, but he was under tremendous pressure to conform, being often attacked by both official Soviet critics and Russian émigrés at the same time. Thus, the émigré critic Iurii Mal'tsev compares Trifonov to the hack of socialist realism Semen Babaevskii, and he accuses him of 'inventing psychology ... In his novel "The House on the Embankment" Trifonov tells us about the times of Stalin, but we will look there in vain for the well-known signs of that epoch.'[68] Mal'tsev ignores, of course, Trifonov's predilection for understatement and the fact that much of what he has to say remains under the surface. Furthermore, much of what Mal'tsev would like Trifonov to write could never be published officially in the Soviet Union anyway.

Trifonov made a rational choice to remain in the Soviet Union, and he paid the price. He could not see himself become an outcast in a world he could hardly fathom. He could not for forsake his roots, which he was still trying to discover, or the city of Moscow, which inspired most of his works. He believed, or seemed to believe, 'that real Russian literature is created by Soviet writers, living and publishing "officially" in their country.'[69]

Paradoxically, as far as Trifonov himself is concerned, the question of a writer's place is academic, because his recent works indicate that he thinks more about death than about life, and it is certainly better to die at home than in a foreign land. This feeling is vividly reflected in one of his stories, in which he describes the anguish of a rich old Russian woman writer, a civil war émigré, who after sixty years in the West is still terrified of dying alone in a foreign country. 'There is nothing more terrible than death in Sicily,'[70] she exclaims, and Trifonov, the narrator, repeats the same.

Trifonov is spared from dying in 'Sicily.' He dies in Moscow. The pressures of growing up in a victimized family, the difficulties of daily, personal, and family life, and the complicated life of a Soviet writer who wants to remain honest in a society that demands submission undermine his health and cause his sudden death.

It is often dangerous to use the life and opinions of an author to explain his work. Yet it is sometimes difficult to separate the artist from his art, particularly the art of one who dwells on the realistic portrayal of his immediate environment and who works in an atmosphere in which extra-literary considerations influence the creative process. In his works published posthumously the personality of Trifonov merges with the images of his characters. The writer's life and his art become one. The narratives reflect his own experiences, feelings, and aspirations; they also foreshadow his tragic fate.[71]

School and Society: Vladimir Tendriakov (1923–1984)

Vladimir Tendriakov belongs to the generation of writers who appeared on the Soviet literary scene in the immediate post-Stalin period. His name is, therefore, closely associated with the 'thaw' in Soviet culture and with the beginnings of the re-evaluation of the canon of socialist realism. His early works are in the mainstream of village prose, dealing primarily with the predicament of the Soviet countryside in the 1940s and 1950s. In his mature works Tendriakov does not limit himself to the portrayal of simple peasant life; he explores more universal problems, setting them in conditions of contemporary urban life. His later heroes, representatives of the urban intelligentsia, are introspective and soul-searching. They search for meaning in life and question their place in this world yet are frustrated by a reality that they cannot fathom and refuse to accept. Some of them evade the dilemma by means of ardent religious faith, while others see the roots of their inner void in the education they received in Soviet schools.

Tendriakov's interest in education is not new; it dates back to the 1950s, when, rather than focusing his attention on the educational system or even the educational process, he was interested primarily in the personality and ability of the teacher. He considered most important the teacher's ability to help students define and distinguish between good and evil, love and hate, selflessness and egoism. Thus, for example, Andrei Biriukov, the narrator-hero of the novel *Za begu-shchim dnem* (On the Heels of Time; 1959),[72] is a teacher of Russian literature and a crusader for school reform. He opposes old teaching methods which stifle the pupils' interest and initiative. He advocates the introduction of 'organized dialogues' to stimulate student involvement in the lesson. The character of Biriukov can hardly be regarded as a successful Soviet hero, for his 'positive' ideals are often at odds with his indecisive nature, and his excellent intentions bear no results. Nonetheless the educational issues examined in the novel were so important to Tendriakov that he waged a broader campaign in the press criticizing many aspects of the state system of education and calling for drastic changes in teaching methods.[73]

Tendriakov's concern did not slacken over the years. In the early 1970s he returned in his fiction to education, this time to the problems of upbringing affecting his young characters. In 'Vesennie perevertyshi' (Spring Turn-overs; 1973)[74] and in 'Tri meshka sornoi pshenitsy' (Three Bags of Weedy Wheat; 1973)[75] he juxtaposes two generations: young, uncorrupted teenagers, who battle for justice and common sense, and their fathers, who represent the corrupt, complacent administrative bureaucracy. The investigation of the relationship between fathers and sons, which is prominently featured in 'Vesennie perevertyshi,' leads Tendriakov to an inquiry into the negative changes in the young, who gradually become malleable, accommodating adults, complacent about everything other than immediate material gratification and personal well-being.

Family, school, and society are the three forces that most influence young people in their formative years. The Soviet school, because centrally controlled, promotes and fosters uniformly values advocated by the state. But the influence that the school exerts is not always commensurate with the needs and ambitions of the individual or with the expectations of his or her family. The objectives of the state often clash with the educational concerns of the individual, leading to conflict between the school and teacher, on the one hand, and the pupil and his or her family, on the other. This incompatibility between the school, which must serve the interests of society in general, and the individual student, who is not always able to sublimate personal cravings through public service, accounts for many of the difficulties Soviet education encounters in its endeavour to prepare young people for the challenges of modern life. These are the problems that most concern Tendriakov, because, according to him, the irreconcilable conflict between the individual and the school is largely responsible for the ethical shallowness, if not moral corruption, of many young Soviet citizens.

The intricate relationship of school, teacher, pupil, family, and society is set forth in extreme, dramatic terms in Tendriakov's trilogy of short stories, 'Noch' posle vypuska' (The Night after Graduation; 1974),[76] 'Rasplata' (Atonement; 1979),[77] and 'Shest'desiat svechei' (Sixty Candles; 1980).[78] The action in 'Noch' posle vypuska' takes place in June 1972, on the thirty-first anniversary of Nazi Germany's attack on the Soviet Union. The plot is set in motion by the valedictory speech delivered by Iulechka Studentseva. The best student of the graduating class admits frankly that though her education opened many different roads for her, all leading to a brilliant future, her schooling failed to teach her what was most important: how to choose. When Iulechka asks, 'What road should I choose?' she replies to her own question: 'School forced me to know everything, except one thing – what I like, what I love ... Now I look around, and it turns out that I love nothing ... and there are a thousand roads, and they are all the same, all indifferent to me ... Do not think that I am happy. I am terrified.'[79]

Iulechka's desperate speech points to the weaknesses and inadequacies of the system under which she studied. Though Soviet schools have a number of admirable qualities – they develop diligence, obedience, and discipline – while stressing the value of good marks and the efficient management of heavy workloads, they also emphasize the importance of the group over the individual and, by their rigorous requirements of uniformity and conformity, discourage students from thinking for themselves. Thus the Soviet school stifles the growth of personality and fosters a conformist psychology which forces everyone to look, to act, and to think as his peers do, as convention requires. Such enforced collectivity can produce dangerous consequences, as is illustrated in the story when the young graduates, after a bitter quarrel, decide to surrender their best friend, Genka Golikov, to a gang that wants to murder him. Only Iulechka, who has already asserted publicly a personal identity distinct from her peers, comes to Golikov's defence. By taking a stand against common treachery she expresses her independence, her ability to withstand peer pressure.

As the title of the story suggests, everything happens in the ominous night after graduation. But the action develops simultaneously in two locations, among two groups of people. While the students begin their graduation celebration in the city square, six teachers, three men and three women, assemble after the ceremony in the teachers' lounge. Both gatherings end in acrimonious arguments and bode little good for the members of these groups. The young people become embroiled in bitter exposure of each other's shortcomings, thus revealing how their enforced camaraderie in school barely camouflaged the jealousy, envy, and hostility deeply rooted in the hearts of supposedly friendly and co-operative schoolmates.

The disputation among the teachers is just as vitriolic. Shocked by Iulechka's valedictory pronouncement, which some teachers view as an impudent act of open rebellion against the school, they argue about the merits and shortcomings of their teaching methods. Zoia Vladimirovna, the sixty-year-old literature teacher, is accused by her colleagues of producing ignorant young people, unable to appreciate a real work of art. Instead of stimulating her students to think and feel and reflect, she requires them to memorize long passages and to repeat the worn-out truths prescribed by the school programs. Zoia Vladimirovna seems to lose the argument, yet she is not prepared to accept her colleagues' accusations. This would be tantamount to a confession of failure, an admission of a wasted life.

The discussion in the teachers' lounge solves nothing. It re-emphasizes only in the form of fiction the opinions many teachers and students have been voicing in Russia since the death of Stalin, views which, unfortunately, have been ignored by the bureaucrats in the upper echelons of the educational system.[80] But Tendriakov's message in 'Noch' posle vypuska' – that the school fails to prepare young people for adult life – is too simple, concrete, and insistent to be easily dismissed. Therefore the story has generated a lively and mixed reaction in Soviet literary criticism. Most critics admit that the story touches on a number of very important issues, but they fail to agree on its relative merits. Tendriakov is attacked harshly for the ideological shortcomings of his work. Thus, for example, N. Shamota decries the fact that Tendriakov poses in his story a number of very important questions but avoids even attempting to reply to them. According to Shamota, 'the literature of socialist realism never shunned the duty of answering the questions posed by life, doing it with a degree of great internal responsibility. A Marxist-Leninist Weltanschauung is a reliable foundation for such cognition.'[81] It is evident that the demands of Shamota sound a retreat from the Chekhovian principles of artistic presentation, according to which it is not the writer's duty to solve problems, but just to present them correctly. It is also a step back from the post-Stalin literary evolution which gave writers relative freedom to present and explore controversial problems, without being required to voice a definite opinion on the conflicts described and the issues discussed.

In 'Noch' posle vypuska' the action is set in motion by an abstract notion, by a statement expressing the failure of the educational system; in 'Rasplata,' the conflict is generated by an act of parricide. A grade-nine student, Kolia Koriakin, shoots his alcoholic father for abusing and tormenting his mother and for destroying their family life. Although an intense family drama is at the core of this story, Tendriakov does little to investigate the family relationship of the Koriakins, nor does he analyse the psychological state of young Kolia before his decisive and terrible act of violence. Instead, he becomes absorbed in the search for the reasons for the crime and for the culprits responsible for it. Among those who take upon themselves the guilt for the murder is, first of all, Kolia's mother, who wants to save her son. Quite surprisingly and quite significantly, Kolia's literature teacher, Arkadii Kirillovich Pamiatnov, is also overcome by a sense of culpability. He is the first at the scene of the crime, arriving even before the police, and from that moment he becomes the main protagonist. And in his search for the causes of the parricide he looks both within himself and at his methods of teaching literature.

Now the murder becomes secondary in the development of the plot as Tendriakov investigates the relationship between teacher and pupil, school and family, and the effect of teaching literature on the sensitive soul of a young man. Pamiatnov greatly influences his students. He is famous for his intense concern with ethics in the classroom. He teaches his students that people are essentially good and that one has to fight evil; at the same time he shelters his students from real life, projecting an idealized reality in which good always prevails. 'Together with other teachers, Arkadii Kirillovich tries to protect his students from the evils of this world. They have been told that there is no alcoholism, no robbery, cheating or self-centred egoism. Instead there are only the achievements of labour, the growing consciousness of the people, noble deeds, and honest relationships.'[82] But the students are not blind. The moment they are dismissed from class they encounter a world vastly different from the one described in their classroom. They are forced to develop new skills and values to ensure their survival in this real and complicated world.

Pamiatnov's notion that one should fight evil is carried to the extreme by Kolia in that he murders for what appears to be an elevated idea. Pamiatnov's conscience may be troubled because he thinks that 'murder and happiness are incompatible.'[83] But his students argue that to 'kill for life's sake, for a better life,'[84] is possible and necessary, and they support their argument with examples previously cited by their teacher in his literature lessons. The question of whether one is justified in killing for a noble cause is not new. It is central to Dostoevskii's famous novel *Crime and Punishment*.[85] It is one thing to discuss these problems on a theoretical plane, as an abstract or historical issue, but totally different to use this argument to justify the murder of one's own father. Pamiatnov is confused and dejected when he realizes that his intent to teach his pupils what is good does not lead to positive results. He also recognizes that supervising the general process of education and upbringing is much more difficult than teaching simple facts and that the ethics of everyday life are often more complicated than an abstract notion of universal morality.

According to Tendriakov, the Soviet school does not give the literature teacher the tools necessary for educating the young. He argues that 'school programs tell the student that he should know the biographies of writers and the ideological essence of their best works. He should be able to determine, in a given stereotyped manner, the essence of an artistic image ... But the programs do not take into consideration that literature describes human relations in which nobleness encounters baseness, honesty faces falsity, magnanimity confronts perfidy, and ethics oppose immorality.'[86] Indeed, the Soviet teacher is given little room for innovation, independence, and imagination in literature classes. From their literature classes the students acquire certain skills; they master many facts and learn to interpret them in the required manner, but they cannot relate the pulsing life of a literary narrative to their own lives.

The story ends inconclusively. Tendriakov does not take the reader into the courtroom for the verdict against Kolia, nor does he make clear who are the main culprits in this human drama. Since Tendriakov tries hard to absolve Kolia of guilt without explicitly revealing who is to blame for the murder, a conclusion is possible that everyone is guilty: the family, its friends, the school, and, last but not least, the whole social system, which often neglects to create conditions adequate for peaceful family life and supports a school system that fails in its task of preparing young people for life.

The hero of Tendriakov's next story, 'Shest'desiat svechei,' is its narrator, Nikolai Stepanovich Echevin, a small-town history teacher. He has just celebrated his sixtieth birthday and the fortieth anniversary of his teaching career. He has been honoured by the town, by the school, and by many of his former students. But among the congratulatory letters is an anonymous threat to kill him for allegedly having ruined the writer's life. The threat has a shattering effect on the teacher, provoking a soul-searching re-examination of his past. Little by little Echevin begins to understand that he has always given in to public pressure and to the 'demands of the times,' choosing consistently the road of least resistance. He finally sees that for years he has been deluding himself that he knows what he is teaching. He realizes that he knows no more about truth than do his students, that the blind have been leading and continue to lead the blind.

Echevin, who appears to be an ordinary and upright man, has been obsessed all his life with the idea of justice and with the welfare of his students. Yet he now recalls painfully that his obsessive drive to put his good intentions into practice has not inevitably led to positive results. He remembers how as a fifteen-year-old student, influenced by youthful zeal and by a young, revolutionary school principal named Sukov,[87] he forsook the girl he loved and denounced and drove to suicide her father, Ivan Semenovich Graube, who was also his former teacher and benefactor. Years later, after the Second World War, he persuaded one of his students, Sergei Kropotov, to denounce his own father, when the old man was wrongly suspected of collaborating with the Nazis. Following this denunciation young Kropotov could not cope with the alienation from his family, and his conscience drove him to alcoholism and ruin. It is for all the ensuing tribulations of a smashed life that Kropotov has decided on revenge against his former teacher by means of an anonymous threat. With these oppressive memories and revelations, Echevin can conclude only that his concerns have resulted in more harm than good.

The encounter between Echevin and Kropotov, however, proves anti-climactic, when the pupil meets a changed and repentant teacher, who nonetheless clings to the belief that his good intentions must be taken into account. Kropotov argues that unconscious delusion is more dangerous than deliberate villainy and then, bidding his teacher to judge himself according to his own conscience, hands over his gun to Echevin. Years earlier, Echevin's teacher, Graube, had poisoned himself after he concluded, 'I have taught him [Echevin] all his life to distinguish between falsehood and truth; to hate evil and to respect the good – but I failed to teach him. I am a wretched bankrupt. I wasted my life.'[88] Echevin, however, does not follow in Graube's footsteps, for he lacks the inner strength and fibre to commit suicide; instead, his guilt, his doubts, and his gnawing sense of his own uselessness condemn him to a life of torment.

Echevin's situation suggests that man is a blind tool of circumstances, no matter how he deludes himself that he is in control of his destiny. Yet his conscience responds to the responsibility that freedom imposes upon man, a burden he is often too ready to relinquish in order to avoid the anguish of being forced to make a choice or take a stand. Echevin wants to be good and just, but in his experience these two are incompatible. It is impossible for him to tell the truth because it would hurt others; therefore to do good means to lie and become a hypocrite in order not to cause pain to himself or to others.

The action in 'Shest'desiat svechei' covers only one day in Echevin's life, but it is not a good day. It is a day of awakening and frustration. Just as Graube, his teacher, had come to realize that he had failed in his educational endeavours, so Echevin learns that his life has been a waste. He knows now that he was unable to instil in his students 'good human qualities and sensitivity. He did not develop in them a sense of independence.' Instead of stimulating their independence and initiative he infected them with his own 'icy indifference to history.'[89]

There are certain parallels in the predicaments of Pamiatnov and Echevin. Both begin teaching by adhering strictly to the requirements of the official school programs. Echevin acts even beyond the call of duty by attempting to influence the private lives of his pupils. The dramatic occurrences that shatter the tranquillity of Pamiatnov's and Echevin's daily lives place their past educational endeavours in a new perspective. Suddenly they recognize the inability of man to judge his fellow man for man himself is fallible and imperfect. They become concerned with the universal problems of the ethics of life and death, discovering that life in itself has a value beyond the noble ideas that advocate and justify war and even murder. By raising these problems the teachers challenge the philosophical foundations of the Soviet interpretation of history and literature as well as the ideological roots of the modern Soviet state. No wonder the teachers find no solutions to their dilemmas. In the contemporary conditions of Soviet life they would get no chance to voice them anyway. All Echevin can say in conclusion to his silent deliberations is, 'Oh, how difficult life is – full of incompatible contradictions!'[90]

Soviet readers have found Tendriakov's later stories compelling, for they not only examine many provocative and relevant issues, but also present their social and ethical content in gripping dramatic fashion. An act of violence or some other dramatic event of great tension precipitates the action, and a Dostoevskian emphasis on the extreme, the unusual, and the criminal, grounded on devices generating intrigue, surprise, and suspense, is constantly maintained. The power of melodramatic events and the moral content embedded in them is offset by a number of aesthetic deficiencies: the actions of the characters are poorly motivated and characterization is often thin. The main characters are introduced primarily to advance certain philosophical and social notions, and their long debates and monologues often hinder the smooth flow of the narrative. Yet despite these flaws, some of which may have resulted from changes demanded by censors and editors uncomfortable with the sensationalistic violence so essential to the stories, the appearance of Tendriakov's recent works is an important Soviet literary event. These works probe the ethical foundation of Soviet education; they disturb the peaceful complacency of the educational bureaucracy and question the moral and social values prevalent in Soviet society.

Since the appearance of his early stories Tendriakov has often been censured by Soviet critics for his artistic as well as his ideological shortcomings, yet he has always remained at the fore of Soviet letters. In the West, Tendriakov was popular with Western readers and editors only in the early 1960s when he was hailed as one of the major figures of the literary 'thaw' in the Soviet Union. J.G. Garrard even suggested that 'technically speaking, Tendrjakov no longer appears to have very much to learn. He is amazingly skillful at structuring his stories and manipulating characters and events.'[91] In the late 1970s, however, the writer's stock declined, and some critics like Geoffrey Hosking addressed the diminishing interest in Tendriakov's work by suggesting 'that this neglect of him is in a way justified. He is important because he is symptomatic rather than because he is a good writer.'[92] But Tendriakov's mature fiction is in no way inferior to his early work, and all his stories demonstrate similar strengths and weaknesses. Though his first works were extolled because they belonged to a minority that espoused liberal, anti-Stalinist views with which many Western readers sympathized, his recent works have been neglected because they are in the mainstream of contemporary Soviet literature, which is generally more critical of its own society.

The spirit of the 'thaw' of the late 1950s had been stifled. Whatever hopes Tendriakov had for a continuation of the post-Stalin relaxation in the arts were shattered by the indifference and complacency of the Brezhnev bureaucracy. His late works, therefore, brood on the over-powering effect of evil and the inability of people to overcome their own failings. No hint of a better future is offered. Most of the characters are negative, and the few protagonists with whom the author identifies and sympathizes roam in the dark without a clear sense of direction or without hope of finding a way out of the darkness. His works seem the outcry of a desperate man who mirrors honestly the contradictions of his age and the absurdity of the human predicament.

The mood of dejection and negativism permeating his late stories found no sympathy in official Soviet circles, particularly at a time when the creation of a new image of a contemporary positive hero was being demanded over and over again. A 1982 resolution of the Central Committee of the CPSU states bluntly: 'The new generations of Soviet young people require a positive hero who is close to them in time and in spirit; a hero who would be perceived as an artistic discovery; a hero who would reflect the fate of the people and in turn influence their actions.'[93] Tendriakov could not produce such a positive hero because he was deeply aware of and perhaps tormented by the incompatibility between the personal demands of his moral nature and artistic integrity and the social requirements of conformity and compromise. And he was oppressed by the chasm between a social reality difficult to change and yet impossible to reject and a personal conscience impossible to alter and yet searingly painful to bear.

Vladimir Tendriakov died in 1984. His life was cut short before the advent of the Gorbachev thaw. His posthumously published works, which could not appear in print while he was alive, bear witness to his constant struggle with censors, with editors, and with himself.[94]

4 The Soviet Countryside

More than three decades have passed since the appearance of Valentin Ovechkin's sketches about Russian village life, *Raionnye budni* (District Weekdays; 1952–6), and the emergence of so-called village prose. The term is still used today by many to denote the literature describing the life of the Russian countryside. Many critics and literary scholars view village prose as a literary trend, but Veniamin Kaverin suggests that there are no literary trends in contemporary Soviet literature because 'writers today are classified by their adherence to a theme, which ... is little connected with the notion of "genre."'[1] In fact, some Soviet scholars suggest that the characters' place of residence is indeed the main common denominator, unifying all works of village prose.[2] Others assert that 'village prose' writers are identified by their support of a certain philosophical and ethical conception of life and adherence to an accepted set of moral values.[3] It appears thus that the term *village prose* is arbitrary and that it may mean different things to different people.

Indeed, literature about the Russian countryside has been written in a variety of genres and styles, but it is not difficult to see that the common feature connecting village prose of the 1950s and 1960s with the works describing the life of the Russian peasant in the 1980s is the setting. To be sure, many contemporary works about the countryside deliver a message similar to that propounded by the practitioners of village prose of the early 1960s, but this message today reflects a different reality. It is also directed at a different audience, because the peasant of the 1950s is a disappearing breed, and so for that matter is the Russian village of the immediate post-war era.

More than a quarter of the Soviet rural population moved from the countryside to the city in the last twenty-five years. Most of those who remained in the countryside have given up collective farming in favour of becoming state employees in agriculture.[4] This mass migration and the transformation of the means and methods of agricultural production have changed the face of the Soviet countryside. In the early 1950s the Soviet Union was basically a rural society in which the countryside population, charged with the responsibility of feeding the city, was scattered in countless villages. In the mid-1980s two-thirds of the Soviet people now reside in cities; the old village is no longer the dwelling place for most of the rural population, nor is it the centre of Soviet agricultural production.

Soviet literature about the countryside reflects these demographic, economic, and sociological changes in different ways. Most works of village prose of the 1950s and 1960s describe the difficult life of the post-war Russian village and the character of the Russian peasant who preserved his inner purity and high moral qualities despite all difficulties. Some of these works are written in the spirit of nostalgia for the past and for the ethical values associated with it. In many works the countryside is contrasted with the city, which is viewed as a repository of evil and as an intruder that unsettles the peaceful and natural life of the village.[5] The pages describing the difficult life of peasants in remote Russian villages belong to the best literature created in post-war Russia. Village prose has been praised by official Soviet critics and Western observers alike, but it has also been subjected, from time to time, to scathing attacks in the Soviet daily and periodical press. The criticism has been generated mainly by sociological and ideological concerns that this literature idealizes old patriarchal values and does not interpret life from the positions of communist and class morality.

Whether under the pressure of official criticism, or under the influence of demographic and sociological change, in the 1970s the subject-matter and the very essence of countryside prose changed considerably, focusing primarily on the portrayal of a disappearing world. Valentin Rasputin's novellas are currently viewed by many as a requiem to this vanishing reality. His 'Proshchanie s Materoi' (Farewell to Matera; 1976) is seen as a logical conclusion to conventional village prose in Soviet literature.[6]

Many Soviet writers, however, continue to concern themselves with current issues of the Soviet village. Some, including Fedor Abramov and Viktor Astaf'ev, whose recent works are set largely in the non-chernozem areas of northeastern European Russia, describe the destruction of old Russian villages, deserted by their inhabitants, and decry the disappearance of the moral and spiritual values associated with the old 'good' life and with 'roots.' Others, like Rasputin, endeavour to analyse the moral damage inflicted upon those who have been forced to abandon their homes in order to make room for new industrial developments in the remote regions of Siberia. Vasilii Belov and Sergei Krutilin have diversified their creative output. Belov investigates the village byt, while Krutilin approaches the farming community as a production unit and emphasizes economic issues. In addition, there are those who concentrate on the relationship of people and nature and deal with countryside issues in purely ecological terms.

Most important, of course, is the discussion of people's relationship to nature conducted from ethical and philosophical perspectives, as rendered in the works of Rasputin and Astaf'ev.[7] D.S. Likhachev points out that the root of the word priroda (nature) is in the Russian language etymologically closely connected with such words as rodina (motherland), narod (nation), rodstvennik (relative), rodnik (spring), rodnoi (native), and rozhdat' (give birth).[8] In fact there is nothing new in the derivation of the word priroda, as Likhachev suggests. But quite new is the emphasis in Soviet literature on the use of nature to propound a certain philosophical conception of life. This conception is based on the identification of nature with the motherland and the nation. It is also connected with the view that nature is the spring of moral wealth which is to save Russia from spiritual stagnation.

In the early post-revolutionary years man was portrayed in Soviet literature in the image of the conqueror of nature. Today this view is seen as a delusion: in conquering nature people have become victims of themselves; that is, the abuse and destruction of nature often harm not only physical well-being but spiritual welfare as well.

Many writers today identify the abuse of nature with the desolation of old villages and the destruction of a way of life. According to Rasputin, 'the village has always been the repository of the nation's moral foundations ... and it was easy for the city to exist when it had a dependable ethical background in the village.'[9] It is obvious that, despite claims to the contrary, Rasputin identifies the urbanization of the Soviet village and the abuse of Russian natural resources with the corruption of ethical values dominant in urban Russia. He warns that 'a time will come ... when people will have to admit that unrestrained indiscriminate technological progress is no progress at all, and that it does not serve man.'[10] Thus Rasputin views real progress not in material quantities but rather in the intangible quality of man's spirit and soul. A similar view on the relationship of nature and progress is expressed by, among others, Andrei Bitov in his 'Les' (The Forest; 1972), 'Ptitsy ili novye svedeniia o cheloveke' (Birds or New Information about Man; 1975), and Pushkin-

skii dom (Pushkin House; completed 1971, US publication 1978, *Novyi mir* 1987).

Among the writers who remain, in some respect, true to the original spirit of village prose, Fedor Abramov stands out most prominently. Valentin Rasputin and Viktor Astaf'ev, remaining true to their old concerns, move on to the analysis of individual evil and its social ramifications in the new conditions of Soviet life in the 1980s.

Fedor Abramov (1920–1983)

Fedor Abramov, one of the most prominent representatives of village prose, is known best for his award-winning trilogy *Priasliny* (The Priaslins; 1958–73). His last novel, *Dom* (The House; 1978),[11] turns his saga about the life of the Priaslin family and the Pekashino village in northern Russia into a tetralogy, which according to the author should be called now *Brat'ia i sestry* (Brothers and Sisters), after the first volume of the book.[12] The action in the third book of the tetralogy takes place in the early 1950s; the events in *Dom* cover one summer in the early 1970s. The novel is set in familiar surroundings: the characters, well known from the earlier volumes, are now joined by a new generation of young people. The intervening twenty years have witnessed a change in the organization of agricultural production, with the collective farm being transformed into a state enterprise. Old Pekashino now enjoys a higher standard of living. People seem to make good use of the new amenities, but except for the selfless and compassionate Liza, ever ready to please others and sacrifice herself for the good of the family, there is little change for the better in the mentality of the villagers. The hero of the tetralogy, Mikhail Priaslin, is now a mature man in his early forties, the father of three daughters. Still dedicated to his family and eager to work for the social good, nevertheless he has become a stubborn, bitter, and angry man.

The tone of the novel is set in its very first pages: in the old tradition of village prose of the 1960s, life in the city is contrasted with village existence. Mikhail returns from Moscow after visiting his sister Tat'-iana, who is married to an antique collector from the capital. Priaslin is happy to be back home, but it is evident that the germ of materialism has already infected him, and although life in Pekashino is now better than before, there is little happiness in the Priaslin family. Constant bickering and tragedy tear the family apart. The mother of the Priaslins is killled in an accident. The brother Fedor is a hardened criminal and in jail. Liza's son, Vasilii, perishes by drowning, but Mikhail continues to reject his sister. He cannot forgive her affair with a married man that culminates in the birth of fatherless twins. Liza suffers in loneliness, forgiving even those who have wronged her, while the well-to-do Mikhail and Tat'iana fail to understand the meaning of compassion. The novel ends in tragedy. Liza and her twin brothers, Petr and Grigorii, are renovating their old family house. She tries to help them raise a carved wooden horse to the top of their ancestral home. An accident occurs and she is crushed by the weight of the wood. Liza is carried off to the hospital with little hope of recovery.

The return to the old house, which is also the family home, symbolizes the attempt to return to old values and to the roots. Indeed, Petr contemplates a return to the village to work on the farm. Fedor will soon be on his way home from jail. This new family abode is to be infused by the spirituality of Liza, who acts as a mother to her brothers. But life in the new village is apparently beyond repair. With the fall of the wooden horse the edifice on which the alleged future happiness of the Priaslins is to be built also collapses. City corruption has already permeated the very existence of Pekashino, and there is no return to the times when hunger fostered sharing, suffering generated compassion, and individual happiness had little in common with material well-being.

A sense of tragic doom pervades the whole novel. The old are ill and dying. Those who are middle-aged are in the process of transition; they are no longer the peasants of the past, but rather farm workers, clinging to new city values. Work in the sovkhoz strips the peasants of collective responsibility. Each tries to contribute as little as possible and receive in return as much as he can.[13] Most of the young, who are supposed to represent the future, are seeking a good and easy life. Abramov contemplates the predicament of the new Soviet man and hints at a conclusion that the easy life deprives people of self-respect and turns them into parasites. The young Rod'ka, the son of Anfisa Petrovna, is a man without honour or moral scruples. Speaking about her son, Anfisa asks the troublesome question: 'Is it then true that a good man can be born only into a difficult life, or that a good life ruins man?'[14] Mikhail's answer to this question is evasive. But the reply is contained in the very essence of the novel. Twenty years of rebuilding have created a richer and stronger country, but, according to Abramov, this reconstruction has also ruined the ethical foundations of Soviet society.

In *Dom* Abramov draws a complete, albeit succinct picture of the Russian countryside in transition. The social and economic changes are reflected in his new characters. They lack the intangible quality of Russianness, the attachment and dedication to the land, characteristic of his earlier heroes. Soviet critics do not fail to note the negative overtones of *Dom*. V. Oskotskii, for example, decries the fact that there is in Pekashino 'everything in abundance, except for peace and happiness.'[15] 'The new houses are invaded by a lack of spirituality which is accompanied by its ever-present fellow traveller – vodka. In no other novel by Fedor Abramov do people drink as much as in this one.'[16] Most critical of Abramov's new novel is Iu. Andreev. He claims that the lack of consistency in the author's opinions interferes with his ability to perceive correctly the complex realities of the current transformation process, thus obscuring the positive vision of the future of the Soviet countryside.[17] Andreev suggests further that the logic behind the negative transformation in the character of Mikhail Priaslin is not very convincing, and he does not accept the changes occurring in the mental life of this hero. The essence of *Dom* is probably best summed up by A. Pavlovskii, who asserts that 'the wooden horse, the traditional ornament of a peasant hut in the north, tumbles down from the roof, denoting by its fall the end of an old way of life, as well as of its beauty.'[18]

Dom concludes Abramov's tale about Pekashino, which covers close to thirty years in the life of the Priaslin family. On the last page of the novel Mikhail seems to admit to his guilt for the terrible fate of his family, and he seeks inspiration in the image of his dead father. But the final chapter of the novel is an afterthought rather than a psychologically convincing ending to the Priaslin family drama. The conclusion of *Dom* is far from optimistic. Symbolically Mikhail has no son to continue in the steps of his father, and his brothers are unmarried and childless. With the death of Liza, the source of uprightness, honesty, and dedication also disappears. The only bond helping to keep the family together is dead.

In *Dom* the house still symbolizes hope – a place to live and a dwelling where the family can gather. In Abramov's later stories the house is usually a symbol of a bygone era. In fact most houses in his recent prose are desolate, deserted, and falling apart. 'Mamonikha' (Mamonikha; 1980),[19] the title of Abramov's short novella, is the name of an abandoned village. Klavdii Sytin, a man in his forties, comes to Mamonikha, for the first time in twenty years, to visit his old ancestral home. He is accompanied by his wife, Polina, and son, Viktor.

Mamonikha presents a sorry sight. There is only one inhabitant in the whole village, the old woman Sokha, who is considered by the local people to be a witch. Sytin is touched by his memories of the past. He is overwhelmed by a nostalgia for the good old days of his youth, but Viktor gets sick and there is no one to turn to for help. In the past Sokha treated the villagers. Now, she says, she has lost all her power to heal because there is no power left in Mamonikha. A place without people is dead. And yet she manages somehow to bring Viktor back to health, something we are led to believe city doctors could hardly accomplish.

Sytin is faced with the dilemma of what to do with the house. He is offered the assistance of a local man, nicknamed Gekha-maz, who is ready to buy it. Gekha-maz is a peculiar hybrid who embodies in equal measure a number of good and bad personal qualities that originate both in the countryside and in the city. He is a mechanic who works in the sovkhoz, but he uses state machinery to earn money on the side. He is thrifty and industrious in managing his beautiful household, but he shows little regard for the preservation of nature or the property of others. He is a speculator whose main income is derived from buying and selling the houses of people such as Sytin. Sytin refuses to sell his house to Gekha; they cannot agree on the price. But Gekha knows that if Sytin does not sell the house today for rubles, he will later give it away for kopecks, because it will be stolen, consumed by fire, or fall apart anyway.

Gekha is a practical man, while Sytin is a dreamer. Overwhelmed by a wave of sentimentality for his ancestral home, he deludes himself into thinking that he will return one day to look after the house. Sytin could have sold the house without difficulty, but he cannot part easily with his family home and the memories associated with it. Together they are the only link that still connects him with his past – his youth and his roots.

Mamonikha is compared by Abramov to a graveyard. Similarly, the setting of his story 'Zharkim letom' (In the Hot Summer; 1982),[20] the old village Lysokha, resembles a cemetery. Only two families remain there. They refuse to move when the order is given to amalgamate the local kolkhoz with another one located somewhere else. For four hundred years Lysokha was able to sustain itself as a prosperous village. All of a sudden, it had outlived its usefulness and its fate was sealed.

The story contains two important themes which are closely intertwined. The first is social, dealing with the economic and demographic changes in the countryside and their effects on the life of the peasant; the second is personal, expressed in the life story of the invalid Arkadii Lysokhin and his relationship with his stepdaughter, Gel'ka. It is a beautiful tale of attachment, dedication, and selflessness which are shaped not by the kinship of blood but rather by an emotional sense of duty and responsibility. Abramov contrasts the external world, which is completely devastated, with the internal beauty of those who grow up in these difficult conditions, and he alludes to the fact that the beauty of human behaviour has little to do with comfort or material well-being. The moral uprightness of Gel'ka is emotional and irrational; she grows up with it, and it becomes a part of her whole being. By contrast, in the materialistic world of the city, sophisticated man has learned to control his emotions and filters them through the prism of his rational faculties. Hence, there are seldom impulsive outbursts of goodness or evil, but rather a calculated and rational approach to everyday life and human relations.

Several general themes permeate most of Abramov's stories of the 1980s: the beauty of nature, the vastness of the Russian land, the decay of the countryside, and the disappearance of a generation of a people who represent a life based on mutual devotion and dedication to a certain ethical spirituality. Even among those who live in big cities, the simple working people are ethically superior to the intelligentsia.[21]

Abramov's prose of the last decade of his life poses a disturbing question: who is to blame for the devastation of the Russian countryside and the destruction of a way of life? The argument between Sytin and Gekha-maz addresses this issue. They blame each other for failing to live up to their responsibilities but cannot agree as to who is the main culprit. Abramov's reply to this question is muted, but it is unequivocally there. The countryside is destroyed and people suffer because they are deprived of the possibility of making their own decisions. Public policy determines where one is to live, and when one is to move. Public policy uproots people, abruptly changing their way of life and shattering their attachment to the land. It is obvious that the government assumes that it knows best what is good for people. But it is also clear that there is a vast disparity between public concern and the interests of individual man. This disparity is further aggravated by the fact that social policy is seldom tempered by public opinion, and still more rarely takes into account the question of personal choice.

Abramov's recent stories are usually prompted by the writer's visits to his native places, by chance encounters, or by passing experiences. Several stories are simple character sketches. Some are narrated in the third person, while in others first-person narration adds a touch of immediacy and authenticity. Abramov's prose flows smoothly, his images are precise, and his language is richly infused with examples of north-Russian dialects. Most of these stories are pervaded by a spirit of gloom and dejection and a sensation of tragic inevitability. In all of them there is a strong and passionate attachment to the land and to its people and a deep sense of compassion for the fate of suffering man.

Valentin Rasputin

By the end of the 1970s Rasputin was regarded in the Soviet Union as one of the most talented and promising writers. His controversial 'Proshchanie s Materoi,' however, encountered severe ideological criticism and placed the direction of his future artistic growth in question.[22] 'Proshchanie s Materoi' addresses the insurmountable conflict between the individual, who is totally self-absorbed, and the impersonal image of the collective state, which presumes to have the necessary answers to all questions. It queries also the basic philosophy of the Soviet state, which is identified with industrialization and technological progress.

Many critics have accused Rasputin of attempting to retard progress by idealizing an old way of life and fostering patriarchal values. Rasputin defends himself by saying that he is preoccupied not with the defence of the old village but rather with 'the spiritual world of millions which is being transformed and is disappearing altogether, and which tomorrow will be different from what it is today.'[23] Rasputin views 'Proshchanie s Materoi' as a work within the broad thematic range of pamiat', which should immortalize the difficult process of transition and leave to posterity an account of the values, hopes, and aspirations of its forbears.

After the appearance of 'Proshchanie s Materoi' Rasputin was silent for close to five years. In 1981–2 he published a few short stories,[24] and three years later the short povest' 'Pozhar' (The Fire; 1985).[25] Rasputin is not a very prolific writer, but the critical reaction to 'Proshchanie s Materoi' may have been one reason for his prolonged silence. Also, in May 1981 the *New York Times* reported that according to unofficial sources Rasputin had been suffering for a year from the effects of a beating that he received in Irkutsk and had been unable to resume writing since.[26] In 1980 Rasputin was beaten into unconsciousness by four thugs. He was hospitalized and operated on several times. The attack was not reported in the Soviet press but was known to his friends and acquaintances.

The four stories published in the 1982 volume of *Nash sovremennik*, 'Vek zhivi-vek liubi' (You Live and Love),[27] 'Chto peredat' vorone?' (What Shall I Tell the Crow?),[28] 'Ne mogu-u' (I Can't),[29] and 'Natasha' (Natasha),[30] defy classification. The first is narrated in the third person; all others in the first. At the centre of each is a trifling occurrence or passing experience that allows the author to explore the relationship of the real and present with the eternal and the intangible. Rasputin muses about the duality of human nature and the connection between the conscious and the unconscious. He searches his soul for an explanation of his own ways, contemplating the difficulties and pitfalls of artistic creation. All the stories are replete with lyrical meditations and permeated by a mood of doubt and a sense of insecurity.

'Vek zhivi-vek liubi' is set in the remote Siberian taiga. The old peasant Mitiai takes along the young and inexperienced Sania on a trip deep into the forest to pick berries. They are joined by another old man, Uncle Volodia. On their way back Volodia points out to Sania that, since his pail is galvanized, his berries are poisoned and have to be destroyed. Volodia has known all along that Sania has wasted his time, but has said nothing. The old Mitiai is furious, but Uncle Volodia shrugs him off coolly by saying that this will be a good lesson for Sania for the future. The boy is devastated. The trip to the taiga is his first trip away from home, but it is also his first lesson in real life. It teaches him that not everybody can be trusted and that there is a price to be paid for everything. Sania discovers in the taiga the real world of nature. It is pure and unpolluted and imbued with an invisible power of spirituality. But Sania becomes also in the taiga the victim of treachery. He learns that one can depend more readily on the surrounding elements than on the corrupt and callous nature of man. The first trip to the taiga is a journey from childhood to maturity, from naive innocence to the vile realities of our world. The title of the story symbolizes the denunciation of Volodia's philosophy of life and the affirmation of Mitiai's natural ways. Mitiai is far from perfect, but he is close to nature, not bent on hurting anyone without reason.

In 'Chto peredat' vorone?' the narrator is away from home and ponders the inscrutable ways of human nature. He relates an episode in which he is overwhelmed by a foreboding of something terrible that is going to happen to his daughter and is overpowered by a sense of guilt when he learns that his premonition was correct. Nature liberates him from the pressures of daily existence, and it sets him free from his mundane concerns. The narrator surrenders his rational self to the overpowering charm of the environment and experiences total freedom of body and spirit in his complete unison with the external world of nature.

The story 'Ne mogu-u' is different. It is set in a train compartment. It is reminiscent of a similar episode in Rasputin's 'Den'gi dlia Marii' (Money for Mariia; 1967), where a variety of people are brought together not by design but by chance, and unexpected encounters and situations can reveal hidden human character traits. At the centre of 'Ne mogu-u' is an alcoholic with an unusual name for a Russian – Harold. The alcoholic is completely devastated by his affliction and suffers terribly. The episode in the train directs the reader's attention to a multitude of personal and social issues connected with alcoholism. Poor health and physical pain, family breakdown, and social alienation are just a few of the problems that befall the alcoholic. It appears, however, that the narrator's main interest is not in the personal predicament of Harold but in the character traits of those who travel with him. Most of the travellers are nameless. They are identified by external signs only; their physical appearance, background, and language reflect their true nature. The narrator, who is a local man, and a tall lanky fellow who is called 'verzila' are compassionate. They want to help the sick man. But an educated man in sweat-pants, who is called 'triko,' and an older woman with a book care for nothing but their own comfort. They insist on throwing the drunk from the train.

It is an old Russian custom to treat drunks with understanding and compassion, and those in the story who are sympathetic to the plight of Harold are pictured as better people. As in many other works by Rasputin, dialogue and language expose hidden features of human character and help contrast the educated and self-centred, spiritually corrupt people of the city with the simple and physically unattractive, but spiritually generous people of remote Siberia. To Rasputin external charm and appearance seldom go hand in hand with inner beauty and in most cases serve to conceal man's inner shallowness.

Rasputin's next story, 'Natasha,' is apparently autobiographical; the narrator refers in the introduction to his hospitalization, surgery, and stay in a strange city. It is a story with a loose narrative structure, in which the author interposes fantasy into a realistic setting – the hospital – to reveal the narrator's psychological and emotional state. Natasha is allegedly a nurse, encountered in the hospital, and apparently an old acquaintance of the narrator's. But her very existence is in doubt, because the narrator's perception is obscure and his thinking muddled. In fact the narrator's mind works in a manner characteristic of someone recovering from the influence of anaesthesia. The story is a combination of reality and fantasy, of the conscious and the unconscious, of dream and the attempt to keep awake, in which it is difficult to discern the limits of truth and imagination.

Some critics suggest that we are confronted in the recent stories by a 'new' Rasputin, one who is unsure not only of his own word but also of himself.[31] Natal'ia Ivanova asserts that the monologue of Sania in 'Vek zhivi-vek liubi' expresses Rasputin's own lack of confidence in rational thought and that Rasputin is attracted to an emotional spirituality that is irrational.[32] Indeed, the stories discussed are distinct from Rasputin's usual mode of creation, but his concerns about the relationship of mind and spirit, and of good and evil, are not new. It is possible, however, to detect in these stories a new understanding of the influence of the irrational on the factors that determine human actions. This new understanding is borne out in his other works of the 1980s.

In 1981 Rasputin published another short narrative, entitled 'Baikal, Baikal ...' (Baikal, Baikal ...),[33] which can be read as an ode or a hymn to the greatness of nature embodied in Lake Baikal. This clarifies to a certain extent Rasputin's approach to the problems of ecology and pollution and man's relationship to nature. Rasputin asserts that from birth man continuously absorbs the air, the salts, and the scenes of his motherland, which in turn form his character and determine his way of life. To Rasputin Lake Baikal is one of the great miracles of nature and sources of inspiration. It is 'famous and holy for its miraculous life-giving force ... for its contemporary spirit, which is not subordinate to time or transformation, for its eternal greatness and might, as well as for the spirit of its natural will and magnetic experiences.'[34] 'The spirit of the Baikal is something peculiar and real; it forces one to believe in old legends and wonder with mystic caution whether man should always be free to act in a manner he may deem necessary.'[35] Rasputin declares without hesitation that the 'Baikal has been created as the crown and mystery of nature, and not for the satisfaction of production needs.'[36]

Rasputin gets carried away and concludes his discourse with a well-meaning statement of questionable merit. He asserts that 'nature in itself is always ethical and that only man can make it unethical. It is, in all probability, to the credit of nature that man is still able to contain himself within certain reasonable limits, which determine his moral condition.'[37] There is no question that nature determines the innate qualities of every human being, which in turn influence one's psychological, mental, and emotional make-up. But nature in itself is not ethical or unethical. Ethics is a philosophical notion and a branch of philosophy that studies the moral principles of human behaviour and, as such, is a logical science. Nature appears irrational to the human mind, because we are still incapable of fathoming completely its inscrutable ways. Natural forces can do good and evil at the same time. They may bring devastation and suffering, as well as happiness and plenty. Rasputin's statement contradicts the basic premisses of Marxist philosophy, according to which moral principles are determined by production relations and social conditions in a given society. Rasputin probably views nature as an ethical force, because it is a positive factor of great magnitude, helping to sustain human existence.

Rasputin's recent povest' 'Pozhar,' for which he was awarded the State Prize for Literature for 1987, falls short of the artistic level that he attained in his prose of the 1970s. It still contains pages of beautiful prose, but it will be remembered primarily for its social significance. In 'Proshchanie s Materoi' the author renders an account of the last summer of the 300-year-old Matera before it is to be flooded to make room for an artificial lake for a new hydroelectric station. In 'Vniz i vverkh po techeniiu' (Down and up the Stream; 1972) a young writer returns to his native village to visit his parents, only to realize that it has been flooded for a similar purpose and that his parents have been moved to a new settlement. In 'Pozhar' we are introduced to a similar settlement, which has become the home for the inhabitants of six villages flooded twenty years earlier in the ruthless wave of industrialization sweeping through Siberia. The main hero of 'Pozhar,' Ivan Petrovich Egorov, is a resident of the settlement Sosnovka. He is a man close to retirement. He comes to Sosnovka from the 300-year-old Egorovka, one of the villages resting at the bottom of the new reservoir.

The connection between 'Vniz i vverkh po techeniiu,' 'Proshchanie s Materoi,' and 'Pozhar' is evident, but whereas in the works of the 1970s the main issue is the change in man's external environment, in 'Pozhar' the emphasis is on the changes occurring in man himself. Rasputin attempts here to investigate the changes in the ethical and psychological make-up of those who have been uprooted and forced to abandon their native homes. The mentality of the people of Sosnovka is influenced by their occupations as well as by the peculiar character of their place of residence. Sosnovka is no longer a village, but neither is it a town. Instead of working the land, people are now employed in forest exploitation. Furthermore, the population of Sosnovka is no longer composed of its original settlers only; most newcomers lack roots and moral commitment and have come to Sosnovka in search of work, money, and good times. The fire that sweeps through the local warehouses uncovers the hidden essence of its inhabitants and illustrates the crippling effect of industrialization on the very essence of man, and on the general quality of life in today's Siberia.

A natural calamity usually unites people in their struggle with the elements. In Sosnovka, while everyone rushes to help put out the blaze, the fire also exposes the true nature and the evil intentions of many who use the occasion to get drunk, steal, and plunder public property. The people of Sosnovka can be divided roughly into three categories: the 'arkharovtsy,' or roughnecks, mostly rootless transients who care for nothing but their own momentary pleasures; the majority of resettled villagers, indifferent to anything that happens around them; and the few who try to salvage whatever possible from the fire, as well as from the universal blaze of social change that seems to destroy everything good in people.

Rasputin looks at the events through the eyes of the hero, who is a positive man in all respects. Unfortunately, at a certain point in the story the author and his protagonist become one, and the hero begins to articulate directly the writer's views and concerns. Ivan Petrovich deliberates on the human predicament and concludes that there are four posts that support man in his life: home, job, friends, and native land, which is the foundation of one's home. But the land has been flooded, and the home has become a place of transition, unsettling not only to man's external tranquillity but also to his internal peace, and in turn affecting the social and ethical underpinnings of life. 'Good and evil are now mixed together, and goodness, in its pure form, has become a weakness, evil in turn becoming a strong force.'[38]

The moral of 'Pozhar' is on the surface and not much different from the message in 'Proshchanie s Materoi.' The povest' is a desperate call to fight evil before it is too late. It is an outcry for a new social communal organization that does not destroy the good in people. In 'Proshchanie s Materoi' these ideas, expressed by old Dar'ia, are part of the conflict and well integrated artistically into the fabric of the novella. In 'Pozhar,' Rasputin the journalist takes the upper hand over the artist, endowing his hero with philosophical notions that seem beyond the level of his capabilities and forcing him to ponder about them at an artistically most inappropriate time. In 'Proshchanie s Materoi' the flood is perceived as a universal calamity, but Rasputin does not hesitate to point at those whom he considers guilty. In 'Pozhar' the fire reveals the evil transformation in those who survive the flooding, but there is no indication as to who is to blame for this horrible change.

The ending of 'Pozhar' is inconclusive. Ivan Petrovich contemplates the possibility of a move to another village, where his son lives and where life is allegedly better, because the people are settled and good. He fails, however, to see that even there he will remain a stranger, without roots. In all probability he will stay in Sosnovka, because there is no place where one can run away from oneself. Some critics interpret the main hero's ruminations, the morning after the fire, as a new positive beginning which usually comes after the symbolic mythological purification by fire,[39] but there is little evidence in the story to support such an inference.

It is obvious that Rasputin sacrifices artistic merit for journalistic effect in 'Pozhar.' Despite the lack of unity between image and idea, and a certain artistic incompleteness, Rasputin's creative talent is evident even here. The intensity of the spiritual anguish and the frustration of Ivan Petrovich, the only fully developed character, reach such heights that they are perceived by the reader as physical pain. The image of the spontaneous fire throws light on the faces of those who are around, but symbolically it also makes it possible to see through their hearts.

Soviet critical reaction to 'Pozhar' and discussion of its relative merits concentrate on the massive infusion of journalism into artistic fiction and on the social relevance of the story as a means of fighting evil and eliminating shortcomings in Soviet life. Most critics see nothing wrong with the proliferation of journalism in artistic prose; others warn that such an approach will certainly lower the artistic quality of prose fiction.[40]

'Pozhar' still contains some elements of old village prose, but the conflicts are different, and the setting is new. The countryside has changed so much that it little resembles the old Russian village, and the mentality of the peasant is different as well. He is no longer a peasant nurtured by his association with the land, but rather a worker with a peasant consciousness. In traditional village prose a man from the city usually goes to the old village to gain inspiration. The new village has little to offer. It has already succumbed to the corrupting pressures of civilization. And the new inhabitants come to corrupt whatever still remains intact from the old countryside.

Viktor Astaf'ev

In the late 1970s Astaf'ev published his well-known narrative *Tsar'-ryba* (Queen Fish; 1976).[41] It is a lyrical and philosophical allegory, set in the Siberian taiga, in which the predatory nature of man is juxtaposed with the tranquillity and infiniteness of the natural world. There are two important negative characters in the narrative. One is Goga Gertsev, a civilized outsider, who uses a sophisticated approach in his abuse of nature. The other is the local fisherman, a reckless poacher called Ignat'ich, who considers the natural resources of Siberia his personal domain. Goga and Ignat'ich are contrasted with the natural man, Akim, who lives according to the rules of collective living and realizes that man by himself is helpless in his confrontation with nature.

Tsar'-ryba is reminiscent of Hemingway's *The Old Man and the Sea*, but Hemingway's hero respects the fish he is out to kill. He views his struggle with it as part of the infinite natural process in which everyone has an assigned place and in which everyone lives at the expense of someone else. And yet when the fish is devoured by hungry sharks, the old man is sorry for the fish. He realizes that he overestimated his powers and abused the balance established in nature. The old man is victorious in his struggle with the fish, but he is defeated by nature. Unlike Hemingway's hero, Ignat'ich is a man without scruples. He is vain and greedy. He catches a huge sturgeon, but he is forced to part with it. The sturgeon overpowers the fisherman, leaving him wounded and dejected. Ignat'ich is destroyed by his greed and punished for his disregard of the laws of nature. The abuse of nature leads to the downfall of man, reminding us that the notion of man as the master of nature is a delusion.

A number of stories published by Astaf'ev in 1978 continue the theme of man's relationship with nature.[42] The leaf in 'Padenie lista' (The Fall of a Leaf) symbolizes the process of constant renewal in the natural world. The dog in 'Zhizn' Trezora' (The Life of Trezor) and the horse in 'Drevnee, vechnoe' (Ancient, Eternal) depend on man's generosity for survival, but they are not angry at man for his superiority; they serve people's needs with diligence and dedication. They submit to the natural course of events and accept the place assigned to them by fate. But humans, the most rational creatures, are seldom satisfied. They struggle continuously for a readjustment in the relationship established by nature in order to make their positions more favourable. Only the haemophiliac in the story 'Gemofiliia' (Haemophilia) is able to accept his lot, because he is close to nature and recognizes his own insignificance in relation to the omnipotence of the natural world. He does not challenge the established order of things or rebel against fate; he accepts life as it is.

In the 1980s Astaf'ev has diversified his creative output. He wrote, among other things, a play,[43] a war story,[44] and a number of meditative narratives, told in the first person and based on his own experience.[45] One of the narratives, 'Slepoi rybak' (The Blind Fisherman; 1986),[46] resembles in spirit Abramov's 'Mamonikha.' Even the name of the village described sounds similar – Muryzhikha. The narrator goes to this remote area with a group of industrial workers to fish. 'There are still a few families left in Muryzhikha, but mostly old single women, the invariable guardians and keepers of the silenced Russian villages.'[47] Life in isolation has turned the old women half savage. They have forgotten how and what to cook or how to do a day of useful work. All they do is gossip, swear at each other, and look for money for drink.

'Slepoi rybak' is a short story, set in the remote Russian countryside. It contains all the ingredients of vintage village prose. There is the juxtaposition of depraved city culture with the old ways of the village, using the comparison of a simple blind peasant with an invalid from the city. Both have been wounded in war, but the peasant accepts his fate without a murmur, while the city invalid is bitter and angry and suffers from empty pride just as much as he does from his physical affliction. The old women in Muryzhikha are far from perfect. They are offended and outraged by the behaviour of the young city fellows, yet when there is need, all the villagers hasten to help those in trouble.

Astaf'ev reminisces about his own childhood. He compares old rituals, traditions, and values of the old village with the physical devastation of the countryside today and the inner emptiness that accompanies it. He asks: 'What happened to us? Who plunged us into the abyss of trouble and evil, and why? Who put out the light of goodness in our soul? ... We lived with a light in our hearts, set for us long ago by men of heroic feats, so that we should not roam in the dark ... Why were we robbed of all we received with nothing to replace it, having created universal unbelief in anything? Who should we pray to? Who should we ask to forgive us?'[48]

Astaf'ev's despair and disenchantment are similar to those expressed by Abramov and Rasputin; so too are his eternal questions, which address the universal problem of the relationship of good and evil in man, and the influence of external circumstances and social conditions on individual behaviour. This tone of anguish is most evident in Astaf'ev's recent novel *Pechal'nyi detektiv* (The Sad Detective Story; 1986),[49] which is, in many ways, a response to Mikhail Gorbachev's new policy of glasnost'. The hero of the narrative, Leonid Soshnin, is an unconventional character. He is a militia officer, wounded and at the age of forty-two put out of service by criminals. He is also an aspiring writer. The novel is set in the Russian provincial town of Beisk. Astaf'ev has employed the device of telling a story within a story. Most of the episodes related in the narrative are part of Soshnin's manuscript, accepted for publication after a five-year wait. In the distant background is Soshnin's own family story.

The novel begins with Soshnin's visit to the local editor, in charge of the publication of his book. Her name, Syrokvasova Oktiabrina Perfil'evna, symbolically bears derogatory connotations. Astaf'ev caricatures her and other members of the local literary intelligentsia, describing them in a tone full of sarcasm and derision. These are mostly ignorant people of little consequence who put down others simply for the desire to put themselves up. And such people determine the future of Russian literature and control the fate of talented writers.

But the main subject of the novel is not literature but crime. In a multitude of fragmentary episodes, some even unrelated to the main hero's life, the author places under a microscope the scum of society and uncovers a number of hideous crimes that overwhelm Beisk. Murder, rape, robbery, and abandoned children left to die by reckless parents are daily occurrences. Astaf'ev does not investigate the social origin of crime or explore the psychology of the criminal. Except for the few instances when he blames alcohol for criminal activity, or when he refers to the murderer's total disregard for the fate of his victim, people and their deeds are dealt with separately. According to Astaf'ev, most crimes are senseless and result from personal rather than social evil. All-pervading materialism, complacency, and destructive self-will make it possible for the inherent, irrational, and evil impulses in man to overcome his inner goodness. A veiled conclusion follows, that man is unable to harness his inner drive for evil and that only strong social measures can assure public order and safety.

Soshnin is a brave officer. He discharges his duties and responsibilities without fear and with dedication, risking his life daily, but he is helpless in stopping the crime wave and unable to influence those who are responsible most for much of the evil. In fact, he cannot affect the mentality even of the town's people – his neighbours and friends. They are outraged and suffer most when a crime is committed, but the moment the criminal is apprehended they beg for his freedom and are ever ready to forgive him. In the end Soshnin is defeated by the dark forces of evil that engulf society. All that is left to him is to seek personal contentment in a renewed relationship with his wife and daughter, because symbolically only a strong family is a reliable foundation for a healthy society.

Soshnin is certainly not the ordinary police officer. When he is helpless in fighting crime on the streets, he turns to study and reading in search for the roots of evil. He criticizes the Soviet school for failing to teach the young about the real world, and he asks: 'Why should we learn about the nature of evil by studying almost in secret Dostoevskii and Nietzsche ... rather than learning about it from our own teachers?'[50] In a lyrical digression, Astaf'ev pays tribute to contemporary Soviet policy on nuclear disarmament and compares human evil with evil in the world. He attacks atom-bomb maniacs and warmongers and reminds them about a book with a prophetic title, *Crime and Punishment*, hinting that crimes of different proportions are committed daily and that punishment and retribution are surely to follow.

Astaf'ev's new novel has a number of artistic imperfections and falls short of the level achieved in *Tsar'-ryba*. Soshnin's family drama is poorly delineated. The images of a number of characters are indistinct. Many episodes and scenes are drawn impressionistically and are little connected with the main plot line of the narrative. The language of the novel is that of its main hero, and it is heavily infused with elements of colloquialism and slang. The ideas of both the narrator and the main protagonist are essentially those of the author himself. The heavy dose of journalism, which is intertwined indiscriminately with the fictional components of the narrative, makes it at times impossible to identify separate voices; this explains why much of the action lacks psychological motivation. We are told what happens, rather than being shown how it happens. It is obvious that Astaf'ev sacrifices artistry for external effect in *Pechal'nyi detektiv*, but it is apparently a calculated risk. He accepts here the challenge of glasnost' and capitalizes on the new 'thaw' by attempting to disclose the 'whole truth.'

Indeed, the message in the novel is direct and on the surface, but the 'truth' presented is not to the liking of all critics. One of them, D. Ivanov, accuses Astaf'ev of portraying a concentration of crime and evil much greater than is common in Soviet society. Ivanov asserts that there is the truth of daily reality, but there is also the ideal truth, which the author is supposed to convey. According to Ivanov, Astaf'ev and his hero are brave enough to uncover the terrible truth, but instead of fighting this horrid reality, they accept life as it is. Alluding to the new leadership of Gorbachev, Ivanov declares that the time has come to fight evil and that it is the writer's duty to lead this struggle.[51] Unfortunately that is easier said than done, and Ivanov is certainly well aware of it. Marxist philosophy propounds a notion that people are essentially good and that only social injustice forces them to do evil. Hence there should be no reason for crime in a social organization without antagonistic classes and in which human interaction is based allegedly on co-operation, understanding, and common interests. With the advent of the new socialist state, crime should have disappeared. But this is not the case. In fact crime is currently more pervasive than at any other time since the revolution.

It is obvious, therefore, that the Soviet writer who searches for the roots of evil finds himself in a paradoxical situation. According to Marxism people are good, and so is the socialist state. In the immediate post-revolutionary years, individual crime was usually attributed to the vestiges of the bourgeois past, but today most criminals are young people who are the products of Soviet life. It seems clear that neither people nor society are perfect and that criminal activity is the result of an intricate combination of personal and social causes which is different in each individual case. Astaf'ev seeks the roots of social evil in the nature of individual man; hence his references to Dostoevskii and Nietzsche. But only if one places individual crime within a social context will one find a solution to this burning problem.

Pechal'nyi detektiv became one of the most frequently discussed works in the Soviet daily and periodical press in the mid-1980s. Those interested in literature for its artistic merits, however, see little positive in the novel. Those concerned with the novel's social and political implications can be divided into two camps. Some appreciate the novel for its daring, openness, and relevance, while others are frightened of its possible repercussions. In fact, the critical reaction sometimes tells us more about the reviewers than about the novel itself. Thus, for example, V. Butorin, a representative of the literary bureaucracy, comes out with a veiled attempt at self-defence by attacking Astaf'ev's portrayal of the editor Syrokvasova. He accuses the writer of turning the woman-editor into a monster and devil in a skirt, and he wonders why so much bitterness, rage, and gall are invested in the portrayal of a secondary character.[52] Butorin chooses to ignore Astaf'ev's symbolic protest against the activity of literary bureaucrats.

Astaf'ev has always concerned himself with social issues, but in the past the ethical quality and the intricate experience of man have always been at the centre of his prose. Astaf'ev has always permitted his characters to act, remaining in the background and limiting himself to meditation and lyrical digressions. In *Pechal'nyi detektiv*, the investigation of personal dramatic conflicts, of human emotions, suffering, and happiness, is replaced by a broad panorama of crime, sin, and transgression. There is little that is positive or optimistic in the novel. The main protagonist speaks with the voice of the author, who himself uses the novel as a pulpit. The voice is charged with a special intensity, created by the deep pain and anguish experienced by the writer.

A number of writers closely associated in the past with the mainstream of village prose have recently diversified their creative output. Vasilii Belov, whose 'Privychnoe delo' (That's How It Is; 1966) has become a classic of village prose, is one of them.[53] Belov continues to write about the countryside, but, perhaps having realized that he would never create a fictional hero to surpass in ingenuity and originality his image of Ivan Afrikanovich, he turned from the artistic portrayal of post–Second World War Russian villages to other historical periods, other subjects, even other genres.

Along with *Kanuny. Khronika kontsa 20-kh godov* (On the Eve: A Chronicle of the Late 1920s; parts I and II 1976, part III 1987) he also published a collection of city prose, *Vospitanie po doktoru Spoku* (Education According to Dr Spock; 1978), in which the hero's adaptation to city life is one of the main subjects. Kostia Zorin is a nice fellow, an engineer, and a capable worker, but his character lacks stability. The same is true of other characters who move from the countryside to the city and whose life is in consequence in disarray.

Belov's next narrative, *Lad. Ocherki o narodnoi estetike* (Harmony: Sketches on Peoples' Aesthetics; 1979–81),[54] is a collection of ethnographic sketches re-creating the countryside byt in north-Russian villages. According to Belov, one has to 'treasure memory ... Without memory, without tradition, history and culture ... there is no individuality. Memory moulds the spiritual strength of man.'[55] Belov's description of the customs and traditions that determine the daily and yearly routine of village life creates a memorable impression of unvarying tranquillity and harmony in the life of the peasant community. This peaceful life can easily be contrasted with the continuous fuss and agitation of city existence. By omitting, however, all reference to the negative aspects of village life, Belov idealizes the countryside mode of existence and invites criticism which accuses him of varnishing reality in order to produce a picture of harmonious existence.[56]

In the 1980s Belov published, among other works, a play,[57] a story about the suffering in remote Russian villages during the war,[58] a journalistic sketch in which he contemplates the history and future of his native village, Timonikha,[59] and finally a city novel in which he denounced the Moscow intelligentsia and expressed opinions similar to those aired in his speeches, interviews, and journalistic writings.[60] *Vse vperedi* (Everything Lies Ahead; 1986) is in a sense an outgrowth of village prose. But instead of juxtaposing the village with the city and showing the superiority of the former, Belov turns to direct criticism of the city family, city morality, and city life in general. Belov has now become one of the main proponents of the struggle against modernity, innovation, and foreign influence in Soviet life. He compares rock music to narcotics and claims that organizers of rhythmic gymnastic performances on Soviet television have lost all elementary sense of shame.[61] He is against drinking, boarding schools, sex education in Soviet schools, matchmaking bureaux, and many other current innovations in Soviet society. He firmly supports big families and strong family ties, attacking young newlyweds who are in no rush to have children and want to live for themselves for a while. According to Belov, 'living for oneself' is a higher form of bourgeois egotism and reflects a consumerist attitude toward life. [62]

Belov is not the only writer for whom the theme of pamiat' or memory, has become the main focus. This theme is popular with many other writers who identify with the current trend of Russian national revival. One of them is Vladimir Chivilikhin (1928–1984), who published a long narrative, entitled *Pamiat'. Roman-esse* (Memory: A Novel-Essay; 1978–85), [63] in which he intertwines accounts of the Russian past with his own biography and attempts to uncover the Russian roots in his own life story.

Sergei Krutilin (1921–1985) was another writer closely connected with the mainstream of village prose. He wrote the well-known *Lipiagi* (Lipiagi; 1967) – a teacher's subtle chronicle, covering thirty years in the life of his native village. After an interruption of some fifteen years, Krutilin returned to the countryside theme, but the new novel, *Grekhi nashi tiazhkie* (Our Heavy Sins; 1982), [64] is artistically a far cry from *Lipiagi*. There is little character analysis or psychological investigation, and the few attempts at philosophizing are at best tentative and not very deep. The narrative pays tribute to the improvements and changes in countryside life since the 1960s, but the central conflict of the novel is reminiscent of Soviet delovaia proza, or business prose, which is usually set in the city. The main hero of the novel, the kolkhoz chairman Vargin, becomes unwittingly drawn into some fraudulent operations. He is removed from his job, put on trial, and expelled from the party. Vargin is shattered. All his interests centred on his job. He gained personal satisfaction and reward by serving a public cause, his personal and family concerns always remaining in the background. Krutilin tells a story that flows smoothly but generates little excitement. It may appear from the novel that life in the countryside is just as slow and dull as the novel itself.

It is clear that the concerns of the writers associated in the past with village prose today transcend local countryside issues and that social problems created by unethical people have greatly influenced their work. The attention of many writers is now directed at the investigation of the relationship of man and nature, mind and spirit, and the roots of evil in Soviet man and society. In many works, ethics and spirituality are connected with physical stability – with a house, *dom* – which is viewed not only as a place of residence but also as a home and a moral base. In this respect the image of dom is similar to Trifonov's image of mesto, or place. It appears also that the old term *village prose* should be used cautiously today when applied to literature describing the Soviet countryside of the 1980s, and it should not be confused with the general designation 'countryside prose.' *Village prose* has become a literary term in the Soviet Union, and this literature is identified by peculiar plot situations, narrative patterns, and symbolic devices that are absent from most recent works about the contemporary village. In fact the Soviet countryside has changed so much since the late 1950s that its social, economic, and ethical problems are vastly different from those encountered by the Russian peasant in the first decades after the Second World War.

5 The Second World War: Forty Years Later

The 1980s ushered in the fifth decade after the Second World War. Although the number of survivors and war veterans dwindles daily, the sheer volume of literature about the Great Fatherland War shows no signs of decline. Some twenty thousand books on this subject have been published in the Soviet Union since the end of the war. 'Five hundred books yearly. Ten every week.'[1] This literature develops and changes; it reacts to the needs of the day, but its main objectives differ little from those in the immediate post-war period. The purpose of war prose is primarily ideological and political. It glorifies the historical and heroic past of Soviet Russia and instils in the young generation a spirit of patriotism and dedication to their Soviet fatherland. This literature stresses the devastation and horrors of war and advocates peace. At the same time it also warns the enemies of the Soviet state that the physical and spiritual potentialities of the Soviet people are boundless and that anyone who dares attack the Soviet Union is doomed to destruction.

Most works of literature appearing in the early and mid-1980s and dealing with war issues were written in response to, and in commemoration of, the fortieth anniversary of the Soviet victory over Nazi Germany. This literature continues the trend, prominent in the 1970s,[2] of combining the portrayal of war with the depiction of contemporary reality. In some works, for example, Iurii Bondarev's *Igra* (The Game; 1985),[3] military confrontation and war scenes remain in the distant background, serving only as a vantage point from which to judge contemporary people and society. In other works, as in Vasil' Bykov's 'Znak bedy' (The Token of Calamity; 1983),[4] new emphasis is placed on the suffering of the Soviet people under Nazi occupation. In addition, there is currently in evidence a strong predilection for documentary literature, which includes war memoirs by military leaders and political personalities alike, as well as documentary prose by well-known writers of fiction. The 1980s have witnessed the appearance of the memoirs and reminiscences of Marshals K. Moskalenko, V.G. Kulikov, and F. Pstygo and Generals B. Utkin, S.P. Ivanov, and A. Egorov, and others,[5] and works of documentary prose such as Aleksandr Kron's 'Kapitan dal'nego plavaniia. Povest' o druge' (The Captain of the Merchant Fleet: A Tale about a Friend; 1983),[6] about the famous Soviet submarine commander Aleksandr Marinesko, and Vladimir Karpov's povest' 'Polkovodets' (The Commander; 1983),[7] about the defender of Odessa and Sevastopol', General I.E. Petrov.

Although most writers who remember the war are already beyond retirement age, the subject of war remains their domain. Of course, some young writers also try to exploit the great possibilities and publication opportunities afforded to war literature. Unfortunately, their works of fiction merit little critical attention.[8] More successful are the young authors who deal with factual accounts of the past. For example, the Belorussian journalist Svetlana Aleksievich taped interviews with five hundred women, participants and survivors of the war, and produced a manuscript about the effects of war on the fate of women entitled 'U voiny ne zhenskoe litso' (The Face of War Is Not a Woman's Face; 1984).[9] This was followed by *Poslednie svideteli. Kniga nedestkikh rasskazov* (The Last Witnesses: A Book of Stories Not for Children; 1985),[10] which relates the reminiscences of men and women who were children during the war. There is little new in these narratives, but the sheer accumulation of factual accounts about lost parents, orphaned children, and human suffering has a shattering effect on the reader. The depiction of the difficult life in territories occupied by the Germans is not limited to documentary prose. Many works of imaginative fiction, including Vasil' Bykov's Lenin Award–winning povest', 'Znak bedy,' deal with similar issues.

The war prose of the immediate post-Stalin era is often designated by such terms as *okopnaia pravda* (the truth of the trenches) and *leitenantskaia proza* (lieutenants' prose). In the 1980s the term *soldatskaia proza* (soldiers' prose) has become popular. It appears that until recently the soldier's difficult lot had usually been presented through the eyes of junior officers. In the late 1970s and the 1980s a number of works began to appear in which war veterans relate the soldier's experiences from a soldier's perspective. 'Sashka' (Sashka; 1979),[11] by Viacheslav Kondrat'ev, is one such work. Two stories by Vladimir Tendriakov, 'Den' vytesnivshii zhizn'' (The Day That Dislodged a Life; 1985)[12] and 'Den' sed'moi' (The Seventh Day; 1986),[13] published posthumously, belong to the same group.

Authors writing about the war approach their subject from one of two perspectives. In some works, events are described as perceived by those participating in battle (Kondrat'ev, Tendriakov); in other works, the same occurrences are portrayed as seen and understood by contemporary man (Bondarev). In the first instance, the invisible and dead heroes pass judgment on those who survived. In the second case, contemporary man often judges those who perpetrated injustices during the war. Though the perspective varies, the theme remains the same, whether contemporaries are worthy of the sacrifices of those who perished in war. This question is seen as an ethical issue, because war with Nazi Germany is now presented not as a conflict of limited significance but as a struggle for a better society and a better life in general.

Many works published in the 1980s, and hailed as great achievements of Soviet literature, were written long ago. Kondrat'ev, a war veteran and a man of over sixty, had to secure the assistance of Konstantin Simonov and wait some twenty years before his 'Sashka' could see the light of day.[14] Although there were apparently some artistic imperfections in the novella, the main obstacles to publication were certainly ideological.[15] The story touches on a number of aspects of the Soviet war effort that historians prefer conveniently to overlook. It tells of unwarranted and useless losses in man-power in the first year of war. It emphasizes the disparity between the difficult and dangerous conditions at the front line and the easy life and complacent attitude of officers and soldiers in the rear. It points also to the lack of subordination to higher authority by some soldiers and junior officers.

'Sashka' is set in the spring of 1942 in the district of Rzhev, just northwest of Moscow. The situation of the Soviet army is desperate. The soldiers are hungry and exhausted. There is a shortage of manpower, ammunition, and supplies. The story covers several days in the life of the simple soldier Sashka. He has been at the front line for two months. He copes bravely with all difficulties and even manages single-handedly to take a German soldier prisoner. But there his troubles begin. The battalion commander instructs him to kill the German. Sashka refuses to obey. He remembers the leaflets distributed among the German soldiers in which they were encouraged to give themselves up and are promised life and peace in return for surrender. To Sashka the German is an ordinary man and a soldier like himself, only one who has been cheated by his superiors.[16] Sashka begins to 'doubt the justice and the need of the order ... He cannot kill an unarmed man.'[17]

Sashka is an excellent soldier. He selflessly helps his comrades and risks his life in order to ease the suffering of others. He is also a good man: compassionate, understanding, and able to forgive. Never before has he questioned the orders of his superiors. But now the affinity between the fates of the captive and of his captor subconsciously fuels his determination to save the German. He is driven by an inner sense of justice and by the innate instinct that life should not be uselessly destroyed. The commander is forced to revoke his order not because he considers himself in the wrong but because he is challenged by a simple man of superior ethical qualities. Refusing to obey an order in time of war is a grave criminal offence, yet the reader sympathizes with Sashka and his sense of higher justice.

The story is told in the third person by a narrator who identifies with the protagonist, but who is also close to the author. Most characters in the story remain nameless or are identified by their first names or physical characteristics. The predicament of Sashka becomes impersonal and can refer to all Soviet soldiers and to all Russian people. Artistically 'Sashka' has its share of imperfections. After the first part, in which the incident with the German prisoner is described, the intensity of narration drops, and the following two parts are anti-climactic. In order to make the behaviour of Sashka believable and in tune with his character, the author idealizes his hero to such a degree that some of his actions are psychologically not very convincing and seem, at times, even naïve.

But 'Sashka' is Kondrat'ev's first published work, and it is difficult to expect perfection from an inexperienced author. The case of Vladimir Tendriakov is different. He is an experienced writer as well as a war veteran, wounded in combat. In the last interview before his death, Tendriakov, who had never dealt with the topic of war in previous works, acknowledges that he intends to write an autobiographical book composed of a number of separate stories and novellas, describing minor episodes of everyday life at the front. The first story, he claims, will describe, almost 'literally, photographically,' his first day at the front, 'a day that dislodged all his past life.'[18] Tendriakov did not live to see the publication of this story. He died in August 1984. Half a year later 'Den' vytesnivshii zhizn' appeared, with an introduction by Daniil Granin.

Like Kondrat'ev's 'Sashka,' Tendriakov's story is also about the daily life of a simple soldier at the front line, but it is told by a subjective first-person narrator, who obviously relates the writer's own experiences. Tendriakov does not resort, as Kondrat'ev does, to the portrayal of major dramatic conflicts between different characters. He limits himself to the description of the narrator's first day at the front. It appears to be an 'ordinary' day, but it abounds in so many shattering experiences and discoveries, so many wasteful deaths, and so much suffering that in other circumstances it would take years to gain such knowledge of life. Tendriakov's prose is fresh. The author observes the smallest nuances in the soldiers' moods. He exposes their hidden thoughts and intentions. Tendriakov does not preach, nor does he glorify the actions of his mates. In a few lyrical digressions he pays tribute to the unheroic daily work of ordinary soldiers. Without their efforts the victory over a superior enemy would remain a dream. To Tendriakov, the signaller's war 'was first of all risky and difficult work; work to exhaustion; work next to death.'[19] Tendriakov wonders how one can romanticize or glorify the death of a man who was killed on his way to fetch a spade.[20]

At the centre of Tendriakov's second story, 'Den' sed'moi,' are all those who survived the first day at the front. The autobiographical hero, Tenkov, continues his saga. For five days his detachment defends a piece of bare ground. On the sixth day there is an ominous silence, and on the seventh day they retreat to the Don River. There is a commotion at the river crossing. Everyone is desperate to run away from the pursuing enemy. The platoon commander, Smachkin, is a professional officer, a man of strong emotions, whose dedication to his fatherland is limitless. He is embarrassed by his helplessness and is ready for self-sacrifice. The officer Zvontsov, who is a bookkeeper in private life, exhibits a pragmatic approach to the situation. He understands that temporary retreat can still lead to victory, that self-sacrifice will lead nowhere. Smachkin is the product of a military school where ideological and political indoctrination equates retreat with treason. Zvontsov is the product of the struggle for existence against uneven odds in daily life, where there is little place for high-sounding but empty theories.

Tendriakov is not interested in the portrayal of active combat or heroism. Rather he observes his characters in defeat and retreat. He describes circumstances in which the sober and practical qualities of Zvontsov are much more important than the blind determination and dedication of Smachkin. Here Tendriakov pays tribute to the many middle-aged soldiers and officers who were drawn into the ranks after the Soviet regular army had been wiped out in the first Nazi onslaught. But 'Den' sed'moi' is primarily a soldier's story. The narrator observes and comments on everything he experiences. Everything in the story is seen and presented through the prism of his perception. Physical and emotional pressure, the fear of death and mutilation, and the incredible hardships of daily existence temper the young and inexperienced character of Tenkov in both stories. It is difficult to do justice to Tendriakov's war stories because they are intended as part of a larger work. All the same, the hand of an experienced prose writer is in evidence.

Another example of the futility of war and the tremendous waste of human resources can be found in Grigorii Baklanov's story 'Naveki – deviatnadtsiletnie' (Nineteen Years Old – Forever; 1979).[21] Nothing extraordinary happens in the life of the main hero, Lieutenant Tret'iakov. He has no time to enjoy life or make a concrete contribution to the war effort. All he manages to do it to get wounded on several occasions, finally being killed in battle. Tret'iakov, according to Baklanov, is one of the unknown war heroes who fulfil their obligations, and even sacrifice their lives, not in expectation of reward, but with an inner sense of patriotic pride. They are guided by a quiet sense of duty and their ethical commitment to life.

An example of documentary war literature can be found in A. Kron, who did not live to see the publication of his last povest'. He died in February 1983, but it took close to ten years for his last work to appear in print.[22] 'Kapitan dal'nego plavaniia' is the story of Aleksandr Marinesko, commander of a Soviet submarine. In January 1945, in the Baltic Sea, the s-13 sank the German liner *Wilhelm Gustlov* and the transport ship *General Shtolbein*, with some ten thousand military personnel on board. The submarine's exploits are well known to Western historians, but they were taboo in the Soviet Union until the early 1960s, because its commander was punished for breach of discipline. Kron takes upon himself the task of correcting Soviet naval history by rehabilitating the memory of one of its heroes.

Marinesko died at the age of fifty. He lived a stormy and eventful life. Originally from Odessa, he joined the navy early and served during the war in the Baltic fleet. Unfortunately, Marinesko's sensitive and hot-tempered nature and his lack of discipline often got him in trouble with his superiors. He was demoted, demobilized, and ended up in prison in the Kolyma. Marinesko was no angel. He drank heavily and abused military discipline, but he was also groundlessly suspected of other transgressions. A night spent with a Finnish woman in a foreign port, and his father's foreign, Romanian extraction, were enough to make him suspected of treason. Before his death in 1963, Marinesko was back in Leningrad, trying to build a new life for himself, but it was already too late to reap the rewards he certainly deserved.

In his book Kron does not draw any generalizing conclusions, but his portrayal of conditions in the Soviet navy, and his analysis of

Marinesko's psychological make-up and behaviour, can lead one to certain inferences, arrived at by Leo Tolstoi many years ago. To Tolstoi military service and war corrupt man's nature. The difficult conditions in the navy, which demand total dedication and tremendous sacrifices, often lead to alienation and mental breakdown. Many individuals are driven to extreme expressions of escapism and alcoholism, to which Marinesko eventually succumbs.

Kron pays tribute to Marinesko's heroism. He seeks to re-establish his fame, but nowhere does he say that the predicament of Marinesko and his tragic fate are shared by other unknown war victims, most of whom never had a chance to sink an enemy ship or even kill a single Nazi. War is an exercise in the survival of the fittest. But Marinesko's disability is not of a physical nature. Military service and war turn him into a mental cripple. Instead of being treated, he is punished. His sensitive nature fails to adapt to the pressures of the outside world, and he begins to disintegrate physically. The story of Marinesko is a sad one. Without being aware of it, Kron raises here the question of the so-called lost generation of soldiers and officers who survived the war but who, for various reasons, could never return to normal life.

Documentary prose strives to uncover the truth about the war, but its impact on the general readership is limited. Similarly, straightforward narratives, relating battle scenes and military confrontation, do not have mass appeal. No wonder experienced writers resort to different artistic tricks and devices to make the subject of war more interesting and entertaining. A case in point is Daniil Granin's 'Eshche zameten sled' (The Track Is Still Visible; 1984).[23] It is a first-person narrative by the Leningrad war veteran Dudarev, but most of the story is revealed in epistolary form through letters by Dudarev's two war comrades, Volkov and Lukin, to a certain young woman from Georgia named Zhanna. Many years after the war Zhanna goes to Leningrad to seek out Dudarev, whose name was mentioned in one of Volkov's letters. Dudarev does not remember Volkov. In fact he wants to forget the war altogether. But the letters that Zhanna gives him to read restore the past. We learn that Volkov, who was a good officer and an honest and upright man, was arrested and sent to jail because he dared to question the appropriateness of a certain operation in which many Soviet soldiers were pointlessly killed. Having read the letters, Dudarev becomes convinced that Volkov was correct in his actions and that he, Dudarev, had contributed to Volkov's undoing.

One of the major themes of Granin's story is memory. Dudarev reflects that 'at times, man becomes completely subordinated to his memory and begins to *suffer* from it.'[24] But memory is selective. The years separating one from the past help create a myth about the war: some imagine things that never happened and accept them as real; others prefer to forget events that weigh heavily on their consciences. Both Dudarev and Zhanna are tormented by their guilty consciences, because both refused to lend a helping hand when Volkov needed it most. Now, the old Zhanna, married twice and unhappy, chases an unfulfilled dream. She wants to rectify her old mistakes. She wants to re-create in her memory not the real past but rather the one that eluded her.

Among the writers dealing with war, Iurii Bondarev and Vasil' Bykov continue to stand out. Bondarev, as a leading literary bureaucrat, is able to introduce thematic innovation and to test new ground. Bykov remains one of the few who write about nothing else but the war; his craftsmanship, dramatic intensity, and sincerity place him artistically above most other Soviet writers dealing with the subject.

Iurii Bondarev

Bondarev's recent novels are no longer in the mainstream of war literature, because most of the space in them is taken up by the discussion of contemporary issues. Nevertheless, the present-day events are engendered by occurrences taking place in the remote days of the Second World War, and the attitudes of the protagonists toward the complex and intricate social issues of the 1980s are determined by their war experiences. In Bondarev's early novels the plots are centred around conflict among several characters, usually soldiers or junior officers, in the background of which is the confrontation between the Soviet and German armies. In Bondarev's novels of the 1980s there are no direct collisions between characters, and personal conflicts are often left under the surface. Instead, there is a constant juxtaposition of motivational factors, of human behaviour, and of the working of fate.

In *Vybor* (The Choice; 1980),[25] Vladimir Vasil'ev and Il'ia Ramzin are two close Moscow friends. In 1941 they are infatuated with the same girl, who later becomes Vasil'ev's wife. They volunteer together for the army and in 1943 serve in the same artillery battery. But fate treats them differently. On a futile mission to retrieve guns previously captured by the Germans, Vasil'ev remains behind to cover the retreat, while Ramzin, with his troops, moves ahead to confront the enemy. The sortie is doomed from the outset, and no one returns. Ramzin is presumed dead, but he remains alive. On the ominous day in July 1943 he was taken prisoner, and he survived. He married a German woman who bore him a son. Now, a widower and terminally ill, he lives in Italy. In the late 1970s Vasil'ev, now a famous Soviet painter, is on a visit to Venice. He is accompanied by his wife, Masha, who in 1941 loved Ramzin. Ramzin approaches the Vasil'evs and asks them to help him secure an entry visa to the Soviet Union. In Moscow he goes to see his old mother, but she receives him coolly and refuses to forgive him. Disappointed and dejected, he commits suicide in his Moscow hotel room.

Ramzin's alleged betrayal symbolically separates him from his roots, and only death can bring him back to mother Russia, which does not forgive him but grudgingly accepts the return of her prodigal son. In his suicidal letter to Vasil'ev, Ramzin begs forgiveness. This note is apparently intended as an expression of sorrow for all the trouble he caused them by his coming to Moscow, rather than as an admission of guilt. Ramzin blames blind destiny for the course his life has taken. He never succumbs to the insinuations that he made a rational choice to defect. It is all a stroke of bad luck, a nightmare in which no minor role is played by his commander, Major Vorotiuk, whose decision to send Ramzin on a mission with no chance to succeed is prompted by ulterior motives.

Vybor, which was awarded the 1983 State Prize for Literature, generated a lively but far from unanimous critical reaction. Most Soviet critics emphasize the philosophical and ideological essence of the novel but pay little attention to its artistic qualities. Literary scholars of the older generation condemn Ramzin for his actions. One of them claims that the novel concerns itself with the cardinal 'notion of the meaning of human existence and with the idea of selecting a true or false objective in life ... By making his choice, he [Ramzin] betrayed everything that was dear and holy to him in his youth: his friends, his mother, and his Fatherland.'[26] Others assert that Bondarev illustrates 'the banefulness of the illusion of neutrality'[27] and that Ramzin returns to Russia 'in order to prove with his death that in the twentieth century there is possible only one choice.'[28]

The title of the novel would have us believe that man is a logical creature, free to determine his own fate, and that human happiness is the result of the right choice. It also alludes to the fact that Ramzin's tragic end is the price he has to pay for the wrong choice made on the fateful day in 1943. It could, however, appear that the title *Chance* would be more appropriate than *The Choice*. Ramzin rejects categorically the notion of rational surrender, and we know nothing about the circumstances in which he is captured. It is clear that most Soviet critics infer here that Ramzin should have killed himself instead of letting himself be taken prisoner.

But as V. Bykov's controversial story 'Mertvym ne bol'no' (The Dead Feel No Pain; 1966)[29] illustrates, even those who urge others not to surrender to the enemy may give themselves up in order to save their lives. The Soviet security officer Sakhno blindly follows orders from above. He does not spare the lives of those under his command, but when he is faced with the enemy, instead of shooting himself as he forces others to do, he gives himself up without regrets and co-operates with the enemy. But Ramzin's predicament is presented in such a manner that the question of his allegiance is not a physical, emotional, or even a national issue but rather a political and ideological one, and in that respect official Soviet criticism admits only one choice. Yet some younger Soviet critics refuse to accept Ramzin as the only culprit in this human drama,[30] while others question the truthfulness of certain scenes, including the one in which the mother refuses to accept her son who has been considered dead for over thirty years.

The character of Ramzin is an innovation in contemporary Soviet literature. He is the first traitor given a chance to return to the Soviet Union and try to defend his position. True, he is not implicated in supporting the Nazis, and there are even allusions to the assistance he renders to Soviet representatives abroad. All the same, he does not return to Russia after the war, and little is know about his activity in the intervening years. In the final analysis Ramzin is defeated. There is no room in our divided world for a Soviet man who wants to accept dual citizenship or dual nationality. Even though the Russian soil accepts its repentant son, to Soviet patriots he remains an outcast.

Ramzin's character is somewhat schematic and created in a certain mould to suit the political role assigned to him in the novel. Much more complex is the character of Vasil'ev, who has much in common with Nikitin from Bondarev's earlier novel *Bereg* (The Shore; 1975).[31] Bondarev is much more generous to Vasil'ev than he is to Ramzin. The latter is faced with the inevitable choice between a life of loneliness and alienation and death. Vasil'ev is spared such choices. Fate decides for him in his favour. Now, many years after the war, his life appears to be full of external tranquillity, yet he is not much happier than Ramzin. He achieves professional fame and material satisfaction, but not much more. He seeks contentment in his love for and identification with his wife, but she eludes him. His daughter, Vika, is raped by two thugs and loses faith in people and life. He is disappointed with his colleagues from the world of the arts, most of whom view their profession not as a calling, which nurtures their creative spirit, but rather as a trade, which satisfies their corrupt, materialistic desires. Vasil'ev is frustrated and disillusioned. He is torn by internal contradictions and haunted by nightmares. There appears to be no direct reason for Vasil'ev's state of mind, but there are many allusions to the deteriorating quality of life in the Soviet city and, in particular, to the pervading consumerism which leads to a spiritual vacuum. Vasil'ev is not a strong character, but he is a decent and honest man who has difficulty in coming to terms with himself and with the society of which he is a part.

Vybor reads well because its plot is engaging, but as a work of art it has its share of imperfections. The action takes place in three different locations and at different times: in Moscow in 1941, in Ukraine in the summer of 1943, and in Venice and Moscow in the late 1970s. But the transition from place to place, and from time to time, is not always as smooth as one could wish. In addition, the narrative is uneven because Bondarev, the experienced author of many war novels, is much better at depicting war scenes and military confrontations than at exploring the intangible qualities of human nature and human relationships.

Bondarev's next novel, *Igra* (The Game; 1985), is close in subject-matter and spirit to his other works, belonging to the trilogy that begins with *Bereg*. The plot of *Igra* hinges on a few melodramatic incidents that lead the hero, the film director Krymov, to soul-searching, metaphysical musing, and reassessment of his relationship with his family, friends, and associates. One incident takes place during the war but fulfils its dramatic purpose in the present. The young lieutenant Krymov is a commander of a reconnaissance platoon. One of his soldiers, the peasant boy Molochkov, is a shameless coward. On one of their missions, Krymov gives in to the entreaties of Molochkov that he be relieved from duty at the front line. Krymov purposely wounds Molochkov in the arm so that he can seek help in the hospital far behind the front lines. Krymov commits a crime by giving in to the weak Molochkov. Many years later, Krymov encounters Molochkov again and helps him secure a position in his film studio. Molochkov acts the toady; he pretends to worship Krymov, who saved his life and provided him with a good job. When Krymov is in trouble, the real Molochkov denounces and blackmails his saviour without hesitation.

The other incident takes place in the present. The famous director Krymov selects the young and talented ballerina Irina Skvortsova, who is injured and cannot dance any longer, to play the lead role in his new film. Skvortsova, who is much younger than Krymov, is presented as a symbol of natural beauty and purity. She is a frail and sensitive flower not fit to survive in the wicked and corrupt atmosphere of society today. She is driven to self-destruction by the envy and jealousy of other actresses who see her as an outsider, a competitor who comes to usurp their rightful place in the studio. It is not clear whether Skvortsova dies by accident or commits suicide. All the same, her departure is a symbolic denunciation of evil and a hint that social apathy and indifference can develop into a horrible force able to undermine the very foundation of any social structure. There is nothing in the novel to indicate that Krymov has been intimate with Skvortsova, but gossip-mongers spread rumours that they were lovers and that he is responsible for her death. Although there are no direct accusations against Krymov as yet, he is interrogated by the police, and most of his colleagues and associates avoid him and treat him with reserve.

Krymov, successful in war and in peace, has been used to fame and public adulation all his life. He loves his wife and children and felt fulfilled in his professional endeavours. Now all this has changed. He is suspected of a crime of which he is not guilty. He is prevented from producing his next film, and the slanderous rumours about his alleged affair finally enter his narrow family circle. His world begins to crumble. His soul-searching leads nowhere, and he finally breaks down and disintegrates, first mentally and later physically.

Krymov does not surrender without a struggle. He searches desperately for the causes of his present state of affairs. He finds strength to fight his difficulties in the determination exhibited by Archpriest Avvakum, and he turns to the contemplation of the 'eternal questions' which trouble Tolstoi and Dostoevskii so much. In a dialogue with the American film producer John Grichmar, in which Krymov attacks the moral degradation of the West, he attempts to identify the evil forces that corrupt and retard social progress. He contends that 'there are too many dull, shrewd, and complacent wreckers, little bureaucrats – from house managers to ministers, who believe in one principle only: live sweetly today, and when we are no more, there may even be a flood.'[32]

When Krymov's son asks him why evil remains unpunished, he tries to explain it by comparing the idealistic generation that perished in the Second World War with his own pragmatic and opportunistic contemporaries. Krymov asserts that 'the flower of the nation perished in war. Only a few of the best remained alive. But the children of those who survived are worse than their fathers.'[33] Krymov declares further that 'contemporary civilization has led the world down the wrong path. Wise men invented machines, but technology ... started to rule people. It pampered them, taking away from them the power of the spirit.'[34]

Despite the fact that Krymov's patriotism, his rabid anti-Americanism, and his dedication to the Soviet state are unswerving, his philosophical deliberations raise a number of controversial ideological questions that can lead to conclusions that run counter to official Soviet policy. On the one hand, Krymov decries the corruption, perversion, and egoism of the Soviet people, who are allegedly influenced by the West; on the other hand, he suggests that Russia will save the world: 'America cannot do that. There, one encounters complete depravity, and total agreement with the devil.'[35] By the same token, Krymov criticizes civilization and technological progress, which are at the root of the economic development of modern Soviet society, while seeking at the same time ethical and spiritual strength in Tolstoi's notion of self-improvement and Dostoevskii's theories of suffering. No wonder some Soviet critics question Krymov's sincerity, by asking what kind of Russia is going to save the world. 'The one that works day in and day out, that develops scientific and technical progress, which Krymov hates so much ... or the half-mystical Russia, with Archpriest Avvakum as its symbol and Tolstoi as its prophet, that exists in Krymov's mind.'[36]

Krymov is a contradictory, confused character who stands very close in his world view and theories to his creator. In a speech at the Sixth Congress of Russian Writers in December 1985 Bondarev expressed views strikingly similar to those voiced by Krymov. Bondarev came out against official plans to reroute some rivers in the Arkhangel and Vologda regions, rich in old cultural monuments, in order to make room for a new hydroelectric system. He asked: 'What is happening? When will patient common sense replace technocratic impatience and local vanity? Indeed, memory and culture are the conscience of generations ... We sometimes confuse civilization with culture. Civilization represents just a small fraction of culture. It is the shadow of its energy which places traps in the path of man, promising him comfort and convenience ... often wrapped in cosmopolitan vogue, feminization and masculinization, money, entertainment, idols of the stage ... and the Russian version of Pepsi-Cola.'[37] It appears that Bondarev, like his hero, opposes civilization and technological progress, seeking spiritual revival in the values of old Russia. It is a view advocated by neo-Russophiles in Soviet intellectual circles and very close to the recipe for a new Russian renaissance prescribed by no other than Aleksandr Solzhenitsyn. It is paradoxical, however, that both Bondarev and Krymov reject technological progress but love the good life and make ample use of its twentieth-century achievements.

The latest three novels by Bondarev – *Bereg*, *Vybor*, and *Igra* – are similar in scope, structure, and methods of narration, but with each novel the place allotted to war diminishes and the protrayal of contemporary reality gradually takes over. Nevertheless, war remains the focal point, serving as a standard by which to judge the actions and behaviour of people today. The three novels are similar in other areas as well. Part of the action in each takes place in a Western country: in West Germany, Italy, and France, respectively, and the dialogues between Soviet and Western intellectuals always emphasize the ethical and spiritual superiority of Soviet Russia over the West. In fact the scenes describing the night life in Paris (*Igra*) and Hamburg (*Bereg*) are identical. There are also parallels between the idealized and not very realistic images of Kniazhko (*Bereg*) and Skvortsova (*Igra*). The death of both characters stresses their ethical superiority over the corrupt majority that surrounds them. The characters serve to remind the reader that there are still people to emulate and that there is hope for a better future. Artistically these three novels are alike. The plots and conflicts are unconventional. Many important scenes and incidents often lack truthfulness to life. Third-person narration, often interspersed with dialogue and internal monologue, predominates in each of the novels. Much of the philosophical discussion, particularly with foreigners, is very general and inconclusive. Most of the notions voiced are not part of a well-developed system of beliefs defended by those concerned but rather a hasty and not always serious reaction to the needs of the moment.

Bondarev makes no use in his novels of legends, myths, or parables. He uses imagery of nature sparingly and attempts to explore the thinking of his characters by describing their dreams, hallucinations, and subconscious. Bondarev's prose is, however, uneven, and his characterization is inadequate. We know little even about the most important characters. The writer masters the portrayal of physical war scenes in which the enemy is always recognizable. But in the scenes of contemporary life most characters wear masks, and enemies are often perceived as friends. Krymov goes down to defeat precisely because he cannot distinguish between those who are good and those who are evil; between those who are his real friends and those who praise and admire him because he is a man convenient to know.

The main heroes in Bondarev's recent novels – Nikitin, a writer; Vasil'ev, a painter; and Krymov, a director – all belong to the creative intelligentsia. All are good family men, successful in their professions, and dedicated Soviet patriots. Yet, paradoxically, all are lonely, unhappy, depressed, and pessimistic and question the ethics of city life.

Nikitin and Krymov disintegrate physically, while Vasil'ev loses his mental equilibrium. Women in Bondarev's recent prose are portrayed impressionistically, and their roles are secondary to those of their husbands. The wives of Vasil'ev and Krymov are independent professional women, loved and respected by their husbands. They fail, however, to reciprocate by giving their husbands the necessary support essential for their survival.

The title *Igra* can be successfully applied to all the recent novels by Bondarev. Most characters play a role in life – they pretend, changing masks according to circumstances. Life is a game in which society sets the rules. Nikitin, Vasil'ev, and Krymov are the losers because they question these rules, without being able to change them. The message is perhaps unintended but unequivocal and far from optimistic, namely, adapt or perish. The novels illustrate convincingly that even strong individuals can be defeated by the invisible stream of daily life which is dominated by the evil impulses of people. This dark, spontaneous tide is slowly grinding away at the very foundations of common social structures, leading to an ever-growing disparity between people and society.

The recent prose of Bondarev does not belong to the conventional Soviet byt literature. The writer attempts to look beyond the immediate physical and material needs of Soviet people. Unfortunately, Bondarev's examination of the creative city intelligentsia intimates that few of them are concerned with anything more. These novels indict the Soviet creative and intellectual élite, along lines similar to the criticism aimed at the urban intelligentsia in the village prose of the 1960s and early 1970s.

Bondarev's recent novels are widely read and discussed in the Soviet Union not because of their artistic quality but rather because they are controversial. The author's leading position in the Soviet intellectual bureaucracy lends them some weight as well. In them Bondarev raises a number of pertinent social issues. He shows the disparity between the unpredictability of fate and the uncertainty that dominates personal life and the social determinism that is at the root of the collective socialist state. His works point also to the disparity between unstable human nature and the one-dimensional character of the social theories that are supposed to guide man's social activity. In fact, as contemporary Soviet literature indicates, evil people corrupt the social institutions, turning deterministic social theories into a sham. No wonder Krymov seeks succour in Tolstoi's theories of self-improvement. He realizes that evil people will corrupt anything they touch and that no perfect society is possible unless its human components are selfless, honest, and ethical.

Bondarev's recent prose is imbued with nostalgia for the past, particularly for the times when young Soviet officers, after having defeated the Nazi invaders, had high hopes for a beautiful, happy, and fulfilling future. Unfortunately, their dreams and hopes did not material- ize. Society did not live up to their expectations. But who is guilty? Surely the parents are, at least partially, accountable for the behaviour and actions of their children. And if that is so, instead of blaming the younger generation, Vasil'ev, Krymov, and Bondarev himself, should accept their share of responsibility.

Vasil' Bykov

Vasil' Bykov's prose of the 1980s retains much of the artistic qualities evident in his earlier works. The imagery is precise, the actions are highly localized, and the heroes are placed in extreme situations. Nevertheless, his recent novellas are structurally, thematically, and even ideologically different and closer to the mainstream of Soviet prose.

'Znak bedy' (The Token of Calamity; 1983) begins with the picture of a burnt-down and abandoned farmhouse. It is a symbol of past troubles. It is a sign for the people to remember that their land was once occupied by the Nazis. This brief introductory passage is followed by the life story of the main characters, the simple peasants Petrok and Stepanida Bogat'ka, former residents of this house. The story is set in the summer of 1942, but narrative flashbacks cover well over twenty previous years, including the period of collectivization. 'Znak bedy' is narrated in the third person, but it is interspersed with flashbacks, lyrical digressions, some dialogue, and internal monologue. The intensity of narration is maintained through a focus on events as well as on the characters' reaction to them.

Petrok is patient but indecisive and quiet. He resists the enemy passively hoping that their troubles will somehow go away. He tries to appease the police by bribing them with vodka, but that does not help much. They drag him away regardless. Stepanida is hard-working, proud, and stubborn. She obstructs and frustrates the Germans who take up residence in her house. She is prepared to share her abode with them, but she will never accept personal abuse and humiliation. Her rebellion is active. When she refuses to give milk to the Germans, they kill her cow in revenge. Then she spites her tormentors by throwing a rifle into the well, and finally she tries to place a bomb under the bridge leading to the village. When the police arrive in search of the explosives, she barricades herself in the house, sets it on fire, and is consumed by the same flame that destroys her house. The behaviour of Petrok and Stepanida is determined by ethical considerations and the demands of their consciences. Their actions are influenced by their psychological make-up and the motivational factors engendered in the process of their long life. Petrok is sixty years old; Stepanida some ten years younger. Both had enough time to learn a thing or two about life.

The present is contrasted in the story with the past, and parallels are drawn. Bykov is not the first Soviet writer to attempt to tell about the excesses in the Soviet countryside in the early 1930s. Indeed, the meeting in 'Znak bedy' of the committee to unmask the kulaks resembles a similar scene in Sergei Zalygin's 'Na Irtyshe' (By the Irtysh; 1964),[38] and the image of the party official, Novik, is reminiscent of Zalygin's Koriakin. It is common knowledge that the Russian peasantry and the Soviet countryside have never fully recovered from the violent damage inflicted upon it in those years. In Belorussia, according to Bykov, there were no kulaks in those years, because no one had much land. Yet it was still required to unmask the non-existent kulaks. The violent process of collectivization generated acrimony and discord, creating a situation in which it was easy to incite people against each other. Bykov's analysis of the social nature of treason leads to the conclusion that injustice usually begets injustice, and evil begets evil. Most collaborators with the Nazis were people unjustly victimized by the Soviet regime, and many joined the police with the simple purpose of avenging themselves on their enemies.[39] Both the Germans and the Belorussian police in the story plunder and murder recklessly, but the local collaborators appear to be even more brutal. They have an axe to grind. The head of the police, Zmiter Guzhov, is the son of a peasant unjustly punished in the early 1930s.

Destroyed houses and burnt-down villages are encountered often in Bykov's works. Belorussia, Bykov's native land, is full of such sad sights. The main characters in Bykov's early works are usually young men, soldiers or partisans, who share a common dug-out rather than a house. These stories focus on a small group of characters and on a single event of extreme intensity. The past of these protagonists, if mentioned at all, is given only sketchily and impressionistically. 'Znak bedy,' in contrast, is a story of a family – of two people who share a common roof. The main characters are civilians, and their lives and the historical past of the Belorussian countryside form the background for the events in the narrative.

The portrayal of pre-war life in the Belorussian village and the investigation of the social and personal roots of the characters of Petrok and Stepanida draw 'Znak bedy' close to village prose. The heroines of village prose are usually hard-working but passive women who accept their difficult lot without a murmur, whereas Stepanida is a strong, active individual. In the past a poor farm-hand, she joins the committee of the poor and promotes collectivization. Justice is her guiding principle, and she does not hesitate to defend those she considers wronged without reason. According to Igor' Dedkov, Stepanida exhibits traits of character that are regrettably lacking in the women protagonists of village prose.[40]

Soviet critics have hailed 'Znak bedy' as an important achievement of Soviet literature. It was awarded the Lenin Prize for Literature for 1986.[41] Stepanida is regarded as a positive heroine in the best traditions of socialist realism. Her background is befitting, and her actions in war and peace are commendable. Yet some wonder whether her philosophical deliberations 'are too complex for a simple peasant woman.'[42] Furthermore, Stepanida's rebellion against her oppressors is not rational but rather impulsive and is doomed from the outset. Hence an incongruity: Stepanida, a seriously thinking, rational woman, acts in a naïve and self-defeating manner. Her attempt to destroy the bridge by setting off an explosion is an act of desperation. She gives away her last piglet to the peasant Kornila, who is hiding the unexploded bomb, but she does not know even how to detonate the explosive substance.

'Znak bedy' is not a story of struggle, combat, or heroism. It is rather a story of oppression and suffering, both in times of war and in times of peace. Bykov claims that war experience 'helps to separate truth from falsehood unmistakably.'[43] Stepanida is a frustrated and defeated truth-seeker. She can do nothing to stop the process of the alleged unmasking of the kulaks, which destroys and damages the lives of her neighbours, just as she can do nothing to stop the same people from joining the police during the Nazi occupation. Stepanida is fighting for her own small truth and dignity. She is swept away by the big 'truth,' which ostensibly has answers to all questions, but to which simple people are of little consequence.

It is assumed that the conclusion of 'Znak bedy' is symbolic and that 'the bomb symbolizes a charge of unprecedented strength, reminiscent of the peoples' anger which will ... come down on the fascists.'[44] Since the bomb never explodes and is still buried under the rubble of Stepanida's house it is also 'a warning and memorial to those who are alive ... This unexploded bomb is waiting for its hour, not only in the ground, but also in the memory of the people.'[45] In the general context of contemporary Soviet war literature the implications of the symbolic ending of 'Znak bedy' are much broader. The buried bomb reminds the Soviet reader of the suffering under Nazi occupation, but it also serves as a warning to all current enemies of the Soviet state that the anger and might of the Soviet people may explode at any time. Soviet writers often endeavour to equate the German invaders in the Second World War with present potential enemies of the Soviet Union, painting them often in tones similar to those applied to the portrayal of the Nazis.

'Znak bedy' is different from most other works of contemporary war prose in that present-day reality is hardly mentioned and contemporary man is not judged according to the standards established in the trying days of war. Instead, the behaviour and actions of Soviet people during the war are a reflection of Soviet pre-war history. Bykov is one of the first in Soviet literature to investigate the full effect of collectivization on the psyche of the peasant. In Belorussia, war and occupation have become a testing ground of collective farming. Deep in Russia, in the regions unoccupied by the Nazis, the peasant had no opportunity to vent frustration openly, and the internal rage and fury remained dormant forever.

Bykov's recent povest', 'Kar'er' (The Quarry; 1986),[46] is one of his longest novellas and in size more like a novel. Bykov claims that he, 'as a reader, does not have much faith in the contemporary novel,'[47] because one cannot write several volumes of prose without resorting to pure belletrism, of which he does not approve. Nevertheless, 'Kar'er' is close to the literature Bykov does not favour, and it is perhaps the least Bykovian work in terms of plot, narrative technique, and even subject-matter. The focus is not on military confrontation or battles with the enemy. Instead, the main conflict is internal, and it centres on an individual's struggle with his own conscience. The main character, Ageev, is a widowed and retired war veteran. We encounter him first in a small provincial town digging up a quarry in search of the remnants of a certain young woman, Mariia, allegedly killed there by the Nazis some forty years ago. In fact, Ageev himself was shot at the edge of the same quarry, but he miraculously survived.

In 1941 Ageev is a young officer of the retreating Soviet army. Wounded and left behind, he finds a place to hide in the house of a certain Baranovskaia, the wife of a priest victimized by the Soviets in the 1930s. Ageev joins the underground, but he is suspected by the police and is forced to sign a note promising to co-operate with them. Mariia, a young woman from Minsk, is hiding in the same house from the forceful advances of the local police chief. She falls in love with Ageev and becomes pregnant. At one point she becomes involved in Ageev's conspirational activities and goes to the station to deliver a basket with explosives. She is caught on her way, and the plot is discovered. The conspirators are shot, but, at the time of the execution, Mariia is not among them. Now, forty years later, Ageev is tormented by a sense of guilt for the fate of the woman he loved and their unborn child. He digs in the quarry, hoping that the rumours about her death are contrary to truth and that he will find nothing, because that would mean that Mariia was not shot and survived the ordeal. The narrative ends inconclusively. Ageev spends several months in a tent digging in the quarry, but he cannot locate Mariia's remains. He is unable to solve the great puzzle of his life, and the fate of Mariia continues to haunt him.

'Kar'er' covers two summers in the life of Ageev: one in 1941, and the other some forty years later. We are told almost nothing of what happens in between, and this makes the reader wonder why Ageev waits so long to begin his search for Mariia. This long delay throws a shade of doubt on the sincerity of his actions, which are, at any rate, self-serving rather than altruistic. This is not the first time that Bykov has combined in his war stories the present with the past, but in 'Obelisk' (Obelisk; 1972)[48] and 'Volch'ia staia' (The Wolf Pack; 1974),[49] for example, the main focus is on the behaviour and actions of men at war, and the few pages devoted to present-day events merely reflect on the influence of the past on contemporary reality. In 'Kar'er' current events are central, and the war is relived and re-created in the memory of those who survived. To others, the war is of little consequence. Ageev's son, for example, is hardly touched by his father's concerns.

'Kar'er' is a third-person narrative in which today's reality alternates with flashbacks, reminiscences, and Ageev's contemplations. Much of the story is taken up with digressions and subplots that have little in common with the main plot. Some of these digressions – for example, the war stories of the veteran Semenov – are interesting but slow the narrative and turn the reader's attention from the main plot. Although the pages describing the events in 1941 are charged with dramatic tension and tragic overtones, the narrative as a whole lacks a compositional focus. The introduction of elements from the detective genre in order to make the story more intriguing does little to alleviate the problem.

Some interesting characters, like Baranovskaia, disappear early in the story, leaving the reader puzzled about their fate. Baranovskaia is perhaps the only character whose actions are guided by a deep faith in both people and god. She claims that one 'should not divide people according to their estates and classes, or professions and ranks, but rather into good and bad ones, because for every good man there are in life ten evil ones, and because goodness is impossible without god.'[50] According to Baranovskaia, 'to believe in god is to have him in one's soul. One does not necessarily have to pray in order to believe, but rather act in a humane and conscientious manner.'[51] In the portrayal of Baranovskaia, Bykov departs from the class approach in the interpretation of Soviet ethics and from the depiction, long accepted in Soviet literature, of religion as a dark force that diverts the masses from immediate political objectives. Bykov asserts: 'Conscience, compassion, and mercy are ethical principles affirmed by man for centuries. Along with its dark sides, which gave reason to consider it as "the opium of the masses," religion preached also general human values, important at all times and to all people.'[52]

Several notions that permeate 'Kar'er' set it apart from Bykov's earlier works. The first is the unequivocal expression of the absolute value of human life. Bykov's early heroes, for example in the story 'Sotnikov' (Sotnikov; 1970),[53] are usually faced with a choice between honourable death, with ethical purity, and treason, with spiritual downfall. No third path is possible. The atmosphere in 'Kar'er' is different. There is a hint that man often finds himself in circumstances that are beyond his control and that young people at war are much too ready to sacrifice their lives without extracting full value for something that is given to them only once and is irreplaceable.

In addition, the notion that fatalism and chance shape human destiny is scattered throughout the narrative. Contemplating his own war experiences, Bykov realizes now that the life of the individual is of little importance in times of war.[54] The fate of most characters, war participants, in 'Kar'er' illustrates this proposition clearly. Some try to outwit the enemy and war itself but are killed in the most unexpected circumstances, while others, including the main hero, Ageev, are doomed to die but survive by sheer chance. 'Kar'er' reaffirms the contention of the unpredictability of human life and the naïveté of the belief that we can harness social forces and control the universal historical process.

Despite its artistic shortcomings, 'Kar'er' is more than a simple story about war. It is a piece of nostalgia for the past and of yearning for lost youth. Veterans of the Second World War are a vanishing breed, and Bykov, himself a war veteran, identifies with Ageev, Semenov, and the other veterans, brought into the narrative sometimes to its artistic detriment.

In his most recent story, 'V tumane' (In the Fog; 1987),[55] Bykov returns to the partisan theme. The conflict in the story is unconventional, but its conclusion is not very convincing. Two partisans are sent to kill a blameless man, Sushchenia, suspected of treason. On their way to execute him, the partisans are killed by the Nazis. Surprisingly, having remained alone, Sushchenia kills himself. His suicide is unexpected but underscores the irony of fate. Chance saves his life from the Nazi hangman, but the suspicion of his neighbours and members of his own family makes life unbearable. It is easier for him to die with dignity than to live with an undeserved burden of guilt.

In the late 1970s Bykov's prose began to mellow. The conflicts presented lack the harsh formulation and solutions characteristic of his early stories. In the 1980s Bykov, himself over sixty, turns to the portrayal of older people, be it at war, as in 'Znak bedy,' or many years after the war, as in 'Kar'er.' Bykov's prose of the 1980s becomes more contemplative and philosophical, but it loses much of the compactness and terseness characteristic of his earlier works.

The Great Fatherland War will continue to be, for the foreseeable future, an important topic in Soviet literature. With time it will more and more reflect the ideological, social, and political concerns of present-day reality. The portrayal of war will shift in step with changes in the official assessment of the events of 1941–5. But the Soviet war archives are still closed to writers and historians, and, with the disappearance of writers who served in the conflict, war prose will turn little by little into historical literature, in which the artistic images reflect the subjective thoughts and feelings of the authors and their views of history, rather than reminiscences and personal experiences.

6 The New Political Novel

Politics and literature are of course intricately intertwined in Soviet society, and political and ideological overtones are part of any Soviet work of art. Hence all Soviet prose is, in a sense, political. Overtly, or under the surface, Soviet literature promotes a certain world-view and a distinct approach to human phenomena. In Soviet literary terminology, however, *political prose* does not refer to internal Soviet politics or issues of local significance. Instead, the Soviet political novel deals mainly with external affairs, foreign policy, and diplomacy.

Contemporary Soviet political prose can be divided into three broad thematic groups. First, there is the traditional political novel, in which the action is set in the recent Soviet past. The central characters are usually diplomats or important political figures, and the main conflicts are between opposing political forces. Second, there is the so-called political detective novel, in which literary quality and artistic mastery are often sacrificed for external effects. The author of the conventional detective novel seeks to unravel a complicated and hidden mystery, which is usually connected with common criminal activity. The political detective novel, in contrast, concentrates on the exposure of real or imagined political crimes committed by enemy security services or political figures. In the Soviet detective novel, the culprits are usually foreigners. Third, there are the new political narratives, which are a mixture of fiction, reportage, and journalism, based on the personal experiences and observations of Soviet politicians, journalists, writers, or travellers. The plots are usually set abroad and reflect the most recent developments in international relations.

The proliferation of political prose in the last years of the Brezhnev era is not accidental. It is connected with the political and military initiatives of the Soviet leadership around the globe as well as with the stalemate in disarmament negotiations and strained Soviet-American relations. Some Soviet critics suggest that in such circumstances 'the need for the arts to participate in the struggle for peace and in unmasking the aggresive aspirations of imperialism and its ideological sabotage is evident.'[1]

Among the most prominent representatives of traditional political prose are Aleksandr Chakovskii and Savva Dangulov. Chakovskii's *Pobeda* (Victory; 1978–81)[2] and *Neokonchennyi portret* (The Unfinished Portrait; 1983–4)[3] are a continuation of his earlier novel *Blokada* (Blockade; 1969–75). All three novels deal with the Second World War and its aftermath. *Pobeda* begins in 1975 in Helsinki. The Soviet correspondent Voronin meets an American journalist whom he had encountered some thirty years earlier in Potsdam. Voronin witnesses history in the making both in Potsdam and in Helsinki. The main subjects of the novel are the negotiations between Churchill, Truman, and Stalin and political and diplomatic confrontation between different ideologies. In *Neokonchennyi portret*, Chakovskii attempts to provide a critical, albeit one-sided portrait of the complex nature and controversial personality of Franklin Roosevelt.

The recent novels of Dangulov, *Zautrenia v Rapallo* (Matins in Rapallo; 1983)[4] and *Gosudareva pochta* (His Majesty's Mail; 1983),[5] deal with Soviet diplomacy and foreign relations in the early post-revolutionary period, as well as with the attempts of Western politicians to isolate the young Soviet state.

The novels by Chakovskii and Dangulov are written in flat and uninspiring prose, but they have received much attention because of their political significance and their authors' positions in the literary establishment. The works of literary bureaucrats are seldom criticized in the Soviet press, because their authors are in control of the editorial boards of publishing houses and periodical publications. An attempt to change this long-established tradition was undertaken at the Eight Congress of Soviet Writers in 1986. In his speech to the congress, the writer and critic Viacheslav Shugaev pointed out that Chakovskii's *Pobeda* is artistically inadequate. To paraphrase Shugaev, *Pobeda* is poor in style, its language lacks expressiveness, and the portrayal of external scenes is colourless. Yet no single negative critical remark has been directed at his work in the last decade.[6]

The most popular and best-known representative of the political detective novel is Iulian Semenov. A specialist in history and Far Eastern studies, he turned journalist and travelled all over the world. In the 1960s and 1970s he visited several countries, including Vietnam, Chile, Portugal, and Spain, to observe at first hand war and political and social upheavals. Semenov describes in his novels the covert activities of intelligence services during the Second World War and the post-war confrontation between the CIA and Soviet security services. Factual material, personal observations, and interviews with past and present political and military personalities form a large part of Semenov's narratives. Real historical figures, such as Hitler and Stalin, appear in his novels, but fiction is at the root of his external intrigues.

One of Semenov's best-known characters, who appears in many of his works, is the Soviet double agent Isaev-Shtirlits, who manages to penetrate Nazi headquarters, hiding his true objectives and identity. In his novel *Prikazano vyzhit'* (An Order to Survive; 1983)[7] Semenov describes the final defeat of Nazi Germany. Hitler is dead, and Germany is occupied by the Allies, but many SS-men survive the war and hide in the West. One of them, the Soviet spy Shtirlits, spends the first post-war year in Spain. On the last page of the novel he is approached by a man representing the American intelligence service with an offer to collaborate. The theme of American co-operation with the remnants of the Gestapo and SS is further developed in Semenov's novel *Ekspansiia* (Expansion; 1986).[8] American intelligence spreads its influence by recruiting past Nazis and sending them to Latin America. Paradoxically, Shtirlits, who continues to work for Soviet security, is one of their new agents. In the concluding pages he is supplied with an American passport, a new name, and a false Paraguayan visa and is sent on his way to South America.

In other novels, such as *TASS upolnomochen zaiavit'* (TASS Is Authorized to Declare; 1979),[9] *Litsom k litsu* (Face to Face; 1983),[10] *Press tsentr. Anatomiia politicheskogo prestupleniia* (Press Centre: The Anatomy of a Political Crime; 1984),[11] and *Auktsion* (Auction; 1985),[12] Semenov continues his denunciation of Western security services and their alleged criminal activities, emphasizing the Soviet struggle for justice and peace.

In *TASS upolnomochen zaiavit'* Semenov describes the CIA's fruitless attempt to undermine the very existence of a Soviet ally, the young state of Nagoniia, which is connected with the Soviet Union by a treaty of friendship and mutual assistance. In *Litsom k litsu*, Semenov describes attempts to recover priceless Russian works of art carried off by the Nazis during their occupation. Semenov develops the idea that despite the assistance of some friendly Germans it is impossible to retrieve these treasures because most have found their way into private collections in the West, particularly in the United States. Semenov suggests: 'It would be worthwhile to investigate the path of the icon, stolen by the Nazis from Tikhvin, which found later its way into the chapel of Cardinal Spelman in New York.'[13] Semenov hints that those who know about these stolen objects prefer to keep quiet, because they are afraid of the Mafia, which is allegedly involved in dealings with stolen Soviet property.

Semenov is popular with the Soviet reading public, and his novels are published in huge editions, but his prose belongs to the kind of popular literature that attracts the reader's attention primarily through identification with the heroic feats of the positive heroes. The action moves fast, but without much explanation or commentary. The language is dry and stylistically deficient. Little attention is devoted to the emotional or psychological state of the heroes. They are all like mannequins. Semenov claims 'that emotions interfere with analysis. The political novel ... should be dry, facts should speak for themselves.'[14] The facts in Semenov's novels indeed speak for themselves, but their selection is determined primarily by political considerations, and his prose reads as political invective rather than artistic fiction. But since the culprits and evil-doers are always alleged enemies of the Soviet people, Semenov's novels serve a purpose: they help shape the Soviet reader's negative perception of the West.

Aleksandr Prokhanov

Aleksandr Prokhanov is a representative of the new political prose. Born in 1938, he graduated from the Moscow Aviation Institute with a degree in aeronautical engineering and worked for a while in a scientific research institute. He soon abandoned his professional pursuits and turned instead to travel and writing. His first published story 'Svad'ba' (A Wedding), appeared in 1967 in *Literaturnaia Rossiia* (Literary Russia). It was followed by the collections of stories *Idu v put' moi* (I Set out on My Journey; 1971) and *Zhelteet trava* (The Grass Becomes Yellow; 1974) and the novels *Kochuiushchaia roza* (Nomad Rose; 1976), *Vremia polden'* (At Noon; 1977), *Mesto deistviia* (The Scene of Action; 1979), and *Vechnyi gorod* (Eternal City; 1981).

Prokhanov's prose of the 1970s is inspired by his travels in remote regions of the Soviet Union, as well as by his journalistic experiences. It illustrates his acute sense of timing and his ability to react to the needs of the day by creating literature of questionable artistic merit but of great social significance. Prokhanov is a prolific and versatile writer who always places his talent at the service of current official political demands. *Mesto deistviia*, for example, deals with new industrial development in a remote Siberian town. The intrusion of technological progress unsettles the local residents. The influx of new workers from outside destroys their way of life. They try to resist but are defeated. Prokhanov identifies with the intruders. He caricatures the leaders of the local intelligentsia. Those representing old values are pictured as dreamers, unable to do much for themselves or for society. In the end industrialization and technological progress are victorious, and the local cultural leaders are so overwhelmed by this powerful transformation that they unwittingly join forces with those they have initially opposed.

In the 1980s we see a dramatic change in subject-matter, but in spirit Prokhanov remains true to himself. Prokhanov's writings of the 1970s affirmed the Soviet way of life and the social changes advanced by economic and industrial development. In the 1980s Prokhanov turned to problems of Soviet foreign policy and international relations, aiming his focus at the Third World, where Soviet involvement is often indirect and purposely kept at a low profile. Between 1982 and 1984 he published four novels set in four different countries in which he delivers a single and uniform message that conforms with official Soviet foreign policy but often advances a one-dimensional and incomplete picture of our troubled world.

The four novels in question are *Derevo v tsentre Kabula* (A Tree in the Centre of Kabul; 1982),[15] *V ostrovakh okhotnik ... Kampuchiiskaia khronika* (The Hunter on the Island ... The Kampuchean Chronicle; 1983),[16] *Afrikanist* (The African; 1984),[17] and *I vot prikhodit veter* (And Here Comes the Wind; 1984).[18] The action in each covers a short span of time and takes place in Afghanistan, Kampuchea, Mozambique, and Nicaragua, respectively. The hero is always a Soviet man of close to forty on assignment. In Afghanistan and Kampuchea the hero is a journalist, in Nicaragua a newspaper photographer, and in Mozambique a movie director.

All four novels are similar in structure, composition, style, method of narration, and subject-matter. The story is usually told in the third person by a narrator who is closely identified with the main hero but who speaks, in most instances, for the author. The main conflict is always connected with the immediate political situation in a given country, but in the background, in the form of reminiscences, meditation, and internal monologue, the narrator muses about his past, about his home, his family, and Russia. He contemplates the human predicament and his own place in this world.

Structurally *Derevo v tsentre Kabula* is placed in a framework of peaceful concerns. It begins with a public meeting before the departure from the Soviet Union of a convoy of tractors that is to reach a remote district in Afghanistan before the sowing season begins. In the last chapter the convoy arrives at its destination and reforms begin. The land of the rich is distributed among the poor and landless peasants. In between, the experiences of the Soviet journalist Volkov, who closely follows the route of the convoy, are related. He interviews a number of important personalities; he visits a local party committee and an Afghan military unit. He witnesses an insurgent attack on Kabul and accompanies Afghan security forces in action. He is also in contact with other Soviet people who have gone there selflessly to help the revolution. The author presents the general secretary of the People's Democratic Party of Afghanistan, Babrak Karmal,[19] as the saviour of his people, and Amin, his predecessor, as a counter-revolutionary and an agent of the CIA. To add a human touch, Volkov's relationship with Marina, a Soviet interpreter in Afghanistan, is depicted.

There is nothing in the novel to indicate that the Soviet troops are invaders. They are there to help in construction, education, and health care. Their main purpose, is allegedly to protect the peaceful lives of the local inhabitants, who appear to support the revolution and its new leadership.

The Afghan communist Said Ismail is a fervent supporter of the new regime; he expresses the official view of the government. In a speech to the masses he declares that 'the enemies of the Afghan people, agents of American imperialism, Chinese hegemonism, and zionism are attempting to destroy freedom.'[20] Prokhanov suggests that the war has been provoked by hirelings of the West and that the fighting is mainly between Afghan detachments loyal to the government and bandits based in Pakistan, trained by the Chinese, Egyptians, and Saudi Arabians. Those who do not support the regime are pictured as a blind mass, lacking in social, political, or national consciousness; in other words, as people who act against their own best interests.

Volkov watches the rebels attack Kabul and meditates on the dark and spontaneous powers that induce the mob to act. 'He understands that sociology and politics have been replaced by a primal force, which is uncontrollable and unthinking. He can feel this force of the mob even through the armour of his car.'[21] The mass is blind indeed, but two different forces endeavour to control it, each trying to use and manipulate it in its own interests, which have little in common with the needs and desires of the local people. The communists, of course, are presented as the progressive and positive force, while their adversaries, supported by foreign, primarily Western interests, are presented as the enemies of the people.

Volkov's antagonist, who is there allegedly to report the truth, is a French journalist from the Paris *Monde*, André Viniar. His main objective, according to Volkov, is to spread lies. Volkov and Viniar observe the same events, but they see and report them from different perspectives. There is an invisible and ongoing struggle between the two; between their ideas and what they seem to represent. On the surface it is a struggle between information and misinformation, but in essence it is between different world-views and political interests. It is paradoxical that no third path is even considered and that no compromising truth is possible. Everything is black or white. In the final analysis, the war in Afghanistan appears to be an extension of the global confrontation between the Soviet Union and the West, with the Afghan people as unwitting puppets.

The action in *V ostrovakh okhotnik* covers a week in the life of the Soviet scholar Kirillov, who is in the final days of a journalistic assignment in Kampuchea. The previous decade had been a time of continuous war, turmoil, and suffering for the people of Kampuchea. In 1975 Khmer Rouge forces, under Pol Pot, the leader of the Communist party, took power with the support of the poorest segments of the peasantry and went on to ravage the country by forcing city inhabitants into the countryside to labour and die in agricultural communes. Pol Pot's government is blamed for the death of millions of people during its nearly four years of rule. In late 1978 Vietnam invaded Kampuchea and installed in Phnom Penh a new anti–Pol Pot, anti–Khmer Rouge communist government. The followers of Pol Pot and those of the non-communist democratic movements were defeated but not totally destroyed. They withdrew to the Thai border and beyond to carry on a guerrilla struggle against the Vietnamese occupiers. The Vietnamese have been supported by the Soviet Union, while those who oppose the regime are supported by most other nations, including China and the United States.

The main hero of the novel, Kirillov, delays his intended departure to Moscow for several days because he is granted the long-awaited permission to visit the devastated regions near the border with Thailand and to witness at first hand the struggle of the Vietnamese with the insurgents. He is accompanied by Som Kyt, from the Ministry of External Affairs, and by Vietnamese security officers.

The novel has little plot. Dramatic tension is maintained with the help of melodramatic tricks and journalistic reports of a dangerous trip into areas infested by enemy bands. The novel ends inconclusively. Prokhanov keeps the reader guessing about the fate of his hero. Kirillov is in a helicopter on his way to visit a captured enemy base, but the craft catches fire and there is nowhere to land in the jungle.

Kirillov, who is a specialist in East Asian studies and fluent in the Vietnamese and Khmer languages, tries to rationalize events by viewing the communism of Pol Pot as a perversion of Marxism. According to Kirillov, 'the appearance of Pol Pot is not rooted in Khmer history, nor in the revolutionary process as such ... It is rather the result of a complex combination of anarchistic and nihilistic ideas, of European bourgeois modernism, and of anti-proletarian doctrines imported from abroad.'[22]

One cannot, of course, defend the regime of Pol Pot. The suffering it inflicted on the people of Kampuchea is well documented. Yet it appears paradoxical that only foreign intervention can save a people from itself. In Afghanistan the Soviet troops are presented as saviours. In Kampuchea the Vietnamese are portrayed as liberators. Western and international help for the starving natives is accepted with mistrust. The Italian woman Lucrecia Cicorelli, from UNICEF, is introduced as a representative of a Catholic fund located in Paris and is suspected by Kirillov of being a CIA agent. Vigilance and suspicion of everything foreign, in particular Western, have become part of Kirillov's nature and personality. He equates those who fight using words to those who fight with rockets. 'He saw real live enemies at press conferences and in journalist cocktail bars, where friendly and charming representatives of American, English, and West German agents exchanged greetings with him. He replied in kind, but he knew well that every one of them had to his credit dozens of well-polished and cleverly written but ruthless publications attacking his country.'[23]

Much of the book is taken up by Kirillov's reminiscences and ruminations. He is overwhelmed by a complex sense of guilt. He feels guilty for the suffering of the Kampuchean people because Soviet life is peaceful. He feels guilty for his father who perished in the Second World War, while he, Kirillov, sees himself as living his father's life. He feels guilty for the death of the Vietnamese officer who is killed protecting him; this sacrifice for the sake of a stranger unsettles Kirillov. He questions the workings of this world, and the unpredictability of death. He realizes that his unquenchable thirst for knowledge and information, which has driven him into this remote region, is a 'kind of psychosis, which afflicted him long ago ... The information acquired grows excessively, but it does not lead to a simple and clear understanding of the truth that could explain life.'[24]

A sad note permeates Kirillov's contemplations. He comes to the conclusion that life is futile anyway, because death destroys everything.

But Kirillov finds a way out of his depression by turning to his roots. He seeks inspiration in his identification with his family, his past, and his country and finds solace in his hope for a speedy return to Russia.

In the third novel, *Afrikanist*, Prokhanov turns to Africa. The action is set in Mozambique, just recently liberated from Portuguese rule. The main hero, the Soviet film director Bobrov, goes to Maputu to observe the situation and to study the mentality and problems of the inhabitants. 'He intends to make a film about a Soviet scholar and explorer of Africa. He arrives in Mozambique where ... another "undeclared war" is still raging and the young state repulses the infiltrators from the South African Republic.'[25] Bobrov is accompanied by Solomau, a former student at Moscow's Lumumba University for foreigners. Now Solomau is a security officer; he supports the Mozambique Marxist regime and fights counter-revolution.

Bobrov goes to Africa as an observer but becomes an active participant in political and military events. He follows Mozambique security forces in their pursuit of South African insurgents and Mozambican rebels. At the end of the novel, Bobrov performs a heroic feat. He rushes from Harare, Zimbabwe, where he has been visiting an old Moscow friend, to Maputu in order to inform the leaders of the African National Congress of an imminent assault on their headquarters. This information is unwittingly passed to him by a South African acquaintance McVillen, who is on his way to Australia. McVillen is a white racist who supports apartheid but finds that life in South Africa has become so difficult and dangerous that he seeks peace and contentment far away.

The struggle of the African National Congress against the South African apartheid regime is portrayed not as a racist struggle between blacks and whites but rather as a battle for socialism which will secure racial equality. Bobrov's attitude to the people he encounters is determined mainly by their political convictions. As opposed to Afghanistan or Kampuchea, in Mozambique many foreigners arrive for different reasons – some to support the new Marxist government, others for purely materialistic purposes. There are Soviet citizens, East Germans, Cubans, and North Koreans, as well as Portuguese communists who return to assuage their guilty consciences by helping the new regime. The English and South African whites are there to make money. They are portrayed as racists who do not hide their preference for white rule in Africa.

South Africa is depicted as an enemy of the Soviet Union, and the United States as a supporter of apartheid. The Americans are allegedly possessed by wickedness, and the CIA, which is the embodiment of

American imperialism, is at the root of the evil. Symbolically the Cuban veterinarian Rafael, a representative of a nation that defeated the devils, is in Mozambique to help fight American poison.

Bobrov's thought is influenced by the notion of global'nost' (globality) – the idea that the fates of Russia and of the Soviet Union are closely intertwined with those of other nations. Progressive people are responsible for the common destiny of all mankind. Universal fellowship and harmony are seen as hampered by American imperialist intrigues and provocations.

The novel ends inconclusively. The wounded Bobrov is ambushed in a house that is set on fire; it remains unclear whether he survives. Just as in *V ostrovakh okhotnik*, Prokhanov here uses melodramatic tricks of suspense and surprise to enliven the plot, but Bobrov's heroic exploits are not very convincing.

The last book in Prokhanov's tetralogy deals with events in Latin America. Unlike in the other novels, in *I vot prikhodit veter* we first encounter the main hero, Gorlov, in Moscow. Gorlov is a famous artist-photographer. When we meet him, he is depressed and dejected; he has lost interest in his craft and reached a dead end in his personal life. In search of new inspiration, Gorlov accepts a temporary assignment in Nicaragua as a photographer for a Moscow newspaper and flies to Managua. His guide there is the Sandinista writer Cesar Cortes. Gorlov claims to be a man of peace, but his art requires the portrayal of war, suffering, and devastation. He travels the country in search of the appropriate sights and emotions. He goes to the Honduran border, where the Sandinistas are fighting the Contras. He travels to the areas where the Miskito Indians rebel against the Sandinista government. He observes enemy planes attack Managua airport. He carries a gun and a camera and photographs everything in sight. In moments of respite, Gorlov visits a Soviet hospital. The doctors treat the local people free of charge, realizing that this is the best form of revolutionary propaganda. It does not take long for Gorlov to fall in love with the nurse Valentina. They plan a reunion in Moscow and a happy life together ever after, but a single bullet kills the Soviet nurse and Gorlov's hopes.

The war in Nicaragua is viewed by Gorlov and the Sandinistas as a war against the United States, but it is also regarded as a fragment of world revolution. The Sandinista officer Ramirez warns the Americans that if they invade Nicaragua 'at first there will be a war in Latin America, but later in the whole world.' He claims that the Nicaraguan revolution 'follows the Cuban but it inspires, in turn, the revolution in El Salvador.' According to Ramirez, by defending its own revolution,

Nicaragua defends also the people of Angola, Afghanistan, Kampuchea, and the Soviet Union.[26] According to Cesar Cortes, 'the revolution in Nicaragua ... rolls ... as a storm, as an eruption. Latin America is a continent of volcanoes that are ready to erupt. El Salvador is a volcano that erupts already! Guatemala is a volcano that exhales smoke and fire! Chile is hot lava!' There is no doubt in Cortes's mind that the Sandinistas will 'wipe out the gringos here and they will become powerless in Europe. Their Negros and Puerto-Ricans are volcanoes in their own home. They will explode and destroy the gringo civilization! Revolution in Latin America ... will take hold of Africa, Asia, and the whole world.'[27]

The young Sandinistas are exalted by the uncorrupted spirit of first-generation revolutionaries. The head of the convoy protecting Gorlov, Sgt Largaespada, exclaims: 'Before I was a Catholic; I believed in God. Now I know God is the revolution. And what is the devil? The devil is the Contra!'[28] But Gorlov appears to know better. He is aware from Soviet experience that taking power is only the first step and that hard work, dedication, and selflessness are required to build a new society. He knows also that when the youthful revolutionary idealism evaporates, scepticism, cynicism, and opportunism set in.

There are many parallels between the four narratives discussed. The main hero in each is essentially the same man. Volkov, Kirillov, Bobrov, and Gorlov live separate, individual lives but share a common past and philosophy of life. They also have a collective father who was killed in the war with Nazi Germany and who imparted to his son responsibility for the future of Russia. The main hero of each novel travels the same route. He is safe in the capital of the country he visits, but his assignment takes him to distant regions, where danger lurks. Typically the enemy is not a local man, but one who hides in a foreign country. In Afghanistan, he comes from Pakistan; in Kampuchea, from Thailand; in Mozambique, from South Africa; and in Nicaragua, from Honduras. But behind all the enemies are the counter-revolutionary forces of the West.

The position of Prokhanov's Soviet man, visiting a friendly foreign country, is the same everywhere. He is treated with the utmost respect. His hosts go out of their way to make his stay pleasant, useful, and safe. At times, one gets the impression that the local people are subservient to Soviet visitors and treat them as their bosses, being ever ready to risk, and even sacrifice, their own lives in order to protect their guests.

Soviet help to a foreign country is always portrayed as selfless and of a peaceful nature. Nowhere is there mention that the Soviets supply arms to their friends. Instead, the tractor 'Belarus', the symbol of bread and peace, appears in all parts of the world; we see it in countries as far apart as Afghanistan and Nicaragua. Evil is inevitably identified with the United States, and most atrocities are inspired by the CIA. The representatives of revolutionary governments are fighting for freedom, progress, and equality, while those opposing them are always bandits and foreign mercenaries. There is no mention anywhere in Prokhanov's novels of Soviet aspirations in Afghanistan, Mozambique, or Nicaragua; yet what he presents as selfless brotherly help can also be perceived as political, ideological, and military infiltration and expansionism.

It is obvious that all four novels are moulded from the same clay and with the same purpose. But some Soviet critics see nothing wrong with this. One of them suggests,[29] and Prokhanov agrees,[30] that the author creates purposely a new type of Soviet hero. He represents a generation of young Soviet people who grew up in times of peace but who have to be ready for war. In Zimbabwe Bobrov visits his old friend the Soviet diplomat Startsev. They are of the same generation and background. They talk about the peaceful times after the Second World War when Russia was recovering, building, and gaining strength. In the words of Startsev 'now ... a new time has come! The world is different. We enter a time of utmost ruthlessness. The respite is over and harsh times are back here ... But we will endure! We will put aside our illusions and our sweet and peaceful song, and if [war] breaks out we will sing "Our Holy War" [*Voina sviashchennaia*] and "Our Armour Is Strong" [*Bronia krepka*].'[31]

Prokhanov calls his novels 'geopolitical or military-political ... war chronicles, novel-probes, novels reportages.'[32] With some reservations all the above designations can be applied to these novels, and this is perhaps their greatest shortcoming. They are inadequate artistically as works of prose fiction and not good enough as serious journalism. For works of art the novels lack compositional balance and psychological truthfulness. The characterization is inadequate, and we learn little even about the main heroes. All we learn about them is usually told by the third-person narrator, who speaks for the protagonist, who is, in turn, the alter ego of the author himself.

The prime objective of Prokhanov's novels is to chronicle political events. The main focus is not human nature or relations, but rather the general flow of historical time. Even the leading characters are passive observers; hence the plots are often monotonous and lack dramatic tension. Prokhanov's prose cannot be regarded as good journalism. First, there is too much fiction. Second, the discussion of social, political, and philosophical issues is shallow. Third, for journalism his works are too long, too general, and too biased. Yet, in today's political circumstances, Prokhanov's novels are probably more important than the traditional political literature of well-established older writers. They reflect the directions in current Soviet foreign policy as it relates to the Third World, and they illustrate Soviet political, economic, and ideological commitments around the globe.

Prokhanov's novels are also a source of valuable information unavailable until recently to the Soviet reader in the daily press. They serve as a source of indoctrination which creates a one-sided and biased view of international relations. Most important perhaps, from the Soviet point of view, the reader acquires patriotic pride by identifying with the positive achievements of his fellow citizens working and fighting abroad. Prokhanov's characters are far from perfect; they have their doubts and weaknesses, but their behaviour in a foreign country is impeccable, and their devotion to the motherland is limitless. For these reasons Prokhanov's novels are promoted and widely published in the Soviet Union and translated into other languages.

Prokhanov's success with the public and with the official bureaucracy does not mean that all critics approve of his writings. In a statement to the Eighth Congress of Soviet Writers, Boris Mozhaev ridicules Prokhanov's use of language in his *Mesto deistviia*, claiming that the author is not familiar with the subject of his portrayal.[33] Another critic, Igor' Dedkov, makes fun of Prokhanov's choice of protagonists in his recent political novels.[34] V. Oskotskii accuses him of repeating the same plots, images, and compositional devices from novel to novel.[35] The most serious criticism is voiced by L. Fink. He calls the novels a combination of reportage and journalistic commentaries, interspersed with some monologues and the portrayal of separate episodes in which the main characters are not participants but simple observers. Fink claims further that the novels lack compositional unity, that they are stylistically deficient, and that most of the secondary characters are poorly drawn.[36] Nonetheless, Prokhanov appears to have secured a safe place in the Soviet literary establishment. He has been recently elected to the Board of the Soviet Writers Union,[37] and *Afrikanist* and *I vot prikhodit veter* were nominated for the 1986 State Prize for Literature.[38]

The political dimensions of Prokhanov's prose are evident, but a distinction has to be made between his works dealing with Afghanistan and those set in other countries. In Kampuchea, Mozambique, and Angola the Soviets have been fighting by proxy, while in Afghanistan they are directly involved in military combat activity. In *Derevo v tsentre Kabula*, written between 1979 and 1981, and published in 1982, Soviet military involvement is portrayed as marginal and most of the fighting is done by the natives. In Prokhanov's later works there are references to Soviet participation in battle as well as to the social implications generated by the invasion within the Soviet Union.

Thus, for example, in *I vot prikhodit veter* Gorlov overhears two men talking in a Moscow restaurant. The older is obviously a veteran of the Second World War, the other fought in Afghanistan and is in trouble. The older man tries to calm the youngster, who nervously relates his story: 'Everything would be fine,' he says, 'but this vile creature upset me. I could not put up with it ... This ugly face started to speak about Afghanistan. I told him quietly: Shut up! You have not been there, so stop it! But he replied with obscenities ... and then something happened to me. I was very offended. I felt sorry for the fellows who remained behind and could not come here to strike this fat mug. I felt sorry ... for Tolia Pishchenko who carried me out on his back, bandaged my side, but was later killed. I remembered all my friends and could not endure it any longer, and then I hit him with such force that he flew out from behind the table.'[39]

In a more recent novella, 'Sedoi soldat' (The Grey Soldier; 1985),[40] Prokhanov relates the story of a Soviet soldier taken prisoner by Afghan guerrillas. When the captured Morozov regains consciousness he is faced by the Englishman Edward Staff, who is a Reuters correspondent fluent in Russian, previously stationed for several years in Moscow. The Englishman urges Morozov to declare 'that he chose freedom; that he left his barracks and ran away from his stern commanders who sent him to death and joined instead the Afghan freedom fighters.'[41] In return, Staff promises Morozov freedom and speedy passage to England. But Morozov does not give in. He seeks internal strength in his recollections of home, family, Moscow friends, and fellow soldiers. He deludes Staff and his vigilant guardians and manages to run away.

'Sedoi soldat' is part of the novel *Risunki batalista* (Drawings of a Battle-Painter; 1986),[42] in which the painter Veretenov is driven by his guilty conscience to Afghanistan in order to find his son, who is a soldier in the Soviet Army. As opposed to Second World War prose, in which the children of veterans usually do not live up to the expectations of their fathers, in *Risunki batilista* the young soldiers are morally superior to their fathers and can be compared to their grandfathers, who fought in the Great Fatherland War. The novel also advances the notion that war develops a number of positive qualities in people. Soldiers participating in action do not take life for granted. They mature rapidly and learn the value of true friendship.

It is evident that the work about Afghanistan is a new war literature, markedly different from that about the Second World War. The war in Afghanistan is localized, with limited objectives; the Soviet troops are strangers in a foreign and hostile country. One of the main purposes of this literature is to glorify the dedication and determination of Soviet soldiers in fulfilling important international obligations and duties. This literature also intends to expose the alleged complicity of Western nations in the war against Afghanistan and its patron, the Soviet Union. No less important is the allusion that all Western correspondents and diplomats stationed in the Soviet Union are foreign agents and spies, enemies of the Soviet people; vigilance on the part of every Soviet citizen is the order of the day.

Furthermore, this literature makes also clear that the war in Afghanistan creates new social problems within the Soviet Union. It is an unpopular war, and Morozov, who grows up in Moscow and is reared for a good and peaceful life, does not hesitate to ask: Why me? It is a question that during the 1941–5 war would have been tantamount to treason. Then conscription and active duty were the rule rather than the exception. Today it is the other way round. The fact that some Soviet youngsters are arbitrarily given life, while others are singled out for death, leads to dissatisfaction and social friction, the more so since a new body of war widows, orphans, invalids, bereaved mothers, and veterans is on the rise for all to see.[43]

The message that emanates from Prokhanov's novels is on the surface. There is global confrontation between American imperialism and the progressive revolutionary forces, supported by the Soviet Union. The Americans and their mercenaries want to stifle the struggle for freedom and equality, while the Soviet Union selflessly helps the subjugated and downtrodden. No wonder Prokhanov's recent political prose is in the mainstream of official literature. It satisfies the party's political and educational goals and supports its internal and external political objectives. Prokhanov creates a new positive hero who is aware of himself and who identifies with his Russian past and its traditions. He is not perfect; he may even question and criticize some aspects of Soviet life, but he is an ardent patriot who upholds, without hesitation, the country's domestic and foreign policy. Soviet critics are prepared to overlook the works' artistic shortcomings because of their political significance.

To summarize, despite numerous artistic shortcomings and the prevalence of khudozhestvennaia publitsistika, the new political prose of the 1980s satisfies Soviet official needs. First, it attempts to show that the interests of the American people are not synonymous with those of its government; that the CIA is an independent institution, operating in a manner contrary to the interests of the American people. It also illustrates the duplicity of the US government and the collaboration of American security services with surviving remnants of the Nazi regime. Second, this literature creates an awareness that imperialist forces in the West pose a constant threat to the peaceful existence of the Soviet Union and other socialist states, and it fosters a sense of constant vigilance in the face of real or imagined enemies. And, finally, it stresses the peaceful objectives of the Soviet Union and its leading role in the struggle for peaceful coexistence between nations, and it glorifies the Soviet Army and Soviet security and intelligence forces as the only reliable protectors of domestic and international peace.

7 The Poet's Prose

The interrelationship and mutual influence of prose and poetry are manifold and intricate. Poets and prose writers use the same language and draw their inspiration from the same roots. The affinity between prose and poetry is even more complex when it is produced by the same artist. It is difficult, however, to generalize about the influence of poetry on the poet's prose because the creative process and its results are highly individualized and different in each particular instance. And yet there is a common understanding that the language and style of a poet's prose contain certain poetic traits. The style of such prose is expected to be figurative, and its language lyrical, laconic, rhythmic, and musical. It is presumed that a poet's prose is usually charged with special emotional nuances and inflections and is imbued with a distinctive mood and atmosphere, characteristic of lyrical poetry.

Russian classical literature offers many examples of the close interdependence between prose and poetry in the creative output of certain artists. Thus, for example, despite the fact that Aleksandr Pushkin and Mikhail Lermontov are considered primarily poets, their artistic genius made it possible for them to create prose and poetry of equal value. Ivan Turgenev, among others, began his creative career writing poetry, but turned to, and became famous for, his prose. Ivan Bunin and Andrei Belyi, in contrast, continued to write both prose and poetry throughout their lives.

There are many similar examples in contemporary Soviet literature. Vasilii Belov started out writing poetry but became famous for his village prose, while Vladimir Soloukhin continues to write both prose and poetry. A similar trend persists in the 1980s. Bulat Okudzhava continues to write intermittently both prose and poetry. Evgenii Evtushenko, who has until recently combined poetry with journalistic prose, writes a novel, and Andrei Voznesenskii produces a narrative of imaginative prose fiction.

It is my intention here not to compare the prose of these writers with their verses and poems but rather to discuss their prose fiction within the general context of Soviet literature of the 1980s. In each case the relationship and parallels between prose and poetry are different, and only a detailed examination of a total oeuvre can lead to detailed conclusions. Nonetheless, even the general reader will notice the rhythmic sentence patterns in Okudzhava's prose, the numerous quotations from Russian and Soviet poetry in Evtushenko's novel, or the fact that Voznesenskii's prose is more transparent, less vague, and easier to interpret than his verse – and sometimes illuminates it. The prose of all three is saturated with poetic imagery and metaphors, but it is also supplemented by the psychological analysis characteristic of prose fiction.

Bulat Okudzhava

Bulat Okudzhava is the most natural prose writer of the three poets. His first significant work of prose, 'Bud' zdorov, shkoliar' (Good Luck, Schoolboy!; 1961),[1] appeared just as he was beginning to make a name for himself as a poet and balladeer. He has continued to write prose throughout his career, producing, among other works, three long historical narratives.[2] There are connections between his poetry and his prose. The poetry relies on prosaic words and incorporates experiments with metre, while the prose makes use of poetic language and rhythmical patterns. Further, both prose and poetry are imbued with similar moods of gaiety and sadness, bitterness and kindness; they contain elements of irony and satire and could be read as allegories of contemporary Soviet life.

Okudzhava's recent novel, *Svidanie s Bonapartom* (A Meeting with Bonaparte; 1983),[3] is written in the spirit of his earlier prose. It is a historical narrative, but not a conventional historical novel. The main characters are not historical figures. Past events are presented through the eyes of what might appear as objective individuals. Reality is projected through the prism of personal experience, and history forms only the background and serves as a springboard for the author's imagination.

The first three parts of the novel are narrated in the first person by three different characters. The fourth, concluding part is composed of letters and memoirs that seem to untangle the complicated plot. The narrator of part I, the retired Major-General Nikolai Opochinin, is obsessed simultaneously by two conflicting emotions. He is overwhelmed by gratitude to Napoleon for having personally saved his life at Austerlitz, but he is guided by a sense of mission to save Russia and is outraged at Napoleon's invasion of his native land. The general intends to give Bonaparte a lavish reception on his estate, but subconsciously he wants also to avenge himself for the suffering of the Russian people and the devastation of the Russian soil.

Opochinin's self-assumed historical mission is a failure, because the mystical bent of his character prevents him from seriously considering the wartime realities of 1812 Russia. Instead of receiving the French emperor in his home, Opochinin faces death at the hands of a French dragoon, at the gates of his own estate. Opochinin's personal life is also a failure. His infatuation with his neighbour, Varvara Volkova, is a hopeless dream. This wilful and enigmatic woman proposes to the general but admits that she loves another man. With the end of part I, Opochinin disappears from the scene.

Part II is narrated by the French singer-actress Luiza Bigar. She lives in Russia for a number of years. She perceives it as her home and is sympathetic to the Russian cause. Yet when Moscow is set free and the mob in the streets finds out that she is French, she is abused and beaten. She decides then to leave Russia and returns to France. Part II portrays Moscow under the rule of Napoleon and gives a graphic picture of the Moscow fire. By sheer chance, fate brings together Luiza Bigar with Opochinin's nephew and heir, Timosha Ignat'ev, his friend Priakhin, and the mysterious Svechin, the very man Varvara Volkova is in love with, as well as with the French Colonel Pastoré, one of those who saw Napoleon save General Opochinin at Austerlitz. Timosha and Priakhin soon abandon Moscow and join the Russian forces fighting Napoleon.

Part III contains the reminiscences of Varvara Volkova. Her life story alternates with authorial digressions in the third person. Varvara's story unites, in a sense, the disconnected plot lines and brings to the fore the heroic nature of Timosha Ignat'ev. Timosha and Priakhin are among the Russian officers who pursue the French and reach Paris. Many young officers, friends of Timosha, become infected by French liberalism and view Russia, upon their return home, as an autocratic monster. Before long they organize a conspiracy against the tsar. Timosha, the youngest and least experienced among them, sympathizes with their cause. Priakhin, a colonel and father of five, never joins the plot. By a strange twist of fate, Priakhin is assigned the task of arresting Timosha and taking him to St Petersburg. Timosha's complicity in the insurrection is minimal, and he is set free, but most of his friends – those who participate in the Decembrist plot – are executed or exiled. Timosha is not a rebel by nature, but he considers himself morally responsible for everything that happens to his friends. He identifies with those who are exiled and executed because he is privy to their secrets. Life becomes unbearable to him. He is tormented by guilt and finally chooses an honourable, self-inflicted death to a life he considers disgraceful.

The setting and the subject-matter of *Svidanie s Bonapartom* are similar to those in Okudzhava's other novel, *Glotok svobody. Povest' o Pavle Pestele* (A Taste of Freedom: A Story about Pavel Pestel'; 1971). It covers the same period of time and deals with the same historical events. But the Decembrist plot, which is in the distant background in *Svidanie*, is at the centre of the plot of *Glotok svobody*, where it is projected through the eyes of the naïve clerk Avrosimov.

Since most of *Svidanie s Bonapartom* deals with Napoleon's invasion of Russia, a comparison with Leo Tolstoi's *Voina i mir* (War and Peace) inevitably arises. Indeed, there are many parallels, and it is obvious that Okudzhava is indebted to his great predecessor. Thus, for example, the predicament of General Opochinin at Austerlitz is strikingly similar to the fate of Andrei Bolkonskii. Similarly, the rebellion of Varvara Volkova's peasants reminds one of the Bogucharovo affair. Okudzhava's novel is also permeated by the Tolstoian unpredictability of fate. People seem to be cast around helplessly in the whirlwind of history, deluding themselves that they control their own destinies. Unexpected encounters and chance occurrences determine the course of everyone's life.

The narrative contains many pages of beautifully written, elegant Russian prose, but the disjointed structure makes it difficult at times to follow the main course of events. Many conflicts and intrigues remain unresolved, and a number of scenes are not quite convincing psychologically. Two of the three narrators disappear just when their fate becomes most engaging.

There is much in the novel that is fateful, enigmatic, and mysterious, and the author makes abundant use of melodramatic devices. Parts of the narrative are written in the mood of the eighteenth-century adventure novel, and some heroes are created in the romantic spirit of eighteenth-century chivalry. The title *Svidanie s Bonapartom* is symbolic, rather than realistic. Napoleon himself is in the distant background. Only twice do characters, by sheer chance, come even indirectly in touch with him. The title relates to the Russian encounter with the values of Bonaparte's France, which destabilizes the tranquil lives of the Russian nobility and leads to the events of December 1825.

As in Okudzhava's previous novels, the allegories of Soviet conditions today remain under the surface, but they are there. Russian officers return home, after defeating Napoleon, with hopes for freedom and enlightment but are faced, instead, by a tsarist autocracy more oppressive than ever before. Similarly, the high hopes for a better life of Soviet soldiers returning home after the Nazi defeat in 1945 never materialize. The parallels between the Decembrists and Soviet dissidents and the allusions to their helplessness before the overwhelming powers of the regime are also evident in both cases. The revolt of the peasants against their masters and their support of the enemies of Russia are reminiscent of many Soviet peasants who did not hesitate to turn against the Soviet state during the Second World War.

Priakhin, a dedicated friend and a good family man, acquiesces with the tsarist regime and betrays his friends for the sake of tranquillity and a promotion. He reminds one of some contemporary Soviet informers who spy on their neighbours not out of conviction but because they are forced to do so by circumstances of life. Only Timosha Ignat'ev has few parallels in contemporary Soviet literature and society.[4] He is a hero of superior moral dimensions, but his suicide saves no one. It only spells an end to Opochinin's dynasty, and it strikes a terrible blow to Liza, Varvara Volkova's only daughter, who is in love with Timosha and intends to marry him.

Okudzhava's novel takes us back to long-forgotten events and reminds us of forsaken and abandoned values, but it also makes one aware that human nature and the intricate unwritten laws that determine human interaction in any social environment have changed very little. Time and civilization change mainly the external forms of human expression, rather than the intrinsic fabric of man's internal world.

Evgenii Evtushenko

Unlike Okudzhava's novels, the prose of Evgenii Evtushenko is contemporary in content, spirit, and form. Like his poetry, Evtushenko's prose deals with burning Soviet problems of the day; it is stimulated by the desire to make a social comment or to deliver a political message. Most of Evtushenko's prose writings of the late 1970s and the 1980s belong to the realm of topical journalism, or publitsistika. Evtushenko makes a distinction between the terms *journalism* and *publitsistika*. 'Publitsistika,' he claims, 'is not a genre; it is a relationship to reality. There is no need to confuse publitsistika with momentary journalism, which can develop into publitsistika only if it deals with important problems of eternity, rather than with momentous issues of the day.'[5] Evtushenko's articles deal with a variety of subjects: the arts, political and social issues, travel impressions from the West, the international situation, and Soviet foreign policy.[6] One narrative, 'Ardabiola' (1981),[7] belongs to the realm of khudozhestvennaia publitsistika – a mixture of reality and fiction with a strong social message and extra-literary connotations.

'Ardabiola' is a fantasy about the biologist Ardab'ev, who produces a miracle cure for cancer by combining a gene of the African tsetse fly with a Siberian plant. This extraordinary remedy is called Ardabiola. The first to be cured by this miracle drug is Ardab'ev's father, who later dies accidentally after a drinking bout. Ardab'ev goes from Moscow to his native Siberian town for his father's funeral. On his way home, after visiting a friend, he is attacked by three young hooligans and robbed of his jeans. He is cruelly beaten on his head with a knuckle-duster and loses his memory as well as the formula of the miraculous drug.

'Ardabiola' is a third-person fantastic narrative placed in a very realistic Soviet setting. It exposes a number of negative aspects of Soviet life, suggesting easy answers to problems for which there are no readily available solutions. Many scenes, incidents, and discussions are included in order to enhance the social significance of the story. Questions of education and alcoholism, hooliganism and crime, abortion and health care delivery are just some of the issues discussed. Even the fantastic notion of a miracle cure for cancer is deeply rooted in reality because it expresses people's dream and hope that cancer will be conquered one day. Evtushenko poses these problems in an eloquent and declamatory manner, but the discussions are shallow and faint-hearted. The opinion is voiced that crime and alcoholism result from lack of faith in anything positive and from a pervading soullessness. People have become indifferent to each other and have replaced the inner search for spiritual fulfilment with constant striving for material goods – or 'veshchizm,' a word derived from the Russian 'veshch,' or thing.

Evtushenko contends that he was prompted to write 'Ardabiola' by the ever-increasing manifestations of veshchizm in all aspects of Soviet life. He asks 'not to confuse this term with the desire to dress well or to have a good flat with all the amenities. There is nothing wrong with that. But it is terrible ... when the desire for things becomes the main objective of one's life. It leads to social cynicism which becomes a public danger ... Veshchizm is dangerous because it is always a potential crime.'[8] Veshchizm assumes different forms in different societies, but the assault on Ardab'ev and the robbery of his jeans by three alienated young hoodlums is not a classic expression of contemporary Soviet veshchizm. For the youngsters the jeans are a status symbol and a sign of belonging to a special clan. They are a token of superiority over all those who wear ordinary Soviet trousers. In fact, the thugs want only American jeans, and they are very disappointed on realizing that Ardab'ev's jeans are of Yugoslavian make. In real life, veshchizm, which is a reflection of a corrupted sense of moral values, is an ailment that afflicts mostly the Soviet middle class, the bureaucracy, and the intelligentsia – people who by Soviet standards have enough of everything but who are not satisfied and want more.

There is, however, another, more probable reason for Evtushenko's writing of 'Ardiabola,' which is referred to in his introduction, when, as he claims, 'three youngsters have cruelly beaten a talented artist. Surely they could have killed him, and together with him all his future creations. And all that for some wretched clothing.'[9] There is little doubt that the talented artist is Evtushenko's fellow native of Siberia, Valentin Rasputin, whom Evtushenko has known for many years.[10]

'Ardabiola' has a plot with much potential but is inadequate as a work of artistic fiction. The reader is little touched by the fate of the heroes because their actions are poorly motivated and there is little connection between their words and their deeds. The conclusion is anti-climactic. In order to end the story on a positive note, the author has Ardab'ev regain his memory and brings him together with his abandoned wife. The forces of life prove victorious; they are stronger than the enemies of the Soviet people. Now Ardab'ev will be able to live a happy family life and go on saving people from the fatal clutches of cancer. It sounds good, but it is not very convincing.

Evtushenko's first novel, *Iagodnye mesta* (Wild Berries; 1981),[11] is close in spirit and style to his khudozhestvennaia publitsistika, and, in particular, to 'Ardabiola.' It also is a mixture of reality and fantasy. It is a montage of disjointed scenes and of little-connected characters and dramatic conflicts, interspersed with much dialogue and discussion of important contemporary Soviet problems. There is little unity in the plot. The main action takes place in the early 1970s, but a time span from the beginning of the century to the present is covered in numerous flashbacks and digressions. The whole novel seems composed of digressions and secondary plots, because there is no single character, or unifying thread of events, to connect all these episodes into one smoothly flowing and developed narrative.

The main locale is Siberia, near Evtushenko's native Stantsia Zima. But just as there is little unity in time, so is there little unity in space. The action moves indiscriminately from one place to another; from Siberia to Moscow and Leningrad, and further to Hawaii, Chile, and Vietnam.

The main cast of characters can be divided roughly into two groups: local Siberians and people from central Russia. But, as a rule, for every positive character the author produces a negative one. The Siberians are represented by people such as the petty and worthless berry commissioner Tikhon Tikhonovich Tugikh, and by the indigenous resident of the taiga Ivan Kuz'mich Belomestnykh, a man of high moral principles, dedicated to his land and to his family. Among the young Siberians, Ksiuta, the beautiful daughter of Ivan Kuz'mich, and the noble, handicapped Kesha stand out.

The second group is composed of members of a geological expedition who arrive in Siberia in search of the rare mineral cassiterite. The expedition is headed by Viktor Petrovich Kolomeitsev, a determined and business-like man of over fifty, and it includes a number of geologists, young and old, men and women. Special attention is devoted to the brave and hard-working Serezha Lachugin, as well as to the envious and egoistic Sitechkin.

A third group is composed of characters appearing in the prologue and the epilogue, which are placed in the novel in reversed order for no obvious reason. This group includes a nameless cosmonaut, who is a native of Zima, the Russian pre-revolutionary scientist Tsiolkovskii, as well as the fantastic invisible creatures Y-Y and I-I, who arrive from a perfect world, the Galaxy of Immortality, to view from above the inhabitants of the Earth, who are still on an extremely low level of development.

Most chapters deal with episodes in the lives of separate characters, but in some parts the geologists are grouped together and interact with the local people. It appears from this relationship that the local residents are spiritually superior to those from central Russian cities. Thus the strong Kolomeitsev seduces Ksiuta, but out of pride and self-respect she refuses to disclose who is the father of her child. Kolomeitsev, in the mean time, goes indifferently about his daily business. Evtushenko somewhat idealizes Kolomeitsev, presenting him as a positive man of action. But his affair with Ksiuta is unwittingly cast in the spirit of village prose of the 1960s, in which the ethical corruption and hypocrisy of the city are contrasted with the spiritual purity of the countryside. The physically strong, but morally shallow and depraved man of the city defiles and abuses an innocent country girl. The dark forces of civilization intrude into the peaceful life of the Siberian taiga, bringing pain and suffering. Kolomeitsev's affair finds its indirect solution in another episode of a similar nature. Tikhon Tikhonovich recognizes in the woman doctor, who treats him in the hospital, his own daughter, an offspring of an affair he had some forty years earlier.

There are few topics that concern Soviet people that are not touched upon in the novel. Problems of war and peace, education and ideology, poetry and music, work and trade are dealt with in the realistic setting of everyday Soviet life. In addition, abstract notions of good and evil, love and hate, ethics and religion, fear and duty are discussed on different occasions by different characters.

In his discussion of Soviet intellectual life, Evtushenko caricatures a poet who denounces everything positive in Soviet and Russian culture. He also ridicules a Russophile essayist who claims that 'the future path of Russia is to be sought in an enlightened autocracy which is united with Orthodoxy,' and that 'the metaphysical spirituality of national values is above the warring cosmopolitanism which hides under the guise of internationalism.'[12] Evtushenko makes fun even of himself. In a superficial discussion about poetry, the names of Voznesenskii and Evtushenko come up, among others. But, according to one character, Evtushenko the poet is already passé. Well, perhaps this is the reason he turns to prose.

Evtushenko may be critical of the Soviet system and even of himself, but he persistently attempts to illustrate the superiority of Soviet society over the West. In order to expose the shortcomings of American education and music he takes the reader to Hawaii. We encounter there a group of young American rock musicians. Some of them have visited the Soviet Union as part of an official student exchange program. Their music is, of course, bad: artistically worthless and inspired only by the desire to make quick money.

Iagodnye mesta, which has sold several million copies in the Soviet Union, received a strong and mixed critical reaction both at home and in the West. The discussion generated by the appearance of the novel tells us more about the Soviet intellectual scene than do the discussions between Evtushenko's heroes. Some ideas expressed in the novel find sympathy with certain critics but infuriate others. Evtushenko tries to satisfy everyone: the mass readership, by exposing the negative and seamy sides of Soviet life; the intellectuals, by paying tribute to or criticizing current ideological trends; and the censors, by trying to balance every negative statement about Soviet life with criticism of the West and by extolling Soviet foreign policy. The net result is that Evtushenko satisfies few critics.

Middle-of-the-road publications, such as *Literaturnoe obozrenie*

(Literary Review) and *Literaturnaia gazeta*, which express official government views, try hard to be fair to Evtushenko; conservative journals, such as *Nash sovremennik* and *Voprosy literatury*, openly voice their unequivocal distaste. In *Literaturnaia gazeta*, Georgii Semenov approves of what he sees as the main idea of the novel, the notion that 'people should live in peace, struggling together to overcome philistinism and spiritual and physical decay.' Though he finds the narrative somewhat disjointed, 'it is a well put-together and thought-out novel.'[13] According to Semenov, Kolomeitsev is a positive hero: 'He is precisely the man that our critics dream of. He is a hero fascinated by his work and a man who scorns all difficulties.'[14]

An opposite view is expressed by Oleg Volkov in *Nash sovremennik*. Volkov abhors the portrayal of 'love' on an animal level, 'the more so since the vulgar seducer [Kolomeitsev] is raised by the author to the level of a strong hero.'[15] Volkov accuses Evtushenko of misrepresenting collectivization in Siberia, of introducing a number of non-realistic melodramatic adventure scenes, and even of corrupting the Russian language. In fact, Volkov says, the book is not, as the title indicates, about Siberia at all. The author is incapable of writing about his native places because he is too far removed from them. According to Volkov, Evtushenko uses the novel as a platform 'for empty philosophizing and the expression of his personal views which are not beyond doubt.'[16]

V. Kardin propounds a similar view in *Voprosy literatury*. He is confused by the immense number of characters, problems, and scenes within the limited confines of the novel. He claims that even historically factual people and circumstances seem unreal.[17] Kardin criticizes the novel and those who support it. He decries some critics' failure to tell the truth about Evtushenko's latest work: 'Criticism of silence' currently finds its home on the pages of *Literaturnaia gazeta*.[18] An editorial in *Literaturnaia gazeta* mildly rebuffs Kardin, acknowledging, however, that *Iagodnye mesta* is far from perfect.[19]

Evtushenko is one of the few Russian poets well known in the West, and the appearance of his first novel in English translation raised high hopes, which have not been satisfied. The Western reader, little enlightened on Soviet internal affairs, judges the novel by its artistic merits and by the scenes set in the West, and he does not approve of either. John Updike expresses the views of many American readers when he asserts that '"Wild Berries," set in the scarcely tamed spaces of the Soviet hinterland, should be a comfortable, rollicking book; but instead it is a book with a bad conscience, by a writer who wants to feel more than he does.'[20] 'The scenes involving Americans, though they show the superficial knowingness of a world traveler, have a patent falsity, a benign corniness, that serves as an index to the falsity of "Wild Berries" throughout: the book is a pastiche, an assemblage of outsides and signifiers with no real insides or unwilled significance.'[21] These are harsh words with much truth in them. Lack of sincerity is a great shortcoming in a work of art. Evtushenko is far from being an accomplished writer of prose fiction, and his novel has succeeded at the cash register because of the name of its author, not its quality. Like his poetry, the novel is topical, and it exudes a sense of mission, but it lacks a sense of measure and psychological truthfulness.

In his introduction to *Iagodnye mesta*, Valentin Rasputin labels it an 'agitational' novel. Indeed, the narrative is replete with ideas that are often little connected with the characters who voice them. The author tries hard to prove the universality of his ideas. The prologue and the epilogue emphasize the universality of human destiny and the fact that values of good and evil transcend national boundaries. The cosmonaut decries universal cynicism. According to him 'all nationalisms are inhuman. It is impossible to believe in one's own country without believing first in mankind.'[22] And yet the universality of mankind and the connection between the past and the future are expressed in the novel by the Russian names of Tsiolkovskii and Gagarin. Tsiolkovskii's dream has been turned into reality by Gagarin. Russia makes possible travel in outer space, and the Russian spirit, expressed in the workings of the contemporary Soviet state, shows universal man the path into the future. There is no reason to doubt Evtushenko's patriotism and his well-meaning ideas, but since the author's omnipresent personality is the only substance that holds the narrative together, the ideas expressed are perceived as the author's rather than his heroes'.

Evtushenko writes in one of his articles that 'mediocrity is inadmissible, and the lack of a world view should place a veto on the use of ink ... A man who calls himself a writer but does not know how to write is far from being modest ... Mediocrity is most often the result of ignorance.'[23] There is no need to accuse Evtushenko of lack of a Weltanschauung or of ignorance. To the contrary. His novel is oversaturated. It contains too many ideas and too many facts, and that is just as bad. In fact, Evtushenko is guilty of the shortcomings that he ascribes to one of his heroes. The young poet Krivtsov, the friend of Serezha Lachugin, is told by the leader of his literary club: 'You have a dangerous mania, Krivtsov. You want to solve all the world's problems in every poem. One thought trips over the next.'[24] Good ideas are important, but they do not make a work great unless they reflect truthfully the lives and the actions of those who profess them. Declamatory statements, unsupported by the simple logic of life, are sometimes good for poetry, but not necessarily for prose fiction.

Andrei Voznesenskii

As opposed to Evtushenko's novel, the prose of Andrei Voznesenskii has limited public appeal and elicits little critical attention. It lacks the declamatory tone of Evtushenko's prose, because it is intimate and very personal; moreover, it is directed at a sophisticated reader.

Voznesenskii's prose is grouped together in a book under the ambiguous title *Rifmy prozy* (Rhymes of Prose). It is not artistic fiction, but neither is it journalism or khudozhestvennaia publitsistika. Most short pieces are impressions and reminiscences of people and events. A special place in Voznesenskii's prose is occupied by his teacher and mentor, Boris Pasternak. Voznesenskii expresses his fascination and respect, paying homage to the man who influenced him most. Kornei Chukovskii, Valentin Kataev, Iurii Kazakov, and Evgenii Evtushenko, among others, are also the subjects of his essays. Evtushenko is discussed in an article symbolically entitled 'Poet i ploshchad'' (The Poet and the Square).[25] In a few subtle remarks Voznesenskii describes succinctly Evtushenko's talent: 'Evtushenko is a poet orator. His gift is enormous. His muse is polemical publicism. He absorbs lyrically the political nerve of the moment.'[26] Voznesenskii says little about Evtushenko's artistry, but he pays tribute to the man without whom Soviet poetry would not have reached the level of popularity it attained in the 1960s and 1970s.

Topical issues come and go, while classical art survives the test of time. This is the subject of Voznesenskii's most recent fictional narrative, 'O' (O; 1982).[27] 'O' is a personal narrative in which reality and fantasy are closely intertwined. It is told intermittently in the first, second, and third persons. The writer is an author-narrator, an outside observer, a story-teller, and a participant in the narrated events. He pretends to be an objective spectator but in fact is the subject and the object of the story. He speaks mostly of his personal experiences and of his perceptions of people, the arts, and life. The story is told on several levels. On one plane the author himself is at centre stage. Reminiscences of his childhood alternate with important events in his literary career; sketchy outlines of important figures from the world of art are followed by discussions about human fate. On the other plane, Voznesenskii shares the spotlight with the British sculptor Henry Moore, with whom he was long acquainted.

The whimsical title 'O' refers to a fantastic black hole which inconspicuously enters the narrator's room. It refers also to the sculptures of Moore, which often resemble huge round bodies with holes. 'O' is the sound uttered by the black hole as well as the physical shape it can assume. But the hole can also be soundless and formless. It is the image of a destroyed civilization and a bottomless pit through which everything can fall. It represents eternity, and it teaches the narrator to reminisce. 'Black holes are lumps of memories and feelings pressed together, not passages into other spaces.'[28] As opposed to nostalgic black holes, which are turned into the past, white holes are turned into the future and represent people full of optimism, who fight for the bright times to come. Picasso, for example, is considered a 'white hole,' because he has overcome death by attaining immortality while still alive.

Within the context of the story, the fantastic black hole becomes a prism through which the author examines his own life and his destiny. Judging by his own words, chance has treated him well. It saved him several times from seemingly unavoidable death, and it made possible his spiritual survival through his works, which others had to risk their safety to publish. The narrative is not too optimistic, but the author appears to have faith in humanity and in himself. He believes in man's creative powers and in the unity of creative artists all over the world.

The philosophical message of the narrative is presented in the final pages. The narrator overhears two voices coming from the bottom of the hole. They ask: 'What is more important – faith or the object of faith? The meaning of life or the life of meaning? Freedom or the road to freedom? The boundlessness of mind or the limits of earthly resources?'[29] The narrator is asked whether he wants to know the answer, but he is told that 'for the answer one has to pay with his life.'[30] It appears thus that in ordinary circumstances man's eternal quest can never be satisfied, because man has to pay with his life in order to learn what he lives for. Thus everyone has to create a meaning for his own life. Yet many waste their lives in idleness, not realizing that they are throwing away the one thing that can bring them closer to the meaning of life. The meaning of the narrator's life is embodied in his art, which assumes an independent existence and gives life to meaning.

'O' is not a conventional povest'; it is not a novella with a traditional cast of characters and conflicts. Voznesenskii speaks much about himself, but he tells us nothing about his personal and family life or about relationships between men and women. He even predicts the sarcastic remarks of a well-informed critic who wonders how the letter

'O' can form the foundation of a narrative plot. But for the author the letter ''O' is a deep breath; it is the oxygen of language.'[31] 'It is the most Russian letter, which is at the same time most common to all European languages.'[32] The letter 'O,' then, is a poetic metaphor that symbolizes the spiritual kinship between creative artists all over the world; it symbolizes the eternal unity of time, which is expressed in the immortal creations of great artists who are people of talent, vigour, and a clear conscience.

The prose of Okudzhava, Evtushenko, and Voznesenskii attests to their desire to diversify their creative output and to reach for a wider audience. In addition to writing poetry, Okudzhava is a singer and performer; Voznesenskii reads poetry, and he works for the theatre; and Evtushenko has tried script writing, directing, and even acting, playing K.E. Tsiolkovskii in the movie *Vzlet* (The Ascent).

The poet's prose is usually a means of self-expression on a subject for which poetry is not a suitable medium. Okudzhava writes novels about nineteenth-century Russia, in the tradition of eighteenth-century literature, which are allegories of twentieth-century Soviet society. Evtushenko writes prose with wide social ramifications. He aims at a large audience and tries to satisfy everyone, but he sacrifices artistry for social appeal. Voznesenskii's prose is subtle, poetic, and intimate, and it is addressed to the sophisticated reader.

All three poets aim in their prose at a universality of ideas. Okudzhava tries to achieve it with the help of history; Evtushenko, by transcending local boundaries and venturing into space; Voznesenskii, by exploring the universality of art.

There is little similarity in the three men's prose, just as there is little in common in their poetry. When asked once to compare the poets Evtushenko and Voznesenskii, Il'ia Erenburg replied with a parable. Once, he said, 'robbers caught two travellers, first one, and later the other. They tied them to one tree, with one rope. Thus they had a common tree, a common rope, and the same robbers,'[33] but not much more. This is a thinly veiled allusion to the creative process in the Soviet Union. All writers and poets belong to the same union. They have the same publishers, editors, and censors, but everyone endeavours to assert independently his creative individuality and write in a manner most appropriate for his art.

8 Women Writers and Women's Problems

The number of Soviet women writing today is indeed small. The index of any history of Soviet literature does not list many female authors who merit critical attention. Among the delegates to the Eighth Congress of Soviet Writers in 1986, there were only forty-four women, or 7.7 per cent of the total. Only 5 per cent of the elected members of the Board of the Writers Union are women. According to I. Grekova, Soviet women have equal rights with men, but far more responsibilities. Hence few women have the time to compete for important positions in the workplace. Among women writers whose works have appeared most often in print in the late 1970s and the 1980s are Galina Bashkirova, Liliia Beliaeva, Maiia Ganina, I. Grekova, Irina Guro, Elena Katasonova, Nadezhda Kozhevnikova, Tat'iana Nabatnikova, Liudmila Petrushevskaia, Mariia Prilezhaeva, Viktoria Tokareva, Tat'iana Tolstaia, and Irina Velembovskaia. Tolstaia, according to some, is the rising star of Soviet prose fiction.[1]

Tat'iana Tolstaia

Born in 1951, granddaughter of the well-known Soviet writer Aleksei Tolstoi, Tat'iana Tolstaia made her first appearance in print in 1983. She is certainly an interesting and original writer, with a personal style and an array of characters outside the mainstream of Soviet life. Tolstaia creates her own fictional world, and she looks at it through the eyes of her heroes, mostly people hurt by nature or abused by life. Thus the main character of 'Noch' (Night; 1987)[2] is a mentally retarded young man with the physical aspirations of a normal human being. All his life he is protected by his mother, but when he ventures once independently into the real world he becomes aware that it is evil. The main hero of the story 'Peters' (Peters; 1986)[3] is another failure. Physical disability combined with emotional inadequacy and poor upbringing doom him to a wasted life, full of unfulfilled cravings.

Many of the female characters in Tolstaia's stories are old and content with their lot; they accept life for what it is and reminisce only about the missed opportunities of youth, deluding themselves that life could have been different and better.[4] There are several strong women characters in Tolstaia's stories, but even they fail to succeed in their endeavours. Zoia in 'Okhota na mamonta' (The Hunt for a Mammoth; 1985)[5] makes a calculated decision to entice a young man into marriage, but fails. Nina, in 'Poet i muza' (The Poet and the Muse; 1986),[6] 'saves' the poet Grisha from his bohemian environment, which she abhors, and marries him. But when he is removed from the atmosphere to which he is accustomed, Grisha's talent withers away, and then he disintegrates physically. Tolstaia's fiction suggests that a mystical power of predestination determines the course of everyone's life and that fate puts people on a certain track, the course of which it is impossible to change. The main hero of 'Krug' (Closed Circle; 1987)[7] tries hard to loosen the grip of habit and break out from the closed circle of fate, but he fails.

Tolstaia's prose is in the turn-of-the-century tradition. Some of her stories are even set in those days. Her prose is cultured but noncommittal. Her language is rich in vivid metaphors, bright colours, and subtle parallels. She is concerned not with the eternal problems of the human condition but rather with the issues that affect people's daily lives and their interaction with their immediate environment. Tolstaia's stories suggest that life is not an easy business, that much of it is determined by unfulfilled dreams and illusions, and that people are essentially lonely creatures, all alone in their attempt to cope with existence. Some Soviet critics reproach her for avoiding contemporary social issues; others find her stories tedious. But Tat'iana Tolstaia has already carved out for herself a special place in Soviet literature – no mean feat for a relatively young woman writer in the Soviet Union.

More important, however, are the works of I. Grekova, unquestionably the best Soviet woman writer of the last two decades. The novels of M. Ganina and L. Beliaeva, the two most prolific contemporary Soviet women writers, are also relevant because they address a number of important women's issues and represent, artistically and thematically, the mainstream of Soviet mass fiction.

I. Grekova

I. Grekova is the pseudonym for Elena Sergeevna Venttsel'. It is derived from the Russian 'igrek,' a mathematical symbol for an unknown quantity. Grekova is a doctor of science, a well-known specialist in applied mathematics, and author of over sixty scholarly publications. She was born in 1907, yet her first work of fiction to be published in a central journal 'Za prokhodnoi' (Beyond the Entryway; 1962),[8] appeared when she was fifty-five – retirement age for most Soviet women. It was followed by 'Damskii master' (Ladies' Hairdresser; 1963),[9] 'Letom v gorode' (Summer in the City; 1965),[10] 'Pod fonarem' (Under the Street Lamp; 1965),[11] 'Na ispytaniiakh' (At the Testing Ground; 1967),[12] 'Malen'kii Garusov' (Little Garusov; 1970),[13] 'Khoziaika gostinitsy' (The Hotel Manager; 1976),[14] 'Kafedra' (The Faculty; 1978),[15] 'Vdovii parokhod' (The Ship of Widows; 1981),[16] *Porogi* (Thresholds; 1984),[17] 'Fazan' (Fazan; 1985),[18] 'Bez ulybok' (Without Smiles; 1986),[19] and 'Perelom' (The Fracture; 1987).[20] She has also published some short pieces for children and articles about the writer's craft in the periodical press.

Thematically Grekova's prose is in the mainstream of byt literature, which concerns itself with the everyday life of the Soviet urban intelligentsia. Most of her attention is devoted to Soviet scientists and scholars and to the workings of Soviet academic institutions. She also explores the predicament of the single woman. Perfect families are rare in Grekova's fiction. The slow process of family disintegration is seldom her main subject; rather she concentrates on its effect on the life of the single woman and her children.

The personal problems of the single woman who is widowed, divorced, never married, or simply deserted by her mate are at the centre of most of Grekova's works. The intimate issues that concern her heroines have far-reaching social ramifications, because love and marriage are most often followed by infidelity and divorce, permissiveness is followed by abortion, and illegitimacy and adoption are the results of child-bearing out of wedlock. Most of Grekova's women are far from perfect. They have been abused by fate. The author treats them with understanding, sympathy, and compassion. She tells her stories from a feminine point of view, but she does not preach or moralize, nor does she offer any solutions to the problems posed. Instead, she lets the facts speak for themselves.

The plots of Grekova's early stories are structured around a single event and are limited to the fate of one or several individuals. Any secondary information is usually related in short flashbacks or internal monologues.[21] Her narratives of the late 1970s and the 1980s are different. They deal with a variety of personal and social issues and involve a number of diverse characters of both sexes. There is, however, continuity in the development of Grekova's prose and a thematic and stylistic unity between her early stories and her more recent narratives.

In 'Malen'kii Garusov,' published in 1970, Grekova relates the life story of a young Leningrad man. He is the product of a broken family. His mother is deserted by her husband and takes to drink. She loves her son but resents his presence; her future would be more promising without him. During the Leningrad blockade (1941–3) Garusov becomes afflicted by some malady which arrests his growth. The boy loses his mother and is evacuated with an orphanage to Siberia. He misses his mother very much. Upon his return to Leningrad he walks the streets for hours in search of a relative, but to no avail. Life goes on. Garusov finishes school, becomes an engineer, and even defends a candidate of sciences dissertation, but he can find no happiness in his personal life. He twice marries and divorces the same woman. He falls madly in love with a young woman, Valia, who uses and abuses him and then discards him when he is no longer of any practical use to her. In the end Garusov is in desperate search of money to buy a flat for another married woman only because she has a difficult life.

Garusov's fate is portrayed through this relationship with a number of single and married women. His unfulfilled love for his own mother is transformed into a masochistic gratification of pleasing and helping other women who are ostensibly in need. It appears that Garusov's childhood experiences cripple his body as well as his soul. The institutional care he received saved him from starvation and made it possible for him to acquire a useful profession and a position in society, but it contributed little to his personal growth. It did not teach him how to cope with the intimate and intricate problems of daily family life. Anatolii Garusov foreshadows Vadim Gromov in 'Vdovii parokhod,' published some ten years later.

In 'Khoziaika gostinitsy,' the main protagonist, Vera Platonovna, is the wife of the domineering Colonel Larichev. who is seventeen years older and has a son from a previous marriage. Their marriage appears solid and based on love, but the love is sustained only by Vera's total submission to her despotic husband. She is a slave in her own home. She loves children, but she is not destined to bear her own child; she likes people and social activity, but she is not permitted to pursue her interests. Vera's marriage survives for twenty-seven years because she has learned to submit without hesitation or distress. Vera is a 'professional' wife: her main role is to please her husband and to obey him. Her marriage survives only because she possesses the innate capacity for happiness, which makes her see and seek the good in everything, rather than torment herself over the difficulties of daily existence. Only after her husband's death does the real Vera emerge. The newly acquired freedom turns her into a socially useful individual, respected by everyone with whom she comes in touch. Her personal and love life respond now to the whims of her heart rather than to the dictates of her husband. Her innate capacity for happiness made it possible for Vera to endure the oppressive atmosphere of her family life and to survive the shock of her husband's death.

Vera Platonovna is the only woman in Grekova's prose who submits to the whims of her husband and whose married life is depicted. Most other female characters are single, by choice or by fate; they are attempting to come to terms with a lonely and often depressing reality.

The plot of 'Kafedra' is centred around the professional life of the faculty of cybernetics of a large Soviet institute. Most of the attention, however, is devoted to the personal lives of those associated with this faculty, teachers and students alike. There is an interesting parallel between the professional life of the faculty as a whole and the personal predicaments of most of the central characters. Both appear to be in total disarray. The faculty finds itself in the process of transition, adjustment, and instability, while individual lives are in a state of confusion, moving toward a certain goal, which is, however, illusory and aimless. The characters perceive the possibility of personal happiness in a blissful union with a mate of the opposite sex, and they find themselves in constant search of a partner. This relentless pursuit leads to the substitution of the imagined for the real, the emotional for the physical, the spiritual for the material, and real love for momentary attachment.

'Kafedra' is narrated intermittently in the third and the first persons by its main character, Nina Astashova. In chapter 1, 'Zasedanie kafedry' (A Meeting of the Faculty), we are introduced to all the members of the department and become acquainted with the educational problems that concern them. The head of the department, kind-hearted Professor N.N. Zavalishin, was a good scholar but is now an unproductive old man. His name, derived from the Russian 'zavalit',' reminds one of his responsibility for the retardation and obstruction in the department's work.

Nina Astashova relates her own life story in the first person. She is a successful professional woman of close to forty. She is independent, hard-working, determined, and aggressive. But she is also a divorced mother with three children, each with a different father: one by her husband, one adopted, and one by her lover. Astashova's image is composed of three independent elements. First, she is a strong and determined dotsent (associate professor) respected by colleagues and students. Second, she is a mother who depends on her older son to be both father and mother to the younger children. At home Astashova is kind and patient, as if hiding her guilty conscience for depriving her children of a happy childhood. And, finally, she is the tender and forgiving mistress of a married and ill man. Nina's unmarried life forces the disintegration of her character into three, often contradictory parts, each of which assumes an independent existence. And the unification of these components could be possible only if Nina – academic, mother and wife, and mistress – could be integrated in one individual. Unfortunately, Astashova is not fit for this combined task. She could never give up work for family bliss. She is not ready to assume, and discharge properly, all the responsibilities connected with organized family life and therefore chooses to remain single. Her character embodies and projects the conflicting position of today's professional woman, who is seldom able to combine successfully work and family, personal life, and children.

The title 'Vdovii parokhod' is a metaphor for a flat with five separate rooms, each occupied by a single woman. The story is told alternately in the third and in the first persons by the invalid Ol'ga Flerova, a war widow. Ol'ga is a professional pianist with higher education, but conditions of life force her to settle for a job in an orphanage. The other tenants cope with their lonely existence. Most of them have little happiness to remember and no hope for a fulfilling future.

Kapa Gushchina was twice given away in marriage by her parents to older men and was twice widowed. Now she seeks succour in religion. Pan'ka Zykova is secretive about her past, but everyone knows that she is a widow. Ada Efimovna, in the past a singer and currently a cashier at the local theatre, is the only one who still deludes herself about the possibility of future love and happiness. She is considered a widow only because her third husband died; the first two are alive and well. Anfisa Gromova was legally married to Fedor, who survived the war but met his death under the wheels of a streetcar. Anfisa returns from the war pregnant and bears an illegitimate son, Vadim, who grows up into a monster with a guilty conscience. His simple mother's misguided attention and his realization that his mother's husband is not his father produce a self-centred character who rebels against society, trusts no one, and alienates himself from everyone, including his mother, thus hastening her premature demise.

The meaning of Anfisa's existence is expressed in the well-being of her only child. She lives in deprivation and gives him more than she can afford, hoping that he will pay her back with diligence and success. But Anfisa obviously expects more than her son can ever deliver and instead of preparing him for a difficult life encourages unjustified expectations in him. Despite Vadim's irrational attachment to his mother, Anfisa's pressure offends his sensitive nature and helps him turn into an angry, bitter, and cynical young man.

Vadim spites his mother for bringing him into this world and placing him in a position that is inferior. His personal world lacks firm foundations, and he questions the social and ethical values of society at large. When he is admonished for mistreating his mother and reminded that she has sacrificed all her life for his well-being, he answers without hesitation: 'I do not need it. Why did she have to bring me into this world? I did not ask her.'[22] Vadim's reply casts lights upon the issues of single parenthood and illegitimacy, and it re-emphasizes the fact that, as hard as a single mother might try to make up to her children for the lack of a legitimate father, they may still reproach her for their fate.

Schematically the fates of the four widows are placed in the corners, while the story of Anfisa Gromova and her family is in the middle. 'Vdovii parokhod' is essentially the story of Vadim, because he is the only character we see grow and develop from early childhood. The past experiences of most of the other characters are related only in flashbacks and impressionistically. Without this structural façade the story would lose much of its meaning, turning into another narrative about the unhappy life of middle-aged widows. By placing Vadim in the forefront and surrounding him with five single women, Grekova shows that being a single woman is not just a personal matter for those concerned but also a social issue of great importance. She suggests that it is dangerous to separate personal problems such as loneliness, alienation, and depression from social issues such as abortion, adoption, illegitimacy, and general health and welfare.

There is a positive note in the concluding pages of 'Vdovii parokhod.' Before Anfisa's death, Vadim tries hard to clear his guilty conscience. He is in constant attendance at the bedside of his paralysed mother. After Anfisa's funeral Vadim has a dream in which he realizes his guilt and cries in his sleep. He wakes up a new man, and a new life is now possible for him. The transformation is reminiscent of the regeneration of Raskolnikov in Dostoevskii's *Crime and Punishment*. Both men fail to repent or atone for their transgressions but regenerate after irrational dreams. In both cases a new future is promised but never shown. Just as the artistic viability of Raskolnikov's regeneration has been questioned for over a century, so is the promised transformation of Vadim Gromov not quite convincing, because it is poorly motivated and not very consistent with his character.

Grekova's first novel, *Porogi,* is a third-person narrative with several internal monologues in the first person. It is composed of over forty small chapters, each dealing with an episode in the life of a Leningrad scientific research institute. The first half of the novel portrays the work of a department developing new means of communication between people and machines and the personal and social interaction of those who work there. The second half describes the effects of a series of anonymous letters denouncing the work of the department and, in particular, its head, Professor Fabritskii.

Structurally the novel is framed between two meetings between the main character, Neshatov, and Fabritskii's associate, Gan. At their first meeting Gan interviews and accepts Neshatov for a position at the institute. Neshatov is an enigmatic individual. He is depressed, indifferent, and withdrawn. His personal life is in disarray. He has deserted his wife, Marianna, and his son, Pasha, because he discovered that she had carried on an affair with his best friend. In the past, Neshatov had been put on trial for criminal negligence at work but was found not guilty. Later he spent some time in what appears to be a mental institution. Gan assumes the role of Neshatov's confessor and spiritual father and helps him become a useful worker and a man able to love and assume responsibility. The last meeting between Neshatov and Gan takes place in the hospital. Gan's role has been fulfilled. Gan returns Neshatov to life, but he himself dies unexpectedly while apparently well on his way to recovery.

Thematically, stylistically, and structurally, *Porogi* is similar to Grekova's earlier prose. She tells her story from a feminine point of view. Men are usually surrounded by many women, and men's private lives are presented through the eyes of women. We know little of what the male characters think, or what moves them. Discussion between men is always business-like and to the point, while there is always a note of intimacy in the dialogue between women. As in most of Grekova's earlier stories, social ills are only hinted at, and personal failings are criticized with due restraint. Grekova remains non-committal to the very end. She does not approve of those who send anonymous letters, but neither does she justify those who are denounced in them. Instead, she is sympathetic to both. She sympathizes, however, not with the actions of those concerned but rather with their human frailty and weakness. She observes them from the sidelines as an objective onlooker and in the wisdom of her old age understands that no one is perfect and that everybody should be forgiven for their delusions of infallibility. This approach removes much of the intensity from a plot that is charged with much dramatic potential, and perhaps even lowers its artistic value.

Like Grekova's earlier works, *Porogi* has an abundance of unfaithful and deserted husbands and wives and many abandoned children. But there is also a new positive note. Along with the broken families there are several exemplary couples who live happily into old age. The secretary of the institute's party organization, Iashin, is a determined but understanding man of high moral principles. Even the evolution of Neshatov's character takes, on the last pages of the novel, an unexpected and surprising twist. He falls in love with a co-worker, but after having learned that his son has been jailed for robbery he is overtaken by a new spell of personal and family responsibility and decides to reunite with his former wife. It is a well-meaning conclusion, but not very convincing.

Grekova's next story, 'Bez ulybok,' is set in a research institute and looks at the psychology and method of a peculiar Soviet phenomenon, 'prorabotka' – a system of groundless insinuations, accusations, and direct attacks on a member of a collective.

The main character of Grekova's most recent povest', 'Perelom,' Kira Petrovna, is a divorced woman physician, the mother of two sons. In the first half of the story she is an active medical practitioner; in the second half, a patient. In the beginning she is a conscientious doctor and a good worker, but emotionally removed from those who are ill and suffer. Later, when she is bedridden for weeks, she becomes aware of the predicament of those who have constantly to rely on the help of others. Grekova deals in 'Perelom' with a number of issues characteristic of Soviet byt literature and discussed already in her earlier works. But along with unfaithful couples, battered wives, and corrupt and lazy young people, she introduced a number of characters who are honest, loving, and dedicated to helping those in need. The title 'Perelom,' refers to Kira's fractured bones, but it also symbolizes a break in the course of her life and a change in attitude caused by illness and suffering.

Grekova's works usually attract the reading public because she explores a number of problems little touched upon in contemporary Soviet prose, and she does so in an original and professionally elaborate manner. Grekova is a woman of advanced age, but her prose is youthful and innovative. Her language is fresh and expressive, with a tinge of irony, and most of her characters appear to be honest with themselves and sincere with others. In her recent fiction Grekova addresses a number of problems candidly, honestly, and without undue sentimentality. She knows well the milieu she describes, and she writes with authority about a number of important issues.

In her discussion of higher education, Grekova does not hesitate to criticize outdated methods of teaching, marking, and granting degrees. Research, she contends, is hampered by red tape, inadequate staffing and difficult working conditions. By pointing out a number of dangerous accidents at the working-place, Grekova expresses her concern for the safety of Soviet researchers, whose work is apparently of great military significance. In 'Za prokhodnoi,' the character Clever Vovka loses his sight in an accident during an experiment. In 'Na ispytaniiakh' Nikolai Tetkin is wounded during tests. In *Porogi*, several people are killed in an explosion at Neshatov's former working-place. Neshatov is pursued relentlessly by the image of the imprint of a bloody hand on the wall, that of a man who tries desperately to save himself during the explosion.

But most of Grekova's attention is devoted to women's concerns. One problem that recurs is abortion. It is the issue on which the plot of 'Letom v gorode' hinges. In 'Malen'kii Garusov,' Zoia, Garusov's wife, cannot bear a child apparently because of the consequences of a previous abortion. In 'Vdovii parokhod,' Vadim's teenaged girl-friend, the grade-ten student Svetka, asks him for money to pay for an abortion. She treats it lightly, as a daily occurrence, as yet unaware of its possible consequences. In 'Khoziaika gostinitsy,' Vera Platonovna is forced by her husband to abort her child. The scene in the hospital's abortion ward is pathetic: 'Every woman has her own trouble, her own pain. If not for need, living conditions, or loneliness everyone would be happy to bear a child ... Except for Vera, all were employed in different professions: there was a cab-driver, a stock-keeper, a librarian, a janitor; there was even a woman judge, and ... an ugly looking book-keeper who had already had two children but not a single husband.'[23] The women are bitter, angry, and humiliated. They are all assembled there for seemingly personal reasons, but abortion in the Soviet Union is also a social issue of great significance. It is one of the prime means of birth control. 'It is estimated that some eight million abortions are performed annually, amounting to more than double the number of live births.'[24] A Soviet woman can expect on average to undergo close to six abortions. Soviet sources indicate that in the 1960s only '25 per cent of birth control was carried out through contraception, and 75 per cent through abortion.'[25] The situation has changed little since.

It is evident from Grekova's prose that single women are affected more than married women by the inevitability of interrupting unwanted pregnancies. But, as is shown in the case of Garusov's wife, Zoia, who had an abortion before her marriage, a hasty decision by a single woman to abort her unwanted child often provides only a temporary solution to what might seem at the time a terrible dilemma. Grekova does not indicate whether she approves of abortion. She presents the problem as objectively as possible, pointing to the dangers of generalization and easy solutions to complex issues.

The subject of illegitimacy and orphanhood recurs in Grekova's works. It affects as much the life of a woman as it does the abandoned, orphaned, or illegitimate child. Single motherhood, which is often connected with poverty, lack of educational opportunities, poor upbringing, or psychological handicaps, can often determine a child's future. Almost 400,000 illegitimate children are born every year in the Soviet Union, and approximately one child in every ten is born out of wedlock;[26] the magnitude of the problem is enormous. But Soviet literature has failed until now to deal with this issue. As shown in 'Vdovii parokhod,' the administration of adoption is far from perfect, and the reader begins to understand why so many orphans and illegitimate children grow into mental and ethical cripples and why children's homes and institutions, despite the obvious dedication of many staff members, often harm those concerned. The fates of Garusov and Vadim Gromov are obvious, if fictional, examples.

An adoption scene in 'Vdovii parokhod' shows that the process often resembles market-place haggling more than a procedure concerned primarily with the child's welfare. Ol'ga Flerova describes what happens in the orphanage where she works: 'People wanting to adopt a child often visited the orphanage ... A show was organized, and the future parents would select a son or a daughter. What a cruel procedure! According to the rules, children were not supposed to know that they were being watched, "selected." But somehow everyone knew beforehand. They even discussed in advance: who will be chosen? To be selected was considered a great success. The children knew that the beautiful, the strong, those with curly hair were selected first ... The children behaved quietly and modestly, begging with their eyes, hands, backs, and with their whole demeanour: "Choose me, choose!"'[27] Such procedures humiliate these sensitive children, already hurt by fate, and contribute only to the disintegration of their personalities, helping turn them into young cynics.

A common denominator unites all the female narrators and most of the female characters in Grekova's stories: they are all single women. But each of them copes with her loneliness in a different way, which depends largely on external circumstances and on the woman's psychological and emotional make-up. The happy and submissive nature of Vera Platonovna makes it possible for her to accept the illusory for the real and seek true love at the mature age of sixty. Nina Astashova is different. Her feminine personality is sensitive and tender, but as a practical, many-sided individual she chooses independence. Rather than marry a man who could become a burden and hamper her professional career, she conducts an affair with him. Except for the unrelenting Ada Efimovna, most women in 'Vdovii parokhod' have given up all hope for future marital bliss and settle for sharing their difficult lot with people of the same sex. These women are subdued by the pressures of everyday life, and, judging from their past experiences, married life to a bad partner is often worse than peaceful loneliness.

Most of the widows in 'Vdovii parokhod' have little education. They hail from the countryside. They are submissive and do not rebel against fate. The intelligent, educated city women are different. They are in constant pursuit of an escape from loneliness. They want to gain, if not real love, then at least some security and contentment through a relationship with an available man. In 'Kafedra,' for example, the relatively young but widowed departmental secretary, Lidiia Mikhailovna, seeks the hand of her boss, the old Professor Zavalishin; the young student Liuda Velichko, who has already had a child out of wedlock, entices the much older Professor Markin. In *Porogi*, Danaia Iartseva, twice married and divorced, falls in love with Neshatov. But when he rejects her, she joins hands with one of the discredited anonymous letter writers.

This relentless chase for a friend and a mate leads to adultery and infidelity, family instability, and divorce, the examples of which are too many to number in Grekova's works. When Vera Platonovna is accused of carrying on an affair with a married man, her friend and neighbour, Honoured Actress Margarita Antonovna, retorts: 'Who does not live nowadays with married men? All solid men are married. Around each unmarried one there are multitudes of youngsters. And what should a mature woman do? Who should she live with?'[28] The young Galia, the secretary of Professor Kovaleva in 'Damskii master,' is also desperate in her efforts to land an eligible man. She claims to have fallen in love with the hairdresser Vitalii Plavnikov, but the latter is not interested in marriage. When asked by Kovaleva what has happened to her previous suitor, Volodia, Galia replies without hesitation or pangs of conscience: 'Well, what about Volodya? Volodya is a married man. He was only going with me while his wife was expecting.'[29] One may wonder why a young unmarried girl of twenty-four would go out with a married man, whose wife is expecting a child. In all probability she wanted to break up Volodia's family and entice him into a new union.

The polemical nature of Grekova's prose and the controversial subjects generate heated discussion in Soviet literary circles. While most critics show respect for this well-educated author and praise her for the compactness of her language, for her truthfulness to life, and for her ability to analyse the emotional and spiritual lives of her characters, others criticize her lack of commitment and her failure to identify with the good in Soviet life. She is chastised for her inability to create an active hero who is a member of the collective and could be emulated by readers. According to G. Brovman, 'There is a mark of poshlost' on all that Grekova tells us in "Letom v gorode."'[30] Sergei Borovnikov attacks Grekova's emphasis on the negative in 'Kafedra' and asks: 'why are all the positive heroes necessarily divorced or ... commit adultery with married men or women? What a disaster! Is family happiness accessible only to the simple man, while a man with intelligence is at best doomed to life in adultery?'[31] Borovnikov criticizes Grekova for writing in language fit only for readers who resemble her negative heroes. He claims that her characters are unable to love; they have no family or relatives, but only acquaintances. 'The depiction of such relationships is often accompanied by indifference or the obscurity of the author's ideological and ethical positions.'[32]

These are serious accusations. They fail, however, to recognize that it is impossible to institutionalize love and affection and that it is absurd even to try to have family life arranged by decree. From the appearance of Grekova's first story, the controversy has never died down. 'She was praised, and she was attacked, while readers read, loved, and looked for Grekova's books. And that is most important.'[33] And yet if one compares Grekova's fiction of the 1960s and 1970s with her works of the 1980s it is possible to conclude that, whether under the influence of the times, or under the pressure of editors and censors, Grekova's prose has somewhat mellowed. She attempts now to infuse a new and positive note in her conclusions. She tries to balance the negative effects of man-woman relationships with the introduction of 'good' and happy families, and in *Porogi* she points to the leading role of the party organization in solving contentious problems at the working-place. The conflicts in her most recent works are as acute as ever, but there is a certain drop in dramatic intensity and a danger that drama and tragedy could degenerate into melodrama.

Maiia Ganina

Maiia Ganina belongs to the generation that first appeared in print in the immediate post-Stalin period. Her first story, 'Pervye ispytaniia' (First Tests), was published in 1954 in *Novyi mir*,[34] but she began writing during the war, at the age of fifteen. Her childhood was not easy. Her mother was eighteen years younger than her father. The marriage was short-lived. Both parents remarried but were soon deserted by their new partners. The young Maiia stayed with her father. She studied in a Moscow machine-building tekhnikum, worked as a technologist, and later took correspondence courses in the Literary Institute.

Ganina's childhood and youth left a lasting mark on her personality, on her world-view, and on her creative output. She states bluntly: 'I do not know how to invent, how to fantasize. Everything I have written … has happened to me or before my eyes.'[35] Ganina's stories are witness to her complicated family life, to her visits to major Soviet construction sites in the Far East, and to her extensive travels in Siberia and India. But most important in Ganina's prose is her peculiar Soviet brand of militant feminism, which she advocates relentlessly in her fiction as well as in her journalistic writings. Most heroines in Ganina's prose are strong, independent women who make their own decisions and determine their own future. They value their personal freedom and independence more than the comfort of marriage and a secure home.

The narrator-heroine of 'Uslysh' svoi chas' (Listen to Your Hour; 1976),[36] Mariia Viktorovna, is an actress of close to fifty. She is a self-made woman who starts out as a simple worker, participates in theatricals, studies acting, and finally becomes a star. She is married to a good man, but she does not love him. Her daughter, Sasha, is also an actress, but her path to stardom is without the obstacles and complications faced by her mother. Mariia Viktorovna falls in love with a cameraman on the movie set. The few days they spend together are the happiest in her life. She leaves her husband and dreams of a new and wonderful future. But one moment of hesitation on the part of her lover prompts her to turn her back on him.

In another plot line, which resembles closely Ganina's own life, the narrator tells us about her relationship with her father. He is now old and ill, but in the past he had the life of a libertine. He had many wives, and many children by younger women. But despite all this, Masha loves him and is attached to him, even in his old age.

The story's message is not optimistic. Masha, a determined and independent woman, has accomplished much in her professional life, but in her personal life she has experienced little happiness. Moreover, she has little hope for a satisfying future. She is getting old; her professional career is coming to an end, and there is nothing she can lean on. She tries to convince herself that it is good to be alone and independent, but she also realizes that one pays a high price for this so-called freedom.

The gloomy mood is offset by a conclusion that is little connected with the main plot. The story ends on a positive note. Masha is abroad; she encounters an old friend who, some thirty years earlier, worked with her at the same plant. Now he is a Soviet specialist, helping a friendly foreign country to industrialize. This final episode is of some social significance to the Soviet reader, but it little affects Masha's unhappy life.

After having achieved a professional position of great stature and an independence envied by many, Masha remained unfulfilled. It is paradoxical that her proud feminine nature, which places her personal freedom above everything else, was the cause of her undoing. She gives up the man she loves because she cannot accept his momentary vacillation, nor can she make the first step toward a reconciliation which she desires so much. Personal freedom is an important component in a relationship between two equal partners. But when it turns into a blind principle, prohibiting compromise, it can ruin one's happiness, even destroy one's life.

At the centre of Ganina's novel *Sto zhiznei moikh* (My Hundred Lives; 1983),[37] is another middle-aged woman, close to fifty. Mariia Nemchinova arrives at a remote construction site in Siberia from Moscow to begin a new life. She leaves behind an unfaithful husband, who married her so that she could look after his household and his old mother. In the first half of this third-person narrative, the action alternates between Nemchinova's present in Siberia and her past in Moscow. The only bright episode is connected with an incredible occurrence when her neighbour, Var'ka, 'sells' or hires out her young drunken husband, Leonid Solov'ev, to Mariia Sergeevna for thirty days. The novel says little about what happens after the thirty days expire, but it is clear that Mariia has become infatuated with Leonid and that this is the only real emotional attachment she has ever experienced. A chance occurrence brings Mariia and Leonid together again. She encounters him in Siberia where he is now head of a major construction project.

The plot evolves around two distinct subjects: Nemchinova's personal life and her relationship with Solov'ev, and social life and working conditions on Siberian construction sites. Ganina does little justice to either topic; she tries to cover too much ground within the limited confines of the novel; the relationship between Nemchinova and Solov'ev remains obscure and psychologically unconvincing, while the work on the construction site is drawn sketchily and the actions of most characters are poorly motivated. The novel portrays working conditions and industrial relations on the construction sites as far from perfect. The workers are greedy and self-centred. They steal, cheat, and deceive the state. Management, short of qualified manpower, gives in to the workers' unjustified demands and closes its eyes to the lack of discipline. False figures report that production plans are fulfilled, at a time when work is almost at a stand still. Party organizations seem powerless to change working conditions and help instead to cover up the situation.

Ganina looks at factors hampering work on the construction projects and discusses Soviet ethics. According to Ganina, in the past, when everyone lived together, young people were educated by the collective, by the street. Now everyone has his or her own place and is out of the neighbours' sight. Being left to themselves, people develop self-centred, philistine traits, which often become destructive. At one point, one of Ganina's young heroines contends even that 'ethics is nothing more than a subordination to habit and a traditional way of action. Most ethical is the one who always makes sacrifices to custom. Free man is unethical because he wants to depend on himself and not on tradition.'[38] Such deliberations belittle people's rational abilities and lower them to the level of beasts. They suggest that without the confines of a definite and strict social structure people are incapable of rising above the level of mediocrity and become a dangerous repository of evil. The conception of people as creatures who must subordinate personal freedom to social demands is a disguised call for totalitarian social organization and suggests that a whip is required in order to bring out the good in the individual, who is basically evil.

In her fiction, Ganina produces an array of hard-working, strong, proud, and vain women, but she demands for them a special place in society without being able to justify her claims. On the one hand, it is claimed in *Sto zhiznei moikh* that Mariia Sergeevna possesses extraordinary skills which qualify her for the position she occupies and make her indispensable. On the other hand, she cannot get along with her fellow workers, and her qualifications and real worth to the enterprise are never explained.

Most women in Ganina's prose are unable to compromise. They are able to secure a superior position in a relationship between supposed equals, but their strength is also their undoing. In 'Uslysh' svoi chas,' Mariia Viktorovna lures away the man she loves from his wife but is unable to keep him. In *Sto zhiznei moikh*, the strong Var'ka maltreats her husband. Her abuse drives him first to drinking and later into the arms of another woman. Valentina, a foreman at the Siberian construction site, beats and intimidates her unfaithful husband, driving him to what appears to be suicide.

In her artistic prose Ganina expresses views similar to those she advocated vociferously in her journalistic writings, trying to make up in her fiction for what is missing in real life. She decries the difficult lot of the Soviet woman, stating bluntly that the ostensible equality between man and woman is a sham. She claims that there are many positions in the Soviet administration to which a woman, regardless of her qualifications, will never be accepted. She reminds her readers 'that the word "emancipation" means freedom from dependence, oppression, and prejudice. The emancipation of the woman means equality in social, professional, and family life. But what kind of equality is it when some "prestigious" institutes accept boys almost without examinations, "failing," at the same time, girls for no reason whatsoever?'[39]

Ganina also carries further Grekova's argument about the ethics of childbirth without a legitimate father, and she questions even the right of legally married parents to bring a child into this world unless they are positively sure that they will stay together.[40]

Ganina's prose belongs to the kind of literature in which the documentary and realistic background and the social significance are more important than the artistic merits. Ganina usually has a story to tell, but her message is often obscure and not very convincing, because her artistic means of characterization and portrayal are often limited and her conflicts lack dramatic tension and psychological truthfulness.

Liliia Beliaeva

Liliia Beliaeva is another writer who focuses on man-woman relationships in Soviet society. Born in the Smolensk region, and having graduated from the philological faculty of the Tambov Pedagogical Institute, Beliaeva started out as a journalist for the Young Communist League press. She travelled to the Virgin Lands, to Siberia, and to the Far East and lived for a number of years on Sakhalin Island. Her first work of fiction appeared in Vladivostok, but her next novella, 'Kvartira s vidom na more' (A Flat with a View on the Sea; 1969),[41] was published in a central journal.

One of Beliaeva's better-known novellas, 'Sem' let ne v schet' (Seven Years Wasted; 1976),[42] was inspired by her Sakhalin experiences. In it, economic conditions and limited possibilities for physical and social mobility destabilize a family. The main plot is simple. Mining engineer Evgenii Prozorov moves to Sakhalin Island in order to earn extra money to arrange a more comfortable life for his family in Moscow. But when he returns home, he realizes that seven years of separation have set him apart from his wife Larisa and that little remains in common between them. His daughter, Alenka, who is the only real bond·between them, refuses to recognize him as her father. The plot is further complicated by the fact that during their long separation Prozorov and Larisa were unfaithful to each other. In fact, Prozorov still loves another woman on Sakhalin, but because of his pressure to abort their child she refuses to see him again.

The plot is composed of two closely intertwined themes: the relationship of the Prozorovs, and the social and economic background of their family drama. The marriage is clearly influenced by economic and social conditions. Family interests are sacrificed to ostensible economic and social needs. In the end, the Prozorovs continue their unhappy marriage, held together by their well-furnished Moscow apartment and their child.

Prozorov's experiences in the rigid conditions of the Far East make him overly sensitive to his wife's life-style in Moscow. He is offended by the pervading materialism and outraged by most of her friends and their philistine approach to life. His own friends from the past are not much better. Most of them are careerists, concerned only with material well-being. Prozorov compares life in Moscow with conditions on Sakhalin. He concludes tentatively that life in the Far East is real, while in Moscow everyone pretends to live. Most things are done for the sake of propriety rather than for their intrinsic value. The juxtaposition of life in Moscow and life in the Far East is conducted in the spirit of 1960s village prose, in which the corrupting influence of urban civilization is contrasted with the spiritual purity of those who reside close to nature and to their 'roots.'

Beliaeva tries to offset the impact of the negative portrayal of the urban intelligentsia by contrasting the spiritless and vacuous relationship of the Prozorovs with that of the Sevast'ianovs. Sevast'ianov is an invalid and a writer, some twenty years older than his wife, but he is a man of set moral principles and is dedicated to his family. Despite their difference in age, the Sevast'ianovs love each other, and their marriage is based on understanding and mutual respect.

'Sem' let ne v schet' implies that a good family requires more than that two people be legally married, have children, and live together. If emotional attachment and affection are lacking, no legal or physical union can help a family survive. Furthermore, a marriage has to be tempered early through forging of a firm bond, able to endure. Unfortunately, Soviet economic and social conditions foster frequent family separations, which can lead to infidelity and alienation and can compel each partner to cater to his own needs and to protect his own interests.

'Sem' let ne v schet' deals with a number of social issues, but as a work of art it has its share of shortcomings. The characterization is inadequate, and the reader fails to become intimate even with the central characters. The narrative is told in the third person, but much of the story is revealed through internal monologue. Unfortunately, Beliaeva's attempt to take the reader into Prozorov's mind is not quite successful. His internal deliberations are vague and inconclusive, and the reader remains puzzled about the course of events. The author tries to make up for these shortcomings by tying together all the loose ends and providing all the missing facts in the last few pages.

At the centre of Beliaeva's major novel *Nesygrannaia rol'* (The Unfulfilled Role; 1982)[43] is a single woman of forty-seven, Elizaveta Petrovna. She is the mother of the actress Lera and secretary, adviser, and mistress of the deputy chairman of the Livensk city council, Poletaev. In the beginning of the novel we are introduced to the heroine. She is in constant pain, dying from an incurable ailment. She is attended by the nurse Mariia Matveevna, who turns out to be the mother of a man Elizaveta Petrovna loved in her youth. He is also ill but on his way to recovery after his third stroke.

The novel covers several days in the life of Elizaveta Petrovna – just enough time to tell her life story. It is the story of a determined, single-minded, and opportunistic woman who acts without scruples or pangs of conscience in order to improve her own life and that of her daughter. In her blind, irresistible drive for the more tangible advantages of this world, she sacrifices love, ethics, even common sense. She dies a bitter, frustrated death. She realizes that she confused her priorities and wasted her life. Elizaveta Petrovna suffers dreadfully. She craves to see her daughter and her lover, the two people mean the most to her. But neither arrives in time. They are occupied with their own affairs, their daily life, which is full of corruption and hypocrisy. All that remains for Elizaveta is to open her heart to the only person present, the nurse. But Mariia Matveevna is devastated upon learning that Elizaveta Petrovna is the very woman who caused so much anguish and suffering to her own son, Aleksei.

Nesygrannaia rol' is a novel original in structure and with a plot of great dramatic potential, but it is also cumbersome, unbalanced, and poorly executed. It is divided into thirty-two chapters of varying length, each set in a different location and dealing with a different group of characters.

But the many secondary plots, with lots of characters connected only remotely with the main story, destroy the flow of the narrative. The composition is complicated further by a method of narration that is far from simple and straightforward. The basic story is told in the third person, but the author employs a range of narrative techniques, including dialogue, monologue, direct speech, quasi-direct discourse, flashbacks, and reminiscences. Most important, however, are the internal monologues of the two sick people, Elizaveta and Aleksei. Their vague ruminations throw a light on their lives, as well as on the lives of those who surround them.

The picture of Soviet life that emanates from these reflections, memories, and stories is far from ideal. It is a society in which most people adhere to a double set of moral values and where infidelity, alcoholism, bribery, and hypocrisy are the rule. The female characters are no better than their male counterparts. A sense of insecurity motivates the actions of some of the women and forces them to behave in a self-protective manner. The young Elizaveta will do anything in order to secure what she considers to be the best possible future for herself and for her daughter. She limits the notion of well-being, however, to its material and physical aspects. She will not give herself away cheaply, but for the right price she will unhesitatingly sell her conscience as well as her body. Beliaeva does not investigate the psychological motivation of Elizaveta's actions, and therefore it is difficult to determine whether her deeds are induced by external or internal factors. But social pressures warp her personality and bring out the worst in her.

Only on her deathbed does Elizaveta Petrovna realize that she has wasted her life. It is doubtful, however, whether she is aware that it is all her own fault. She is responsible for the education and upbringing of her only daughter. She is also the one who most influences her boss, Poletaev, and helps shape his indecisive nature. She moulds both people in her own image and gives them her own attributes. Now they pay her back in kind.

Beliaeva's prose is in the mainstream of byt literature, but the main emphasis is not on the psychological intricacies of human relationships but rather on the social and economic factors that determine people's actions. There is, however, a common denominator that unites Beliaeva's fiction with other works of byt literature, namely, the total lack of ethical motivation in the action of most heroes. Most of them are moved by material considerations only and are ready to sacrifice family and friends for their narrow materialistic goals. They exchange emotional and spiritual fulfilment for material well-being, and love and affection for physical intimacy.

The female writers discussed here do not limit themselves to investigating their heroines' feminine peculiarities but usually place the personal and social problems that confront the heroines at the centre of their works. These works vary greatly in subject-matter and level of artistic mastery, but underlying concern for the fate of Soviet women gives them a certain thematic unity.

Grekova's prose is sincere, true to life, and well balanced. She devotes equal attention to personal dramas and to social background. In her works, social conditions influence human relations, but they do not determine the outcome of human actions or decide the course of people's lives.

In the prose of Ganina and Beliaeva, the social aspect appears predominant, and psychological motivation is often sacrificed to external effects. Most of their conflicts are between men and women who are usually in adverse positions. Ganina's female characters are strong women who take charge of their own destinies and try to solve these conflicts in their own favour.

Grekova is understanding and compassionate; she blames no one for the predicament of her lonely women. Ganina's strong voice demands justice for her female characters; she criticizes men's superior aspirations and blames them for the suppression of women's drive for equality. Beliaeva attempts to play the role of an impartial observer of man-woman relationships. Accordingly, she blames the difficult conditions of daily life for the behaviour of her female characters, which is much too often far from commendable.

Conditions in the Soviet Union have emancipated the modern woman, but this newly acquired liberty does not necessarily make her equal and turns much too often into a burden too difficult to bear. The Soviet critic D. Tevekelian points out aptly that as a rule 'the heroine of contemporary books is a nervous and self-assertive individual who takes the initiative in breaking up her family ... Nevertheless without a family she feels inferior and strives toward constancy and stability in a new marriage.'[44] This paradoxical situation is illustrated well in the works of Ganina. The victories of her female protagonists are illusory, because both parties in her male-female conflicts are losers. Ganina's women are liberated and independent; they refuse to accept male support, but that does not make them any happier, because a lonely, single life is a poor substitute for an open and trustful relationship between two equal individuals. It appears from contemporary Soviet literature that when a marriage breaks down, or when a child is born out of wedlock, it is usually the woman who accepts responsibility for the children and suffers most.

There are many reasons for the precarious situation of the single woman in the Soviet Union. There are more women than men: women compose 53.1 per cent of the population.[45] For every 1,000 women between fifteen and forty-nine there are only 855 men. As well, women live much longer than men. The average life-span of a woman in the early 1970s was seventy-four years; for a man, only sixty-four.[46]

The predicament of single womanhood is shared in equal measure by women in the Soviet Union and in the West. There are also many parallels in the motivation behind the struggle for women's equality all over the world. But the means and objectives of this struggle are determined in different societies by different social values, a different mentality, and different conditions of daily life.

For the first time in generations, Soviet literature begins to broach the subject of single womanhood candidly, honestly, and seriously. Unfortunately, there are no ready-made solutions to the problems posed. And yet, by focusing on the problems of women, the reader learns that social achievements and collective success seldom alleviate personal hardship and individual suffering.

9 Innovation and Experiment

In the 1970s innovation and experimentation in Soviet literature were in most cases limited to language, style, and structure. Some writers included elements of folklore, myth, and parable in their works. Others made use of a variety of symbolic devices and supplemented their narratives with fantastic subplots, placing them in a realistic setting. In the early 1980s many prose writers abandoned traditional psychological prose and turned to phantasmagoria, the grotesque, and hyperbole. They explored new vistas by creating allegorical narratives in which they drew hidden parallels between the fantastic world and Soviet reality.

In the mid-1980s artistic experimentation has given way to thematic innovation, often coupled with the introduction of new unconventional heroes and controversial plot lines. Attempts are being made to turn literature into an artistic reflection of political transition that aims to transform Soviet society. The spirit of transition is articulated in party documents and official speeches by political figures and cultural bureaucrats alike. The social transformation is to be illustrated in works of prose fiction.

The appearance of a number of books, by writers such as Chingiz Aitmatov, Vladimir Orlov, Anatolii Kim, and Veniamin Kaverin, in which reality is mixed freely with myth, fantasy, and the grotesque, has been influenced by the so-called magic realism of Latin American Nobel laureate Gabriel Garcia Marquez. Marquez, a leftist writer and friend of Fidel Castro, is highly regarded in the Soviet Union, and many of his works have been translated into Russian. But Soviet critics try to unravel his 'magic realism' in order to separate the surreal and the bizarre from the social essence allegedly hidden behind the ornamental façade of his novels. The notion of ultimate loneliness and nostalgia for something indefinable permeate Marquez's *One Hundred Years of Solitude* (1967). Solitary existence and unhappiness are almost synonymous in the novel;

hence the critics conclude that happiness and the escape from solitude should be sought in the creation of a social environment conducive to collective living. *The Autumn of the Patriarch* (1975) is regarded as a study of the cult of personality in which hyperbole serves as a magnifying glass and a tool of creative analysis.[1]

One of the first novels of the 1980s to follow in the steps of Marquez and Mikhail Bulgakov is Vladimir Orlov's *Al'tist Danilov* (Danilov the Violist; 1980).[2] Orlov, a middle-aged writer largely ignored by critics, is a minor figure in Soviet literature. Yet, to the dismay of many official critics, his new novel generated much interest among the reading public. *Al'tist Danilov* has a fantastic plot and a realistic setting. Its main hero, the musician Danilov, is half-man and half-demon and therefore little trusted by his masters on high. He is sent to Earth to create as much evil as possible but is constantly watched and in danger of disappearing into nothingness. The novel deals with the peculiarities of the creative process, the place of the artist in society, and his fate in a totalitarian system. When Danilov's masters disapprove of his music they remove his viola, depriving him of his main means of expression. *Al'tist Danilov* is an allegorical satire in which the demonic world, its institutions, and its order of things are strikingly similar to Soviet reality. The emphasis in the demonic world is on theory and ideology and the belief in the importance of political manipulation and power. Paradoxically, many in high positions there do not believe in the dogma, clinging instead to power by any means.

Al'tist Danilov has imperfections. Many ideas, images, and even scenes are replicas of similar notions expressed by other writers. For example, the theory of tishizm, developed by Danilov's fellow musician Zemskii, is an elaboration on the 'genre of silence' advocated by some Soviet writers in the 1930s. A number of plot lines remain unfinished and inconclusive, and many characters mentioned in the novel never appear in person and are given no chance to act. *Al'tist Danilov* is certainly not a masterpiece; it is, however, symptomatic of the interests of the Soviet reading public, which had become tired of the flat and didactic prose appearing in most Soviet journals and looked for any signs of originality, freshness, and change in Brezhnev's stifling last years.

The realistic background of Anatolii Kim's first fairy-tale novel, *Belka* (Squirrel; 1984),[3] also includes artists. Four school friends dream of becoming great painters but are forced by circumstances to forsake their aspirations and settle for whatever fate has in store for them. The most important character, who narrates most of the story, becomes a lowly bureaucrat of the arts. But *Belka* is far from being a realistic story. It is a narrative in which folklore, myth, fantasy, and everyday reality are indiscriminately mixed together. Many characters have the ability to become transformed into animals, and the main hero, allegedly saved from death in his childhood by a squirrel, acts alternately as man and animal, being also able to penetrate the hearts and minds of others and recognize other changelings.

In his novel, Kim muses on the essence of art in modern society, on the relationship of life and death, eternity and temporariness, good and evil, as well as on the bestial essence of human nature and its relationship to innate goodness. The central character attempts to become good by killing his animal double, the squirrel, thus destroying his own animal origins. According to him, 'in order to transform death into immortality one has to fashion one's life in a *human manner.*'[4] But the killing of an unsuspecting squirrel does not turn him into a real human being or bring him any closer to immortality. One cannot prolong one's existence by taking away the lives of others. On the contrary, murder affirms the bestial essence of human nature and severs the connections with natural roots. Kim seeks an answer to this dilemma by creating the cumulative image of MY (we), which represents the collective goodness of all mankind as well as the infinite existence of humanity in time and space.

Kim is a relatively young writer whose first works appeared in the early 1970s, but he has already secured a place in Soviet literature.[5] His art is rooted in his Korean heritage, but it is blended with his experience of a Russian environment. His perception of life is emotional and intuitive, rather than rational and logical. His language is lyrical in tone and infused with irony. His prose is often likened to the etching of a painter, but his style does not make for easy reading.

Kim has many admirers among Soviet readers and critics alike, but his world of changelings and the style in which the voices of different characters often blend in the same sentence make his narratives vulnerable to official criticism. Furthermore, the lack of a direct social message is also regarded as a serious shortcoming.[6] Thus G. Markov suggests that the plot of *Belka* is composed of 'endless transformations of different people into different animals. This is probably permissible in the selected manner of narration. The shortcomings of *Belka* are somewhere else, namely, in the abstract discussion of notions such as evil, philistinism, and egoism.'[7] Kim's works are different in language, style, and content from the works of most other Soviet prose writers. Unlike authors whose creative experimentation is a reflection of the times, Kim is always true to himself, and what is innovation and experimentation to others is the norm to him. His style and subject-matter are not a mark of the times, but rather a reflection of his own creative personality.

Veniamin Kaverin is one of the oldest surviving Soviet writers (born 1902) and was a member of the Serapion Brotherhood of the 1920s. Some of his early works are experimental fantastic tales. In the 1980s Kaverin returns to the themes of his youth by creating the fairy-tale povest' 'Verlioka' (1982).[8] 'Verlioka' is a fantastic story in which the main hero, the boy Vasia, is imbued with superhuman powers which he applies skilfully in his struggle with evil. On the surface 'Verlioka' is a conventional fairy-tale, but just as in the works of Orlov and Kim, so the story is placed in a contemporary time-frame, and the parallels between the fantastic world of plants, animals, and superhuman creatures and Soviet reality are too obvious to be overlooked by the sophisticated adult reader.

'Verlioka' is about the struggle between good and evil. Vasia manages to destroy his antagonist, the old Verlioka, who is the source of all human suffering, but Verlioka's offspring have already been born, and they are ready to create new evil. Evil seems prevalent in this world, and miraculous powers are required to weed it out; destiny seems blind and responsible to no one, and hence man has to take fate into his own hands and fight for a better life. But since ordinary people do not possess the skills and abilities ascribed to mythological characters, they are doomed to submission, the inevitable victims of chance, fate, and the dark forces of nature. Kaverin's fairy-tale is a refreshing piece of prose in which the imagined and fantastic come into proximity with the interests of modern people, reminding them of their own complexity, vulnerability, and responsibility for the creation of a better world.

The works discussed here, as well as prose by writers such as Kataev, provide examples of current Soviet attempts at artistic diversity and experimentation with genre, style, and subject-matter. Most characteristic of the changes of the last decade is the prose of Chingiz Aitmatov.

Chingiz Aitmatov

In 1978 Chingiz Aitmatov celebrated his fiftieth birthday. By that time he reached the pinnacle of Soviet and world literature. According to figures supplied by UNESCO, his works are among those most widely translated into foreign languages.[9] From 1978 to 1982 alone his books were printed and distributed by ninety publishing houses all over the world.[10] Aitmatov's success is not accidental. First, Aitmatov is an accomplished and mature craftsman. His prose is expressive and rich in poetic elements. His conflicts are charged with dramatic tension, and his themes transcend local confines and address ethical issues of universal significance.[11] Second, the Kirghiz-Turkic-Muslim origins of his art make his works appealing to readers in Islamic and Third World countries. And, third, his prose embodies the officially promulgated fusion of ideological uniformity and linguistic and cultural diversity within the Soviet Union.

Aitmatov is perfectly bilingual, and he considers the Russian and Kirghiz languages equally native to him,[12] making it at times difficult to determine what he has written in Russian and what in Kirghiz. He says: 'It makes little difference to me in what language I write. Everyone is aiming at perfection, which is difficult to achieve. Good literature is difficult to write in any language.'[13] Aitmatov's bilingualism is often greeted with suspicion by both Russian and Kirghiz critics. Some Kirghiz accuse him of catering to the tastes of Russian readers, while some Russian critics, particularly those close to the neo-Russophile tradition, are concerned with the infiltration of foreign elements into the Russian cultural heritage.

Aitmatov's fiction of the 1980s is in the tradition of his earlier prose, but with a difference. In the 1960s and 1970s he worked mainly in the genre of the povest'. In the 1980s he began writing novels. Formerly, most of his works were set in Kirghizia and most of his characters were simple Kirghiz people. Beginning in the late 1970s Aitmatov diversified the locale of his action and the ethnic identity of his heroes. The events in 'Pegii pes, begushchii kraem moria' (Spotted Dog by the Sea's Edge; 1977)[14] are located on the northern shores of the Okhot Sea in the Far East. In *I dol'she veka dlitsia den'* (The Day Lasts More Than a Hundred Years; 1980),[15] the action takes place in the central Asian republic of Kazakhstan, and most of the characters are local people; in *Plakha* (The Execution Block; 1986),[16] one of the main protagonists is an ethnic Russian, and one of the main themes is the parallel between the Christian ethic and the ethics of contemporary Soviet life. Kirghiz legends and myth are here replaced by the Christian myth of resurrection.

Aitmatov is a writer with an acute sense of timing. Both of his novels of the 1980s are, in a way, a reaction to the political needs of the moment. In the stifling atmosphere of the final days of Brezhnev's rule a new positive hero was required, and Aitmatov creates a character, in the old tradition of socialist realism, who is a dedicated, honest, and decent workman, worthy of being emulated by his readers.[17] In 1986, in response to Mikhail Gorbachev's policy of glasnost', Aitmatov published his controversial *Plakha*, in which he uncovers the evil and corruption prevalent in Soviet society. Both novels are innovative, experimental, and challenging. Both also a raise a number of important issues which were, until recently, taboo.

I dol'she veka dlitsia den' is a narrative composed of a number of separate dramatic episodes occurring in the lives of a variety of characters. At the centre of the novel is the image of its main hero, Edigei, a worker at the railway siding Boranly-Burannyi, in the Kazakh steppe. The novel covers two days of actual time, and close to forty years of narrated time, in the life of Edigei. One of the two days is devoted to the task of burying his old friend Kazangap at the distant cemetery of Ana-Beiit. The cemetery is legendary in Kazakh mythology. Composed of six people, the funeral procession includes Kazangap's son, Sabit-zhan. On the way to the cemetery Edigei reminisces. The story of Edigei's life and of those he has come in touch with unfolds in the form of third-person quasi-direct discourse and internal monologue.

The realistic plane of the narrative is closely interwoven with legends from Kazakh mythology, which form the compositional centre of the novel and which have become part of Edigei's life and his world outlook. One of the legends relates the story of some young local warriors driven into slavery by Zhuan'zhuan invaders. In order to secure the boundless devotion of the slaves to their new masters, the warriors were turned into mankurts, individuals without memory of their past or awareness of their true identity. Changing men into mankurts was a gruesome process. First, the prisoner's head was shaved and then a tightly fitting cap, made from the udders of a killed camel, was fitted on the head. The prisoner was then taken to the desert, where the heat of the sun would dry out the cap, squeezing the victim's head mercilessly, subjecting him to excrutiating pain, and depriving him of the use of his mental faculties. Most mothers would lose hope of ever finding sons who had been taken prisoner by the Zhuan'zhuans. One of them, Naiman-Ana, did not lose hope and searched for her son ceaselessly, only to be killed by her offspring, who had been turned into a savage mankurt by his captors. The cemetery of Ana-Beiit, the final destination of Kazangap's funeral procession, is the alleged burial-place of the legendary Naiman-Ana.

But it is not Edigei's good fortune to be able to fulfil Kazangap's final wishes and bury him at the Ana-Beiit cemetery. Upon arrival, Edigei realizes that the whole area has been cordoned off to make room for a cosmodrome and an adjoining settlement. The earthly cosmodrome represents, in a way, the intrusion of technological progress into the remote steppes of central Asia, perpetrated without regard to Kazakh custom and tradition or the will of the local people. The image of the secluded cosmodrome connects the legendary past with a fantastic subplot which illustrates the inherent insecurity of humanity, the fragility of earthly institutions, and the disparity between different socio-political systems.

The fantastic subplot was conceived in the spirit of détente of the mid-1970s, when the novel was being written. It relates the story of a joint us-Soviet space mission to bring to Earth minerals and energy resources from other planets. The astronauts make contact with human-like creatures from another galaxy and visit their planet. They are impressed with the social organization and interpersonal relations in the newly discovered civilization. When the astronauts return they are refused readmission to Earth and are doomed to annihilation in the vast emptiness of outer space. The development of the joint space program was stimulated by common interests and hopes for mutual benefit. But when the fragile balance between the superpowers is threatened by an invasion of representatives of a superior civilization, insecurity, fear, and a morbid sense of self-preservation set in, leading to isolationism and protection of the status quo.

The mankurt motif, taken from central Asian lore,[18] is the dominant idea of the novel and connects the different narrative levels and time sequences. It relates directly to the theme of pamiat', or memory, and to the relationship of past, present, and future. The son of Naiman-Ana is forced to forget his past because he is a slave, but Sabitzhan is, in the understanding of Edigei, also a mankurt, because he forgets the customs and traditions of his people and shows no respect for his forbear.[19] Aitmatov does not investigate the socio-psychological make-up of a Soviet mankurt, or the ways and means of his development, but the novel contains veiled, yet strong insinuations that the Soviet system of education helps to develop self-centred, materialistic, and unethical individuals who live for the day, caring little about their people's past or their children's future. The non-memory of Sabitzhan can be contrasted with the memory of Abutalip, a friend of Edigei's and a tragic victim of Stalinist persecution. Sabitzhan's memory is selective, because the Soviet school that educates him determines what one is to remember. Abutalip, in contrast, wants to retain and pass on to his children everything. He writes down the old legends from the peoples' lore, as well as reminiscences of his prison and partisan experiences during the war. And that is his undoing, because the Stalinist system of mind control does not permit one to learn whatever one chooses.

Thus the cap that makes the mankurt forget his past is a metaphor for the Soviet school, which makes the student remember only what is required, as well as for the ring of rockets, placed around the Earth, which is to protect it from the superior wisdom of another civilization. The Zhuan'zhuan invaders turn slaves into obedient but passive savages; the Stalinist school turns its pupils into individuals with a selective knowledge of their past and only a limited capacity for intellectual inquiry; and the ring of rockets prevents all mankind from learning the truth about the universe. In its own way, and with its own means, each civilization or system of government tries to protect its own narrow interests by controlling the minds of its subjects and feeding them with the information most expedient to those in power.

The action narrated in the novel covers some forty years, but most of the events take place in 1944, 1952–3, 1956, and the late 1970s. More than two decades, between 1956 and the late 1970s, are left out altogether. There are indications in the novel that some individuals have been punished for their transgressions and their abuse of power in the days of Stalin. Nonetheless, the hopes and optimistic expectations expressed after 1956 by Edigei's Russian friend, the scholar Afanasii Elizarov, never materialize. Indeed, most members of the young generation seem much worse than their fathers and not much better than those representing the Stalinist regime. Elizarov obviously expresses Aitmatov's views when he speculates on the motives prompting Stalinist interrogators. He searches for the roots of human evil. He asserts that evil is 'possibly an illness, an epidemic that strikes mankind in different periods of its history. Or, perhaps, a destructive quality that is an original part of human nature.'[20] Aitmatov avoids directly blaming the system of government for the abuse of power or social injustice in Soviet society, but he observes that anyone ready to sell his soul to the devil is a kind of mankurt and that every social system creates its own mental cripples who serve its purpose.

As in Aitmatov's earlier works, the novel is full of natural imagery, striking symbolic parallels, and personal tragedy. The novel begins with the symbolic description of a fox searching for food along the path of the railway tracks. The animal fights for survival. In the concluding pages, a kite, a bird of prey, is soaring over the funeral procession. His target is Edigei's unsuspecting dog. The dog also fights for survival. He feels secure among people, but this security is deceptive because people themselves are not safe anywhere. At that very moment, the rockets, which are to protect the earth, are launched from the cosmodrome, and Edigei, his dog, and his camel all flee in terror. There is a symbolic parallel between the kite and the rockets. The kite fights for personal survival; the rockets allegedly fight for the survival of our earthly civilization. The former can succeed only at the expense of another living creature; the latter, only by endangering the existence of the old cemetery which symbolizes memory and the survival of the human spirit.

There are in the novel a number of telling allegorical parallels that relate to contemporary Soviet reality. Thus the recurring image of the train, moving continuously from east to west and from west to east, is a symbol of infinite motion and of mutual interdependence in a shrinking world. The Chinese-sounding name of the Zhuan'zhuan invaders is a subtle hint about Chinese-Soviet relations, which reached their lowest ebb in the late 1970s. The legend about the old singer Raimaly-aga, who falls in love with a young woman but is looked on by his relatives as out of his mind and in need of medical treatment, is reminiscent of those subjected to forced psychiatric treatment for their unconventional political and ideological opinions. Sabitzhan's view of individuals' responsibility for their actions is similar to that of Osipbai in Aitmatov's 'Voskhozhdenie na Fudziiamu' (The Ascent of Mount Fuji; 1975). Both blame time and history for whatever happens in society and absolve individuals from all accountability.

I dol'she veka dlitsia den' is most reminiscent, in structure, imagery, and characterization, of Aitmatov's 'Proshchai, Gul'sary!' (Farewell, Gul'sary!; 1966). Old Tanabai sits beside the dead body of his best friend, the horse Gul'sary, and reminisces about his life. So Edigei accompanies the body of his dead friend, Kazangap, and recollects his past. Both Tanabai and Edigei are close to nature. Tanabai devotes his life to tending horses and sheep, while Edigei would not hurt a living creature, refusing to kill even the fox that trespasses on his property. The relation of Tanabai to his horse, Gul'sary, is similar to Edigei's dedication to his camel, Karanar. Tanabai is furious when he learns that Gul'sary has been gelded by evil people. Edigei puts up with his camel and refuses to castrate him. Both Tanabai and Edigei come from hard-working, simple stock; they are dedicated family men, yet both fall in love with other women. In both cases, the wives appear superior to their unfaithful husbands and help them overcome their harmful infatuations. Tanabai is a party member, and the party's cause gives meaning to his life, but he is also restless, irritable, and rebellious and in haste to make the promised beautiful life a reality. Edigei is different. He also seeks truth and justice, but he is patient and tolerant. His ideals for the future are rooted in the past of his people, and, in this sense, he has much in common with Momun from 'Belyi parokhod' (The White Steamship; 1970).

The characters of Edigei and Kazangap were conceived in the

tradition of Russian village prose, in which the spiritual nature of the parents is often contrasted with the unethical and materialistic life of their children. Aitmatov is deeply concerned with the growing cynicism and unethical behaviour of the young, and he wonders 'whether the generation of those who have fought in the war see their ideals realized in their children and grandchildren. Aren't they contaminated ... by a certain "opportunism"?'[21] Aitmatov sympathizes with the simple, uneducated, and hard-working Edigei, because he does not equate education with spirituality, and he acknowledges that material well-being often leads to ethical shallowness: 'If material things become the only objective of man's existence ... they lead to degradation. The very essence of man is lost.'[22]

Edigei's trip to the Ana-Beiit cemetery is a failure. He is not admitted to the cosmodrome area and is forced to bury Kazangap in the nearby steppe. But Edigei does not give up hope of saving the old cemetery, and we are told in the last paragraph that he is visited by his daughters and is on his way to see those in charge of the cosmodrome. Some critics view this ending as an optimistic conclusion. Katerina Clark suggests that 'Aitmatov is careful not to end his novel on ... [a] pessimistic note. He tacks on a later incident in which Edigei's daughters and their families come to visit. Thus he invokes in a somewhat limp way the mandatory theme of generational renewal and arrives at a happy ending.'[23] M. Bolkhovskii sees nothing optimistic in this conclusion, and he asserts that only 'naïve readers and critics, or sworn optimists, can imagine that the old Kazakh with his noble heart ... can get to the *truth* ... and save the tribal cemetery, forgotten by all the Sabitzhans. Unfortunately, Edigei's attempts are doomed. There is no "happy ending" in Aitmatov's novel. *I dol'she veka dlitsia den'* is a tragedy.'[24] Indeed, the novel may conclude on a positive note, but there is little positive in store for Edigei. He is old and worn out. He asks his fellow worker, Edil'bai, to bury him, when he dies, next to Kazangap, but there is no return to Ana-Beiit, just as there is no return to the past.

In his prose of the 1970s Aitmatov developed a style suitable for the integration of past with present. Reminiscences, flashbacks, and internal monologue, as well as myth and legends from folklore, are intertwined with daily reality, creating an image of people whose ethics are determined by their memory of, and adherence to, the ways and means of their ancestors. *I dol'she veka dlitsia den'* was created in the same tradition, but it also contains an innovation: the fantastic subplot. This innovation emphasizes the conflicts and tragic contradictions of our age and stresses global interdependence in the struggle for survival.

While the fantastic story reminds the reader of science fiction, where action is usually set in the distant future, this fantasy is played out in our own time. Hence a certain incongruity between the realistic and the fantastic and between the different sequences of time. Furthermore, the introduction of scenes in outer space often disrupts the flow of the narrative because it necessitates the use of journalistic language, which is vastly different from the language in other parts of the novel.

Most Soviet critics have hailed Aitmatov's new novel and praise the character of his positive hero. Edigei is a hard-working and decent human being. His life story suggests that one has to do nothing that is extraordinary in order to live a heroic life, because any human being who retains his decency in our terrible world is a hero of sorts. The same critics point out, however, that while the introduction of the fantastic subplot may have some ideological justification, it destroys the artistic and linguistic unity of the novel. Moreover, Aitmatov is accused of failing to make a clear distinction between the policies and ideologies that motivate the actions of the two sides participating in the joint space venture.[25]

Aitmatov perhaps anticipated a mixed, not necessarily positive reaction to his new novel. To forestall criticism he supplied the novel with an introduction in which he explains its artistic, ideological, and political objectives. He also wrote an article in *Voprosy literatury*, which appeared almost simultaneously with the novel, in which he places the narrative in a broader social and political perspective and elaborates on the motives inducing him to create the character of Edigei. Aitmatov states bluntly that the 'image of Burannyi Edigei expresses ... [his] relationship to the basic principles of socialist realism'[26] and that 'man without memory ... is deprived of the experiences of his own people as well as of those of others, remaining outside any historical perspective and being able to live only by the day.'[27] Aitmatov defends his fantastic story by saying that he created it only with the purpose of 'intensifying in a paradoxical and hyperbolic form the existing situation which is fraught with potential danger to all mankind ... Fantasy is a metaphor of life which makes it possible to view it from a new and unexpected angle.'[28]

Aitmatov set a precedent by interpreting his own novel before it even reached the public. There is no doubt that he does so to influence the reader, and that in itself makes his intentions suspect. A work of art may be perceived by different people in different ways, and it should need no explanation. In other words, a novel has its own narrative rules and artistic confines, and it comes to life regardless of its author's intentions.

Aitmatov's introduction should, therefore, be viewed as an ideological document rather than as a preface of artistic significance. A novel by a master of Aitmatov's stature needs no introduction; his art speaks for itself.

Aitmatov's novel *Plakha* is an artistic commentary on the social ills of Soviet society, articulated in the spirit of Gorbachev's reforms. Aitmatov attempts to maintain the structural and compositional unity of the plot by placing it within the framework of a story about the life of a family of wolves who are victims of the human assault on nature and are driven from place to place for shelter and security. The novel is composed of three parts. Parts I and II form the first half, and part III, the second; each half deals with different issues and characters. The wolves Akbara and her mate, Tashchainar, are the only images connecting the two halves. In the first half the main character is Avdii Kallistratov, a religious seeker and an ethnic Russian. The second half centres around the fates of two Kirghiz herdsmen, Boston and Bazarbai.

There are several distinct narrative lines in the novel. In the first half the emphasis is on drug trafficking, crime, corruption, and the destruction of nature. One major episode describes the process of picking and transporting hemp and other plants of high narcotic potency from central Asia to Russia. Another episode portrays the mass slaughter of antelope in the steppes of central Asia, undertaken to cover up inefficiency and economic failure in meat production. The hemp is gathered by a gang of young people who come from different corners of the Soviet Union and meet in Moscow. The other gang, which gathers the killed and wounded antelope, is composed of local outcasts, alcoholics, homosexuals, and criminals.

The story of Avdii Kallistratov is closely intertwined with these segments of the narrative. After being expelled from the seminary for his attempt to modernize Orthodox religious dogma, he continues to act as a lay preacher. He joins the gang and undertakes a trip to central Asia as an undercover freelance correspondent for a youth newspaper in order to study at first hand the problem of drug addiction among the young. On another trip to central Asia Avdii unwittingly joins the criminal hunters and moves into the steppe with them. But instead of co-operating with them, in order to fulfil his undercover assignments, Avdii tries to convert them to his own faith. His sermons fall on deaf ears; he becomes suspect and is severely punished. The drug traffickers beat him and throw him from a moving train. Members of the other gang torture him and leave him hanging between trees in the steppe. Miraculously Avdii survives, but he achieves nothing.

In the second half of the novel the fate of the wolves is closely intertwined with the fate of the human characters. Bazarbai, an evil man, created in the image of Orozkul in 'Belyi parokhod,' comes upon the hiding place of Akbara and her family. The cubs are all alone, and Bazarbai steals them with the intention of selling them for drink. On his way home he stops at Boston's place. Boston is away on business. An excellent worker and a good family man, Boston is respected by everyone. Bazarbai is envious of his neighbour and hates him for his success. When Boston returns home, he is furious. He knows that stealing the cubs without killing their parents is a crime against nature. The wolves will never give up the search for their offspring, hurting in turn anyone they come in touch with. Indeed, the wolves come every night to Boston's house and howl in wailing voices. Boston offers to buy the cubs, but Barazbai refuses, selling them out of spite, to strangers. Bazarbai complains to party officials that Boston opposes the fight against predators and wants to set the cubs free. The secretary of the local party organization, Kochkorbaev, hates Boston for his innovative approach to work and to life and supports Bazarbai. In the end Boston decides to kill the wolves. He puts away Tashchainar, but Akbara eludes him. One day Akbara comes near Boston's house and carries off his little boy to replace her own missing cubs. Boston chases Akbara into the hills, but before losing sight of her he shoots and kills her together with his own son. Then he goes and kills Bazarbai his enemy. The ultimate fate of Boston is unknown, but there is a hint at possible suicide in the waters of Issyk-Kul.

In addition to the plot lines connected with the main conflicts in the novel, there are several secondary subplots, the most important being the story of Jesus and his dialogue with Pontius Pilate. When Avdii is in a state of unconsciousness, he hallucinates that he has become transformed into a disciple of Christ who wants to save his master. Aitmatov departs from the Gospels and ascribes to Christ ideas close to those expressed by Avidii himself. Avdii asserts that traditional dogma is outdated. In order to save humanity, religion will have to bring forth the 'figure of a God-contemporary with new ideas that will corresponds to the needs of the day.'[29] Avdii deplores the rigid essence of religious dogma and ritual and believes that human beings will discover this contemporary God within themselves, through free inquiry. He claims that there is no monopoly on truth, because dogma equals self-deception.[30] According to Aitmatov's Christ, the collective image of man is the expression of God on earth, and since man himself is supposed to be the creator of his future, every human being is a particle of the God-Tomorrow.

The dialogue between Jesus and Pilate is similar in form to the dialogues of Avdii with Grishan, the leader of the drug traffickers, and Ober-Kandalov, the leader of the other gang. Both Jesus and Avdii dispute the actions of their antagonists with the hope of saving their souls, but both fail. Their efforts are futile. Jesus sacrifices himself for mankind and is crucified. Metaphorically Avdii is crucified twice. Both men are resurrected, but according to Aitmatov their way is not the way to redemption. To save man from himself, not words but deeds are needed. And yet it appears from the novel that there is nothing to replace religion. Avdii contemplates the failure of religion to move people today, but he also alludes to the inability of the materialistic sciences to take its place, drawing thus a veiled parallel between religion and Marxism. Avdii asks whether there is now anything new and superior to old religion, and he asserts that 'surely the new should be better than the old. Indeed there is ... a new and mighty religion – the religion of superior military power ... and the gods are those who possess this power.'[31]

Failure to replace religion with new ideals and a new spirituality leads, according to the novel, to alienation, corruption, distortion of social values, and a spiritual vacuum that drives many young people to alcoholism and narcotics. *Plakha* is the first major Soviet work of prose fiction that deals openly with these burning issues. Until recently the problem of drugs was taboo to Soviet readers.[32] Avdii decries the fact that the editor of his newspaper is afraid to publish his article, which openly describes his experiences among the drug traffickers. He admits that only a small segment of young people is experimenting with drugs, many of them under the influence of the West, yet he is amazed that bureaucrats are afraid that this information will harm the prestige of the Soviet Union. He asks: 'Who needs such prestige if its price is so high!'[33]

Aitmatov's concern for the ethics of Soviet youth is placed in extreme terms. In an interview that appeared at the time of the novel's publication, Aitmatov said: 'I do not feel comfortable among young people today ... One cannot be complacent, hoping that nothing terrible happens: today they are callous, heartless, and vain, and when they grow up we will be able to change them for the better ... It is difficult to change anyone, and to assume that by providing for mass secondary education we solve all problems is, at best, naïve.'[34] According to Aitmatov the school is one of the main culprits responsible for the moral decay and cynicism of the young. In the days of Stalin strict programming, fear, and lack of intellectual stimulation produced mankurts like Sabitzhan. The post-Stalin school is in the process of continuous structural and organizational change, but the ideological essence of education remains the same. The school fails to attract the interest of the student, because he experiences daily the disparity between what he is taught and what he sees in real life.

Aitmatov makes a lame attempt to inject some optimism into the novel by creating a young party instructor who objects to the conservative views of the party official Kochkorbaev. Twenty years earlier, in 'Proshchai, Gul'sary!' Aitmatov created a similar young party official who struggled with the vestiges of Stalinism in Soviet life. It appears, however, that as they get older, these young and progressive individuals turn into dogmatic bureaucrats who care for little more than their own peace and security.

Avdii identifies three principal evils as the scourge of Soviet society: 'Man is torn between the temptations of greed, vanity, and conformity ... There is no force on earth, including religion, that could overcome the all-powerful ideology of this philistine world.'[35] Judging by the novel, as well as by Aitmatov's journalistic statements, the author agrees with his hero: no social ideology, including Marxism, can overcome the deep-seated instinct for evil in human nature.

Parallels with Bulgakov's *Master i Margarita* and Dostoevskii's *The Idiot* and *The Brothers Karamazov* can be seen in *Plakha*. The dialogue between Jesus and Pilate was apparently inspired by, and modelled on, a similar story in Bulgakov's novel. Avdii, whose initials remind one of Alesha Karamazov, is as naïve as Prince Myshkin is, in his hope that good intentions can change the world. The reality in which Avdii lives is just as terrible as the world of Myshkin, and both fail because they are too decent and honest to survive in a world full of evil.

The animal world is always part of Aitmatov's imagery. But in most of his earlier works there were no predators, and the fate of the animal was closely intertwined with human lives and actions. In *Plakha* the family of wolves is an independent unit that lives its own life. Moreover, Aitmatov contrasts here humans and wolves and views reality through the eyes of the predator. The juxtaposition of people and wolves illustrates the unquestionable superiority of the latter. The wolves are a close family with a highly developed sense of duty and responsibility. Most of the men in *Plakha* are lonely and alienated, responsible to no one but their own inflated egos. According to the novel the morality of the predatory animal is much higher than that of 'civilized' man. The wolf is a natural creature who will kill only when hungry and even then will never touch one of his own kind. Man is different. He indiscriminately destroys nature, including his fellow man. People are the cruellest living creatures. Ivan Karamazov says that to 'speak of man's "bestial cruelty" ... is very unfair and insulting to the beast: a beast can never be so cruel as man, so ingeniously, so artistically cruel.'[36]

Akbara and her family are driven from place to place by the excesses of people who place themselves above the laws of nature. There appear to be certain unwritten rules that determine the workings of the natural world, and no one oversteps them without risking punishment. Bazarbai starts a chain reaction. He abuses nature, and Akbara avenges this abuse on other people. Boston pays the price for Bazarbai's transgression, but he avenges himself in turn on the perpetrator of his own suffering. Both Akbara and Boston pay for their revenge, Akbara with her life, and Boston with spiritual desolation, which is surely to be followed by physical punishment. The moral of the story is simple. Evil man, when supported by those in power, can destroy nature and create much hardship and suffering for his fellow man. But ultimately those guilty are also punished. The death of Bazarbai symbolizes the facts that no one is permitted to overstep the basic laws of nature, which govern the cohabitation of all living creatures in this world, and that after each crime against nature retribution will necessarily follow. A parallel can be drawn between the fates of Avdii and Boston. Both, in their own different ways, struggle for truth and justice, and both voluntarily take up the cross and are ready to suffer for what they believe in. But society does not appreciate their sacrifice, and they remain all alone in their struggle for justice. The title of the novel, *Plakha*, symbolizes their readiness to suffer and to risk their own lives in the struggle with universal evil.

Plakha is a novel of great social and ideological significance, but artistically it has a number of shortcomings. Initially Aitmatov intended to write a large, synthetic novel under the title 'Krugovrashchenie' (Closed Circle), but later he changed his mind and decided to limit it to the story of Avdii.[37] *Plakha* is a complex and uneven novel, composed of a number of narrative segments apparently hastily carried over from one plan to another and placed within the structural framework of the story of Akbara's family. But whereas there is a strong connection between the fates of the wolves and of Boston and Bazarbai, the relationship between the stories of Avdii and of the wolves is at best tenuous. The fates of many heroes, including that of Avdii himself, are not brought to any logical conclusion, and some characters, for example, Inga, the girl Avdii falls in love with, are brought into the narrative with the sole purpose of moving the plot.

The novel combines a realistic story, philosophical dialogue, and parable with portrayal of the animal world. But the inclusion of different, little-connected plot lines often leads to stylistic complications. Third-person narration alternates with narration in the first person, as well as internal monologue, dialogue, reminiscences, and epistolary passages. Some passages are written in beautiful, elegant, and dramatic prose, while others, particularly those devoted to philosophical and religious dialogue, are written in flat, journalistic language, which blends poorly with the main tone of the narrative. The story of the tragic predicament of Boston is written in the spirit of Aitmatov's earlier works and is superior in style, language, and dramatic tension to the first half of the novel. It is a self-contained story that gains little from its inclusion in the novel.

Aitmatov the moralist comes through in *Plakha* stronger than in any of his previous works. Many passages are written in the spirit of didacticism, but for all Aitmatov's efforts the real perpetrators of social evil are never identified. The instigators of the merciless slaughter of the animals in the steppe remain anonymous. Nor do we learn about the causes of the spiritual void among the young or about those who stimulate drug trafficking by creating a demand for narcotics.

Soviet reaction to *Plakha* has been mixed and guarded. Some hail it as an outstanding and timely work.[38] Others 'do not predict a long life for the novel.'[39] The editors of *Literaturnaia gazeta* are afraid that the novel may lead the reader to the wrong conclusions. They state bluntly: '*Plakha* is a novel about social evil. But is one to fight this evil only with individual ethical feats and sacrifices? And where are the social forces that will oppose Kochkorbaev and Ober-Kandalov? It is possible to get the impression that the novel counsels the struggle with injustice not on the plane of social collisions but rather with a call to "faith."'[40] Aitmatov explains, however, that his recourse to Christianity is an attempt to reach out for the universal cultural heritage and that Avdii is a seeker and fighter and therefore a challenge to the inertia of the Soviet young.[41]

Plakha is not a call for a return to faith. It is rather an artistic statement to the effect that contemporary social ideals are inadequate as a substitute for religion. Any dogma, whether religious or ideological, is doomed because it subverts the dialectical process and affirms the status quo. The novel alleges that the myth about the old god of the past has been destroyed and that the practical god of today, expressed in the pragmatism and the ethics of Boston, has been demolished. Symbolically the only hope for the future lies in the god of tomorrow, envisaged as a new social organization based on an ethical revival, which combines the spirituality of the past, as embodied in the values of Avdii, with the practical vigour of the present, as exemplified in the character of Boston.

Lawlessness and evil are victorious in most of Aitmatov's works. But whereas in 'Proshchai, Gul'sary!' and *I dol'she veka dlitsia den'* most of the evil is identified with the Stalinist regime, and in 'Belyi parokhod' it is connected mainly with the deeds of one vicious character, in *Plakha* it is the result of an intricate interaction between society, state, and individual, all infested by the same germ of corruption. One has to add, however, that Aitmatov, to his credit, does not pretend to have any solutions to the problems posed.

Aitmatov's two most recent novels differ from each other in spirit and subject-matter. Edigei is a role model to be followed. His life is difficult, but he survives. Boston, the positive hero of *Plakha*, faces evil head on, but he perishes fighting it, while the Kochkorbaevs, Ober-Kandalovs, and Grishans remain alive and well and continue their dirty work. There is an attempt to attach a positive ending to *I dol'she veka dlitsia den'*. No such attempt is made in *Plakha*. All is bleak. Both novels deliver important, but different social and political messages, pertinent to a given political situation. Aitmatov knows that literature in the Soviet Union is a vehicle of ideology, but he is also aware that the 'task of innovating ... , of moving the development of Soviet literature ahead ... , is entrusted to those who have reached a high level of artistic mastery and have proved beyond doubt their dedication to ... [the] cause.'[42] It is clear that Aitmatov assumes the mission of artistic and thematic innovation because he considers himself among those who can be trusted. That does not mean, however, that innovation and experimentation lead necessarily to a rise in the artistic level of a work. Aitmatov's recent novels fall short of the artistic level reached in 'Proshchai, Gul'sary!' and 'Belyi parokhod.'

Conclusion

Literature is an important cultural, intellectual, and political factor in everyday Soviet life. Its social function outweighs all other artistic considerations. The Soviet people pride themselves on being the nation that reads the most. They follow developments in Soviet prose, which they view as a barometer to gauge the social atmosphere in the country. The Soviet literary scene of the 1980s is dynamic, vibrant, and changing. It reflects the political transition and social transformation of the last decade. It mirrors the values and attitudes of the Soviet people.

The last years of the Brezhnev era are identified with economic and intellectual stagnation and with official pressure to create a new positive hero who could imbue the reader with a new spirit of optimism and faith in the motherland. Artistic experimentation and innovation were used as an escape and as a means of allegory, satire, and Aesopian language which helped keep much under the surface. In the mid-1980s, in response to Gorbachev's policy of glasnost', a number of issues previously taboo became the subject of literature. One of the objectives of glasnost' is social and economic renewal through the efforts of individual man, invigorated by a new spirit of decency and dedication to the Soviet state. The role of literature is to assist in the process of economic revival and moral regeneration.

The thematic range of Soviet literature today is diverse. Many writers stress the negative aspects of Soviet life but as a rule do not probe into the reasons for these shortcomings. An attempt is made to reassess the legacy of the Brezhnev past, placing blame for the sluggish economy and moral decay on his administration. In countryside prose, Abramov, Astaf'ev, and Rasputin examine the spiritual effects of the intrusion of technological progress into the remote Russian countryside. City prose explores the disintegration of the urban family, the workings of the

service industries and the underground economy, and the manifestations of the all-pervading values of consumerism, philistinism, and
self-gratification. Female writers concern themselves with such issues as
loneliness, divorce, abortion, illegitimacy, and the delusory nature of
sexual equality in a society with total legal emancipation of women. The
literature about the Second World War evolves slowly from subjective
prose, rooted in the authors' personal experiences, into historical
fiction. And the new political novel, set in exotic and remote locations, is
witness to the global confrontation between those who support socialism and world revolution and the so-called reactionary forces of the
West.

The 1980s are also witness to the appearance of a number of works by
Platonov, Zamiatin, Pasternak, and others, written many years ago but
previously not approved for publication in the Soviet Union. These
works are little connected with the general literary process of the last
decade and reflect a different age, but exposure to work of such superior
quality may encourage the development of artistic taste and raise the
expectations of the reading public.

In reaction to the 1986 Chernobyl' disaster, many Soviet writers today
express anxiety for the survival of humanity, and particular despair for
the spiritual and ethical health of the Soviet nation. They fight also for
the protection of nature and the physical environment. These concerns
are, of course, voiced within the requisite political and ideological
context. New emphasis is placed in literature on the allegedly humanitar-
ian and freedom-loving basis of Soviet foreign policy and international
relations.

Most Soviet prose is realistic, little changed in style over the last
decade. Some writers are experimenting by varying narrative technique
and by introducing elements of fantasy, myth, parable, and symbolism.
Some resort to the application of melodramatic contrivances and devices
from the detective novel: others experiment with structure and language, infusing their conventional prose with archaisms, colloquialisms,
and figurative speech. In the 1970s the povest' was the leading genre of
Soviet prose fiction. In the 1980s the multi-volume novel has reappeared,
and many talented authors, such as Grekova, Aitmatov, and Evtushenko,
have made their début in the genre of the novel.

The relationship between literary theory and practice has changed
little in the last decade. Theory has lost much of its previous significance
and can no longer prescribe how good literature is to be written. It has
also lost its ability to explain literature, because one finds little
uniformity in the interpretation of different theoretical notions. Socialist

realism remains the official 'method,' but there is no agreement on what this term means. Party resolutions and daily ideological and political guidance now determine cultural activity and the development of intellectual life. The notion of socialist realism has, for all practical purposes, been squeezed out by the notions of partiinost' and narodnost', as well as by such concepts as *grazhdanstvennost'* and *sovetskost'*, which denote a new brand of patriotism and special attachment to the Soviet motherland.

The emphasis on the negative aspects of the Brezhnev era, and the overriding concern with social issues, lead to the penetration of journalism into artistic prose, and thus to a general decline in the artistic quality of prose fiction. The deaths of a number of gifted and prolific writers such as Kataev, Abramov, Trifonov, and Tendriakov, have also contributed to the decline in quality. The generation that has come along to replace these authors does not measure up either in talent and skill or in integrity and civic honesty. The most gifted of today's writers, such as Aitmatov and Rasputin, continue to explore the intricate inner world of man and his relation to nature, to his past, and to his social environment, but even their works are influenced by topicality, where artistry is often sacrificed for social effect. Most works of prose project the image of a Soviet man who has learned to adapt to changing political and social conditions. He is no longer the builder of a beautiful future but a survivor, concerned only with his daily affairs and his personal well-being. Today's literature seldom inspires the reader with a positive faith in a glorious future; instead it stresses the imperfection of individual man and criticizes his social institutions.

More than at any other time, Soviet writers are involved today in shaping public opinion and social policy. In their fiction and journalistic writings, as well as in their public appearances, many writers advocate isolationist, nationalist, and anti-Western sentiments. Some, under the guise of glasnost', defend Stalin and his cultural policies. Speeches at the Sixth Congress of Russian Writers in December 1985, and at the Eighth Congress of Soviet Writers in June 1986, as well as at the Nineteenth Party Conference in June 1988, convincingly illustrate this proposition. Some writers seek a solution to the predicament of Soviet people in a return to the roots, to old Russian spiritual values, while others seek salvation in enlightenment, civic honesty, and liberal ethical revival. Most writers, however, affirm the Soviet way of life and the superiority of the Soviet system over the West.

Among the most important works of prose fiction of the pre-Gorbachev period are Aitmatov's *I dol'she veka dlitsia den'*, Trifonov's

Vremia i mesto, Bykov's 'Znak bedy,' and Bondarev's novels. The spirit of glasnost' is expressed in the literature of the mid-1980s in two different ways. On the one hand, it has made possible the publication of a number of significant works about the Stalinist past, such as Rybakov's *Deti Arbata* and Bek's *Novoe naznachenie,* previously rejected by the censors. On the other hand, it stimulated the appearance of works such as Astaf'ev's *Pechal'nyi detektiv,* Rasputin's 'Pozhar,' and Aitmatov's *Plakha,* which deal candidly with current issues. There are still flashes of good writing in these works, but the explicitness of the social message ultimately depreciates their artistic value.

The new emphasis on social issues is a response to the political changes of the 1980s. It leads to a decline in the significance of literature as a means of artistic re-creation and self-expression and to the view that prose fiction is most important as a mirror of social interaction and as a tool to transform human nature. Literature does have a social function to play, but it is doubtful whether an art infused with a heavy dose of journalism and a didactic message can ever bring about the expected changes. Instead, such literature kills artistic taste, aesthetic perception, and the appreciation of beauty in art and in life.

The current situation in Soviet literature raises the important and provocative issue of the relationship between liberalization and freedom of expression, on the one hand, and artistic quality and talent, on the other. But it appears that it may take years before a new generation of writers, free from the shackles of the past, will appear. With the exception, perhaps, of Tolstaia, who has already developed a theme and style of her own, there are few young names deserving positive mention.

The Soviet literary scene is today volatile, and prose is at a cross-roads. Its future evolution will depend on the political and economic situation. In the pre-Gorbachev era the reader looked in prose fiction for information unavailable in the daily press. Today newspapers write openly about the shortcomings of Soviet life and the failings of the Soviet system. There is no longer any need to look in prose fiction for information unavailable in the periodical press. It is possible only to surmise that since the supply of previously unpublished works is drying up, the new situation will stimulate the development of several diverse thematic tendencies in Soviet literature. Some writers will probably turn to the analysis and portrayal of new social types, until recently ignored. Others may turn to the investigation of glasnost' and perestroika, criticizing those who try to undermine Gorbachev's reforms. Still others may oppose the current changes in Soviet society and decry the fact that there is little improvement in the daily life of the Soviet people.

It remains to be seen whether the established Soviet writers will be able to rid themselves of the psychological shackles of the past, as well as of the ideological and political constraints and narrow group interests of the present, in order to be able to produce good literature. One can only hope that the new spirit of glasnost' will extend into the realm of artistic creation, so that it will be possible for the most talented Soviet writers to produce works of imaginative fiction of great artistic value, in response to their genuine creative impulses rather than to a set of prescribed social needs. There are many examples in the Soviet literature of the 1960s and 1970s that attest to the possibility of producing prose fiction that is both socially relevant and of high artistic quality.

Notes

Chapter One: Decade of Transition

1 Robert Chandler, translator's introduction to Vasily Grossman, *Life and Fate* (New York 1985), 10
2 *Pravda*, 11 May 1988, 2
3 Vladimir Karpov, 'Otvetstvennaia rol' literatury,' *Literaturnaia gazeta*, 26 Nov 1986, 1–2
4 Aleksandr Nikitin, 'Trevozhno za perestroiku,' ibid, 25 May 1988, 10
5 Evgenii Evtushenko, 'Priterpelos',' ibid, 11 May 1988, 13
6 Viacheslav Gorbachev, 'Perestroika i podstroika,' *Molodaia gvardiia*, 1987, no. 7, 235
7 V. Gusev, *Literaturnaia gazeta*, 1 Jan 1988, 5
8 *Pravda*, 11 May 1988, 2
9 *Literaturnaia gazeta*, 25 June 1986, 6
10 Ibid, 21 Oct 1987, 1–2
11 See I. Skachkov, 'Ne tol'ko tovar ... ,' ibid, 12 Aug 1987, 3; D. Evdokimov, 'A voz i nyne tam ... ,' ibid, 11 Nov 1987, 3; and A. Salynskii, 'Avtor: prava i bespraviia,' ibid, 24 Feb 1988, 3.
12 *Nash sovremennik*, 1986, no. 5, 123–41
13 Timur Pulatov, 'Luchshe pozdno ... Luchshe vovremia,' *Literaturnaia gazeta*, 26 Nov 1986, 3
14 V.V. Karpov, 'Sovershenstvovanie natsional'nykh otnoshenii, perestroika i zadachi sovetskoi literatury,' ibid, 9 March 1988, 3
15 G. Alimov and R. Lynev, 'Kuda uvodit "Pamiat'",' *Izvestiia*, 3 June 1987, 3
16 Valentin Rasputin, 'Zhertvovat' soboiu dlia pravdy. Protiv bespamiat'-stva,' *Nash sovremennik*, 1988, no. 1, 171
17 A. Shavkuta, 'Ne byt, a bytie,' *Literaturnaia gazeta*, 20 Nov 1985, 3
18 Danilo Kiš, 'The State, the Imagination and the Censored I,' *New York Times Book Review*, 3 Nov 1985, 3–4

19 Vl. Gusev, 'Liubov' i tainaia svoboda ...,' *Literaturnaia gazeta*, 13 May 1987, 3

20 Ibid., 2 July 1986, 14

21 L. Lavlinskii, 'Diagnozy i retsepty,' ibid, 9 July 1986, 4

22 Ibid, 26 March 1986, 2

23 Viacheslav Gorbachev, *Molodaia gvardiia*, 1987, no. 7, 242

24 See Vadim Kozhinov, 'Pravda i istina,' *Nash sovremennik*, 1988, no. 4, 160–75, and Stanislav Rassadin, 'Vse podelit'?' *Ogonek*, no. 20 (May 1988), 14–16.

25 B. Sarnov, 'Kakogo rosta byl Maiakovskii,' *Ogonek*, no. 19 (May 1988), 14–16, and F. Kuznetsov, ' "Stenka na stenku" ili detskaia bolezn' "levizny" v kritike,' *Literaturnaia gazeta*, 18 May 1988, 3

26 A. Neverov, 'Nado li dinamitom?' *Pravda*, 9 June 1988, 6

27 A. Bocharov, 'Pokushenie na mirazhi,' *Voprosy literatury*, 1988, no. 1, 72

28 Galina Belaia, 'Dialog vo imia nashei obshchei kul'tury,' *Knizhnoe obozrenie*, no. 20 (13 May 1988), 4

29 *Znamia*, 1986, no. 4, 210. For an attempted theoretical substantiation of khudozhestvennaia publitsistika, see Iu. Surovtsev, 'O publitsistike i publitsistichnosti,' *Znamia*, 1986, no. 4, 208–24, and no. 10, 215–26.

30 V. Kataev, 'Dusha i slovo,' *Literaturnaia gazeta*, 16 April 1986, 3

31 Miklós Haraszti, *The Velvet Prison: Artists under State Socialism* (New York 1987), 13

32 Ibid, 19

33 G.A. Belaia, 'Ne sotvori sebe kumira,' *V mire knig*, 1987, no. 5, 76

34 Ibid, 77

35 Vasil' Bykov, 'Na urovne, no ne bolee ...,' *Literaturnaia gazeta*, 21 Nov 1984, 5

36 Ibid, 3 Sept 1986, 3

37 Ibid, 25 June 1986, 6. Many young writers and poets are, in a sense, 'amateurs' and not admitted, for a variety of reasons, to the Writers Union. Only members of the Writers Union are not required to be gainfully employed elsewhere and can devote all their time to creative writing.

38 Viktor Astaf'ev, 'A zhizn' idet ... ,' ibid, 11 Dec 1985, 3

39 Vladimir Krupin, 'Chtob sluzhba medom ne kazalas',' ibid, 21 May 1986, 3

40 Ibid, 2 July 1986, 5

41 Valerii Kozlov, 'Paradoksy massovosti,' ibid, 5 Dec 1985, 5

42 Ibid, 2 July 1986, 10

43 For an analysis of the socialist realist canon see Katerina Clark, *The Soviet Novel: History as Ritual*, second edition (Chicago 1985).

44 For a discussion of socialist realism in the 1970s see N.N. Shneidman, *Soviet Literature in the 1970s: Artistic Diversity and Ideological Conformity* (Toronto 1979), 3–14.

45 D. Markov, 'Sistemnoe edinstvo sotsialisticheskogo realizma. Problemy poetiki,' *Voprosy literatury*, 1983, no. 1, 9
46 *Literaturnaia gazeta*, 13 Juiy 1983, 6
47 N. Anastas'ev, 'Dialog,' *Voprosy literatury*, 1983, no. 3, 104
48 Ibid, 1983, no. 1, 12
49 Iurii Andreev, 'Dlia chego literatura,' ibid, 1983, no. 9, 47
50 Ibid, 62
51 S.M. Petrov, 'Vse o nem, vse o realizme …,' *Russkaia literatura*, 1984, no. 2, 138
52 Ibid, 145
53 Ibid, 146
54 Ibid, 144
55 I. Baskevich, 'Tvorcheskii metod ili "sistema" sotsialisticheskogo realizma?' *Voprosy literatury*, 1983, no. 4, 15–16
56 Iu. A. Andreev, 'Metod zhivoi, razvivaiushchiisia,' *Russkaia literatura*, 1982, no. 1, 131–2
57 P. Nikolaev, 'Doverie k teorii,' *Voprosy literatury*, 1985, no. 9, 18
58 S. Shermailova, 'Chto v realizme glavnoe?' ibid, 1985, no. 4, 32
59 *Novyi mir*, 1980, no. 11, 3–185
60 Iu. Bogdanov, 'Teoriia – opyt razvitiia literatury,' *Voprosy literatury*, 1984, no. 1, 19–20
61 *Literaturnaia gazeta*, 12 March 1986, 7
62 The interviews took place in Moscow, Leningrad, and Vilnius in May–June 1987 and May 1988.
63 V.A. Kovalev ed, *Russkaia sovetskaia literatura. Uchebnik dlia 10 klassa* (Moscow 1987), 356–7
64 Ibid, 357
65 See, for example, N. Groznova, *Voprosy literatury*, 1988, no. 1, 271; S. Lomidze, 'Teoriia v dolgu,' ibid, 1987, no. 12, 4; and V. Zakharov, 'Sotsialisticheskii realizm: spornye problemy,' *Literaturnaia gazeta*, 13 April 1988, 3.
66 Mikhail Epshtein, 'Teoriia iskusstva i iskusstvo teorii,' *Voprosy literatury*, 1987, no. 12, 18
67 Vl. Gusev, 'Otkazyvat'sia li nam ot sotsialisticheskogo realizma?' *Literaturnaia gazeta*, 25 May 1988, 3
68 *Moscow News*, 8 May 1988, 3
69 See D. Markov, 'O nekotorykh voprosakh teorii sotsialisticheskogo realizma,' *Voprosy literatury*, 1988, no. 3, 3–22, and I. Volkov, 'Otkazyvat'sia li nam ot sotsialisticheskogo realizma?' *Literaturnaia gazeta*, 25 May 1988, 3.
70 Iu. N. Verchenko, 'O proekte novoi redaktsii ustava Soiuza pisatelei SSSR,' *Literaturnaia gazeta*, 9 March 1988, 10
71 Max Hayward, 'The Decline of Socialist Realism,' *Survey*, 18 no. 1/82 (1972), 96
72 See, for example, *Slavic Review*, 43 no. 4 (winter 1984), 573–87.

73 Edward J. Brown, *Russian Literature since the Revolution*, revised and enlarged edition (Cambridge, Mass, 1982), 343
74 Maurice Friedberg, *Russian Culture in the 1980s* (Washington, DC, 1985), 62
75 Geoffrey Hosking, *Beyond Socialist Realism: Soviet Fiction since Ivan Denisovich* (London 1980), 199
76 'On Literary-Artistic Activity' (1972), 'About Work with Creative Youth' (1976), and 'On the Creative Ties between Literary and Social Journals with the Practice of Communist Construction' (1982)
77 See P.A. Nikolaev, 'Kritika kak nauka,' *Literaturnaia gazeta*, 22 Oct 1986, 4.
78 Ibid, 14 March 1985, 5
79 I. Volkov, 'Chuvstvo sotsial'noi otvetstvennosti,' ibid, 14 Sept 1986, 3
80 Vasil' Fashchenko, 'Rovesnik veka,' ibid, 19 Dec 1984, 2
81 M.S. Gorbachev, 'O perestroike i kadrovoi politike partii,' ibid, 28 Jan 1987, 1
82 Ibid, 23 July 1986, 1
83 Ibid, 8 Oct 1986, 1
84 Ibid, 2
85 Igor' Zolotusskii, 'Toska po idealam,' ibid, 23 July 1986, 3
86 L. Anninskii, 'Oglianis' na povorote,' ibid, 23 July 1986, 3
87 V. Oskotskii, *Voprosy literatury*, 1983, no. 10, 14

Chapter Two: The Literary Scene

1 For a discussion of contemporary countryside prose see chapter 4.
2 For a discussion of contemporary war prose see chapter 5.
3 For a discussion of contemporary political prose see chapter 6.
4 For a discussion of women's issues and the prose of I. Grekova see chapter 8.
5 Iurii Nagibin, 'Terpenie,' *Novyi mir*, 1982, no. 2, 25–53
6 For a discussion of the works of Maiia Ganina and Liliia Beliaeva see chapter 8.
7 For a discussion of Soviet schools and society in the works of Vladimir Tendriakov see chapter 3.
8 Georgii Semenov, 'Loshad' v tumane,' *Nash sovremennik*, 1980, no. 7, 34–78
9 Il'ia Shtemler, *Taksopark* (Moscow 1980)
10 Il'ia Shtemler, *Univermag*, *Novyi mir*, 1982, no. 8, 82–125, no. 9, 110–83, and no. 10, 170–200
11 Il'ia Shtemler, *Utrenee shosse*, *Neva*, 1983, no. 9, 6–72, and no. 10, 73–136
12 Il'ia Shtemler, *Poezd*, *Novyi mir*, 1986, no. 8, 7–86, and no. 9, 67–129
13 F. Chapchakhov, 'Kogda geroi v plenu obstoiatel'stv,' *Literaturnaia gazeta*, 27 March 1985, 2

14 Il'ia Shtemler, *Univermag* (Moscow 1984)
15 Liudmila Zemliannikova, 'Glavnyi geroi nashego vremeni,' *Literaturnaia gazeta*, 17 Oct 1984, 3
16 Liudmila Zemliannikova, 'Posviashchaetsia cheloveku truda,' ibid, 11 June 1986, 2
17 Aleksandr Pletnev, *Shakhta, Oktiabr'*, 1979, no. 8, 14–85, and no. 9, 78–141
18 *Oktiabr'*, 1979, no. 9, 136
19 Sergei Zalygin, *Posle buri, Druzhba narodov*, 1980, no. 4, 5–59, no. 5, 32–236; 1982, no. 5, 7–115; 1985, no. 7, 3–70, no. 8, 80–132, and no. 9, 7–107
20 Initially Zalygin intended Kornilov to disappear without indicating his future fate, but he changed his mind. See A.A. Nuikin, 'Fenomen Zalygina,' *Voprosy filosofii*, 1986, no. 4, 115.
21 Arsenii Gulyga, 'Mudrost' tragediinogo eposa,' *Literaturnaia gazeta*, 25 Feb 1987, 3
22 Mikhail Alekseev, *Drachuny* (Moscow 1982)
23 *Novyi mir*, 1987, no. 8, 6–81
24 *Don*, 1987, nos. 1–3
25 *Druzhba narodov*, 1987, no. 4, 3–133, no. 5, 67–163, and no. 6, 23–151
26 *Znamia*, 1986, no. 10, 3–72, and no. 11, 3–66
27 *Oktiabr'*, 1988, no. 1, 3–127, no. 2, 27–103, no. 3, 25–150, and no. 4, 3–143
28 *Druzhba narodov*, 1987, no. 1, 6–95
29 *Neva*, 1987, no. 1, 6–111, no. 2, 62–132, no. 3, 3–77, and no. 4, 18–124
30 Lev Gudkov and Boris Dubin, 'Literaturnaia kul'tura: protsess i ratsion,' *Druzhba narodov*, 1988, no. 2, 179
31 A. Anninskii, 'Otsy i syny,' *Oktiabr'*, 1987, no. 10, 185–92; A. Latynina, 'Dogovorit' do kontsa,' *Znamia*, 1987, no. 12, 211–20; and Genadii Murikov, 'Pamiat',' *Zvezda*, 1987, no. 12, 166–76
32 Vadim Kozhinov, 'Pravda i istina,' *Nash sovremennik*, 1988, no. 4, 160–75, and A. Lanshchikov and D. Urnov, 'Kritika-87: mneniia i somneniia,' *Literaturnaia gazeta*, 27 Jan 1988, 3
33 Aleksandr Bek (1903–1971)
34 Vasily Grossman, *Life and Fate*, translated from the Russian by Robert Chandler (New York 1985), 21
35 *Literaturnaia gazeta*, 2 March 1988, 2–3
36 For a discussion of the prose of Bulat Okudzhava see chapter 7.
37 Valentin Pikul', *U poslednei cherty. Roman khronika, Nash sovremennik*, 1979, no. 4, 19–152, no. 5, 62–145, no. 6, 79–120, and no. 7, 34–127
38 Valentin Pikul', *Favorit. Roman-khronika vremeni Ekateriny II* (Leningrad 1984)
39 V. Kaverin, 'Vzgliad v litso,' *Literaturnaia gazeta*, 18 June 1986, 12
40 G.A. Belaia, 'Ne sotvori sebe kumira,' *V mire knig*, 1987, no. 5, 77

41 E. Sidorov, 'Prodolzhenie sleduet,' *Voprosy literatury*, 1976, no. 6, 34
42 Viktor Kamianov, *Literaturnaia Rossiia*, 29 May 1987, 5
43 For a discussion of the prose of Chingiz Aitmatov see chapter 9.
44 For a discussion of the prose of Evgenii Evtushenko see chapter 7.
45 Anatolii Anan'ev, *Gody bez voiny, Novyi mir*, 1975, no. 4, 12–113, no. 5, 118–70, and no. 6, 83–118; 1979, no. 1, 3–63, and no. 2, 11–175; 1981, no. 1, 3–106, and no. 2, 11–126; 1984, no. 2, 7–92, no. 3, 25–107, and no. 4, 8–51
46 For a discussion of the prose of Anatolii Kim see chapter 9.
47 Vladimir Krupin, 'Zhivaia voda,' *Novyi mir*, 1980, no. 8, 26–106.
48 Vladimir Krupin, 'Kolokol'chik,' ibid, 1981, no. 4, 30–5
49 Vladimir Krupin, 'Sorokovoi den',' *Nash sovremennik*, 1981, no. 11, 72–117
50 Ibid, 79
51 Ibid, 88
52 Ibid, 89
53 Ibid, 83
54 'Za zhivoi vodoi,' *Literaturnaia gazeta*, 26 May 1982, 5
55 Georgii Bazhenov, *Vozvrashchenie liubvi. Povesti* (Moscow 1982), 147–233
56 Ibid, 326–74
57 Ruslan Kireev, *Podgotovitel'naia tetrad'*, *Znamia*, 1981, no. 4, 7–71, and no. 5, 68–128
58 Vladimir Makanin, 'Gde skhodilos' nebo s kholmami,' *Novyi mir*, 1984, no. 1, 68–102
59 'Velenie vremeni,' editorial, *Literaturnaia gazeta*, 7 Aug 1985, 2
60 Vadim Sokolov, 'Nachinaetsia s publitsistiki,' *Literaturnaia gazeta*, 16 Jan 1986, 3
61 *Novyi mir*, 1987, no. 5, 39–81
62 'Dva rasskaza. Bilet. Novyi zavod,' *Novyi mir*, 1987, no. 6, 128–39
63 Daniil Granin, *Kartina, Novyi mir*, 1980, no. 1, 3–132, and no. 2, 85–176
64 Daniil Granin, 'Zubr,' *Novyi mir*, 1987, no. 1, 19–95, and no. 2, 7–92
65 Boris Mozhaev, 'Poltora kvadratnykh metra,' *Druzhba narodov*, 1982, no. 4, 105–57.
66 Bitov is one of the few writers whose works have been published in the Soviet Union as well as in the West at the same time. His novel *Pushkinskii dom*, completed in 1971 and published in the United States in 1978, appeared in *Novyi mir*, 1987, nos. 10–12.
67 Andrei Bitov, 'Chelovek v peizazhe,' *Novyi mir*, 1987, no. 3, 64–99
68 Ibid, 96
69 Georgii Semenov, 'Literatura – doroga lichnosti,' *Literaturnaia Rossiia*, 12 June 1987, 9

Chapter Three: The Passing Generation

1 *Novyi mir*, 1978, no. 6, 3–146
2 Ibid, 1980, no. 6, 122–56
3 Ibid, 1982, no. 10, 9–105, and no. 11, 162–227
4 Ibid, 1985, no. 1, 83–96
5 Ibid, 1986, no. 1, 8–42
6 Ibid, 1966, no. 5, 3–66
7 Ibid, 1967, no. 3, 3–129
8 Valentin Kataev, 'Beskonechnost' proshlogo, beskonechnost' budushchego … ,' *Literaturnaia gazeta*, 7 Nov 1986, 4
9 *Novyi mir*, 1978, no. 6, 44
10 V. Kardin, 'Tochka obzora, tochka otscheta,' *Voprosy literatury*, 1978, no. 10, 72
11 Ibid, 73
12 *Novyi mir*, 1980, no. 6, 122
13 Ibid, 156
14 Ibid
15 In *Trava zabveniia* the autobiographical hero appears under the name of Riurik Pchelkin.
16 *Novyi mir*, 1982, no. 11, 195
17 Ibid, 1982, no. 10, 68
18 Ibid, 1982, no. 11, 226. Since Pchelkin is a soldier in the tsarist army and participates in what is termed in the Soviet Union an 'imperialist war,' one should be careful in equating his anti-war sentiments with those of a Soviet soldier during the Second World War or with Kataev's own approach to contemporary political issues.
19 Ibid, 1982, no. 10, 13 and 74
20 Ibid, 25
21 Deming B. Brown, *Soviet Russian Literature since Stalin* (Cambridge 1979), 256
22 *Novyi mir*, 1978, no. 6, 6
23 Ibid, 1982, no. 10, 36
24 Ibid, 1978, no. 6, 11
25 Valentin Kataev, *The Holy Well*, translated from the Russian by Max Hayward and Harold Shukman (New York 1967), 101
26 See, for example, Robert Russell, *Valentin Kataev* (Boston 1981), 113–17.
27 Valentin Kataev, 'Ne povtoriat' sebia i drugogo,' *Literaturnaia gazeta*, 1 Jan 1972, 7
28 Valentin Kataev, *Pochti dnevnik*, second, enlarged edition (Moscow 1978), 381–2
29 *Novyi mir*, 1978, no. 6, 139
30 N. Krymova, 'Ne sviatoi kolodets,' *Druzhba narodov*, 1979, no. 9, 236
31 *The Holy Well*, 128

32 *Pochti dnevnik*, 291
33 Violetta Iverni, 'Sotsrealizm s chelovecheskim litsom,' *Kontinent*, 1976, no. 7, 413
34 *Literaturnaia gazeta*, 7 Nov 1984, 4
35 *Novyi mir*, 1986, no. 1, 36
36 For a discussion of Trifonov's early works see, among others, N.N. Shneidman, *Soviet Literature in the 1970s: Artistic Diversity and Ideological Conformity* (Toronto 1979), 88–105, and Geoffrey Hosking, *Beyond Socialist Realism: Soviet Fiction since Ivan Denisovich* (London 1980), 180–95.
37 *Novyi mir*, 1981, no. 7, 58–87
38 *Druzhba narodov*, no. 9, 72–148, and no. 10, 11–108
39 Sigrid McLaughlin gave a paper at the Third World Congress of Soviet and East European Studies, 30 Oct–4 Nov 1985, in Washington, DC, in which she compared the Russian edition of *Vremia i mesto*, published in *Druzhba narodov*, with a slightly longer, evidently uncensored version that appeared in German translation, in both East Germany and West Germany.
40 All the letters quoted here are from my personal correspondence with Iurii Trifonov. The letters are in my possession.
41 *Voprosy literatury*, 1982, no. 5, 76; originally published in *Weimarer Beiträge*, 1981, no. 8
42 See, for example, Hosking, *Beyond Socialist Realism*, 195
43 From my interview with Trifonov, Moscow, 16 April 1976
44 Valerii Golovskoi, 'Nravstvennye uroki trifonovskoi prozy,' *Russian Language Journal*, 37 no. 128 (fall 1983), 158
45 M. Bakhtin, *Problemy poetiki Dostoevskogo*, third edition (Moscow 1972), 49
46 For a detailed discussion of time in *Vremia i mesto*, see S. Eremina and V. Piskunov, 'Vremia i mesto prozy Iu. Trifonova,' *Voprosy literatury*, 1982, no. 5, 34–65.
47 *Druzhba narodov*, 1981, no. 10, 85
48 Ibid
49 Ibid, 96
50 Ibid, 97
51 Ibid, 99
52 *Novyi mir*, 1981, no. 7, 63
53 Ibid, 75
54 A. Bocharov, 'Listopad,' *Literaturnoe obozrenie*, 1982, no. 3, 45
55 *Novyi mir*, 1981, no. 7, 70
56 Ibid, 71
57 Iurii Trifonov, *Prodolzhitel'nye uroki* (Moscow 1975), 12
58 *Novyi mir*, 1981, no. 7, 62
59 The author of this letter was an intimate friend of Iurii Trifonov's for many years. His letter from Moscow is dated 8 August 1982 and is in my possession.

60 From a letter dated 11 Aug 1978
61 *Druzhba narodov*, 1981, no. 10, 77
62 Ibid, 1981, no. 9, 78
63 Ibid, no. 10, 107
64 *Novyi mir*, 1970, no. 12, 123
65 From a letter dated 4 Dec 1978
66 *Druzhba narodov*, 1981, no. 10, 49
67 *Prodolzhitel'nye uroki*, 28–9
68 Iurii Mal'tsev, 'Promezhutochnaia literatura,' *Kontinent*, 1980, no. 25, 302
69 Iurii Trifonov, 'Interv'iu o kontraktakh,' *Inostrannaia literatura*, 1978, no. 6, 25
70 *Novyi mir*, 1981, no. 7, 68
71 Trifonov's story 'Nedolgoe prebyvanie v kamere pytok' (A Short Stay in the Torture Chamber) was published in *Znamia*, 1986, no. 12, 118–24; his unfinished novel *Ischeznovenie* (Disappearance) appeared in *Druzhba narodov*, 1987, no. 1, 6–95. These works change little in the general evaluation of the writer's creative work.
72 *Molodaia gvardiia*, 1959, nos. 10–12, and in Vladimir Tendriakov, *Sobranie sochinenii v chetyrekh tomakh*, ii (Moscow 1979), 233–612
73 See Vladimir Tendriakov, 'Vash syn i nasledstvo Komenskogo,' *Moskva*, 1965, no. 11, 143–59. Tendriakov's article sparked a heated discussion on the pages of *Moskva*; see *Moskva*, 1966, nos. 1, 4, 10, and 11.
74 *Novyi mir*, 1973, no. 1, 118–71
75 *Nash sovremennik*, 1973, no. 2, 3–80
76 *Novyi mir*, 1974, no. 9, 82–130
77 Ibid, 1979, no. 3, 6–99
78 *Druzhba narodov*, 1980, no. 9, 91–165
79 *Novyi mir*, 1974, no. 9, 83
80 For a discussion of programming and methods of teaching literature in the Soviet Union, see N.N. Shneidman, *Literature and Ideology in Soviet Education* (Lexington, Mass, 1973).
81 N. Shamota, 'Chitatel' i literaturnyi protses,' *Znamia*, 1976, no. 8, 232
82 *Novyi mir*, 1979, no. 3, 62
83 Ibid, 72
84 Ibid
85 In his article 'Uchitelia i ucheniki,' Ark. El'iashevich points out a number of parallels between 'Rasplata' and *Crime and Punishment* and between the characters of Koriakin and Raskol'nikov, placing an exaggerated emphasis on the affinity between Tendriakov and Dostoevskii. See *Novyi mir*, 1982, no. 7, 240–1.
86 *Novyi mir*, 1979, no. 3, 14
87 The name Sukov can be interpreted as a derogatory symbol because it is etymologically related to the word 'suka,' which means 'bitch.'
88 *Druzhba narodov*, 1980, no. 9, 114
89 Ibid, 144

90 Ibid, 165
91 J.G. Garrard, 'Vladimir Tendrjakov,' *Slavic and East European Journal,* 9, no. 1 (spring 1965), 2
92 Hosking, *Beyond Socialist Realism,* 84
93 'O tvorcheskikh sviaziakh literaturno-khudozhestvennykh zhurnalov s praktikoi kommunisticheskogo stroitel'stva,' *Literaturnaia gazeta,* 4 Aug 1982, 1
94 'Chistye vody Kitezha' (The Clear Waters of Kitezh), *Druzhba narodov,* 1986, no. 8, and *Pokushenie na mirazhi* (The Assault on Illusions), *Novyi mir,* 1987, nos. 4–5

Chapter Four: The Soviet Countryside

1 Veniamin Kaverin, 'Portret zhanra,' *Literaturnaia gazeta,* 10 Dec 1986, 3
2 A. Vil'chek, 'Vniz po techeniiu derevenskoi prozy,' *Voprosy literatury,* 1985, no. 6, 36
3 Viktor Chalmaev, 'Vozdushnaia vozdvigalas' arka … ,' ibid, 1985, no. 6, 75–9
4 In 1951, 40 per cent of the Soviet population resided in the city and 60 per cent in the countryside (*Narodnoe khoziaistvo SSSR v 1974*g [Moscow 1975], 7). In 1985, 65.3 per cent lived in cities and only 34.7 per cent in rural areas (*Narodnoe khoziaistvo SSSR v 1984*g [Moscow 1985], 5). There were in 1949 some 250,000 collective farms (kolkhozy), with an average of 557 sawn hectares of land, and approximately 5,000 state farms (sovkhozy), with an average of 3,000 hectares each. In 1984 there were 26,200 collective farms, with an average of 9,900 hectares each, and 22,515 state farms, with an average of 21,000 hectares each (*Narodnoe khoziaistvo SSSR v 1984*g, 294–5 and 304–5).
5 For a discussion of village prose of the 1950s–1970s see Geoffrey Hosking, *Beyond Socialist Realism: Soviet Fiction since Ivan Denisovich* (London 1980), 50–83, also Deming B. Brown, *Soviet Russian Literature since Stalin* (Cambridge 1979), 218–51.
6 Vil'chek, 'Vniz po techeniiu derevenskoi prozi,' 71, 73
7 For a discussion of 'Man, Nature, and the *Roots* in Recent Soviet Russian Prose,' see S.D. Cioran, W. Smyrniw, and G. Thomas, eds, *Studies in Honour of Louis Shein* (Hamilton, Ont, 1983), 125–33.
8 D.S. Likhachev, 'Zametki o russkom,' *Novyi mir,* 1980, no. 3, 12
9 Valentin Rasputin, '… prezhde vsego vospitanie chuvstv,' *Literaturnaia gazeta,* 26 March 1980, 5
10 Ibid
11 *Novyi mir,* 1978, no. 12, 3–164
12 Fedor Abramov, 'Dom i ego khoziaeva,' *Literaturnaia gazeta,* 22 March 1978, 3
13 *Novyi mir,* 1978, no. 12, 31
14 Ibid, 130

15 V. Oskotskii, 'Chto zhe sluchilos' v Pekashine?' *Literaturnoe obozrenie*, 1979, no. 5, 46
16 Ibid, 48
17 Iu. Andreev, 'Dom i mir,' *Literaturnaia gazeta*, 7 Feb 1979, 4
18 A. Pavlovskii, 'V nachale vos'midesiatykh godov,' *Russkaia literatura*, 1984, no. 3, 45
19 *Neva*, 1980, no. 9, 3–27
20 *Novyi mir*, 1982, no. 5, 11–20
21 See, for example, the story 'Novogodniaia elka' (The New Year Tree), *Neva*, 1981, no. 1, 112–13.
22 On Rasputin's early works, see N.N. Shneidman, *Soviet Literature in the 1970s: Artistic Diversity and Ideological Conformity* (Toronto 1979), 75–87; also Hosking, *Beyond Socialist Realism*, 50–83.
23 Valentin Rasputin, 'Byt' samim soboi,' *Voprosy literatury*, 1976, no. 9, 146
24 Valentin Rasputin, 'Rasskazy,' *Nash sovremennik*, 1982, no. 7, 15–55
25 Ibid, 1985, no. 7, 3–38
26 Anthony Austin, 'Soviet writer, beaten year ago, still can't work,' *New York Times*, 3 May 1981, 13
27 *Nash sovremennik*, 1982, no. 7, 15–34
28 Ibid, 34–44; first appeared in the almanac *Sibir*, 1981, no. 5
29 *Nash sovremennik*, 1982, no. 7, 44–9
30 Ibid, 50–5; first published in *Sovetskaia kul'tura*, 10 March 1982
31 Natal'ia Ivanova, 'Vol'noe dykhanie,' *Voprosy literatury*, 1983, no. 3, 208
32 Ibid, 212
33 Valentin Rasputin, *Izbrannye proizvedeniia v 2-kh tomakh*, ii (Moscow 1984), 436–43; originally published in *Sovetskaia kul'tura*, 15 May 1981
34 Ibid, 438
35 Ibid, 441
36 Ibid, 443
37 Ibid, 442
38 *Nash sovremennik*, 1985, no. 7, 33
39 Evgenii Sidorov, 'Ispytanie ognem,' *Znamia*, 1985, no. 10, 229
40 For a discussion of the above see Vadim Sokolov, 'Nachinaetsia s publitsistiki,' *Literaturnaia gazeta*, 15 Jan 1986, 3, and Natal'ia Ivanova, 'Nekhochu byt' chernoi krest'iankoi ... ,' *Literaturnaia gazeta*, 29 Jan 1986, 3. Sokolov and Ivanova express diametrically opposed views on this issue.
41 For a detailed discussion of Astaf'ev's early work see N.N. Shneidman, 'Viktor Astaf'ev: The Soviet Bard of Siberia,' *Russian Language Journal*, 33 no. 114 (1979), 99–107.
42 Viktor Astaf'ev, 'Chetyre korotkih rasskaza,' *Novyi mir*, 1978, no. 10, 124–35

43 'Prosti menia' (Forgive Me; 1980)
44 'Tam v okopakh' (There in the Trenches), *Pravda*, 25 Sept 1985
45 'Mesto deistviia,' Rasskazy (Place of Action, Stories), *Nash sovremennik*, 1986, no. 5, 100–41
46 Ibid, 111–23
47 Ibid, 112
48 Ibid, 118
49 *Oktiabr'*, 1986, no. 1, 8–74
50 Ibid, 27
51 D. Ivanov, 'Vremia prishlo,' *Ogonek*, 1986, no. 14 (March), 25–6
52 V. Butorin, 'Chtoby eta rabota byla vidna,' *Literaturnaia gazeta*, 1 Oct 1986, 3
53 On the early works of Belov, see Hosking, *Beyond Socialist Realism*, 50–83
54 *Nash sovremennik*, 1979, no. 10, 117–58, and no. 12, 85–96; 1980, no. 3, 60–84; and 1981, no. 1, 160–74, no. 5, 145–71, no. 6, 143–53, and no. 7, 125–64
55 Aleksandr Bragin, 'Puteshestvie v budushchuiu knigu,' *Nash sovremennik*, 1979, no. 10, 112
56 Chalmaev, 'Vozdushnaia vozdvigalas' arka ...,' 116
57 Vasilii Belov, 'Raionnye stseny' (District Scenes), *Moskva*, 1980, no. 8, 128–56
58 Vasilii Belov, 'Takaia voina' (Such Is the War), *Iunost'*, 1985, no. 11, 75–80
59 Vasilii Belov, 'Razdum'ia na rodine' (Native Land Ruminations), *Nash sovremennik*, 1985, no. 6, 100–60
60 Vasilii Belov, *Vse vperedi*, Nash sovremennik, 1986, no. 7, 29–106, and no. 8, 59–110
61 *Literaturnaia gazeta*, 18 Dec 1985, 6
62 *Sovetskaia kul'tura*, 11 Feb 1986, 3, quoted in *The Current Digest of the Soviet Press*, 38 no. 9 (2 April 1986), 18–19
63 *Nash sovremennik*, 1978, no. 2, 62–103; 1980, no. 8, 10–43, no. 9, 3–57, no. 10, 135–72, no. 11, 113–58, no. 12, 27–153; 1983, no. 5, 21–129, no. 6, 32–120, no. 10, 17–101, no. 11, 25–100; 1984, no. 3, 98–128, no. 4, 90–130; and 1985, no. 9, 97–121
64 (Moscow 1982); originally published under the title *Polovod'e* (High Water) in *Molodaia gvardiia*, 1982, no. 1, 33–129, no. 2, 60–128 and 161–83

Chapter Five: The Second World War: Forty Years Later

1 Anatolii Bocharov, 'Lichno prichasten,' *Pravda*, 17 Feb 1985, 3
2 For a discussion of Soviet war prose of the 1970s, see N.N. Shneidman, *Soviet Literature in the 1970s: Artistic Diversity and Ideological Conformity* (Toronto 1979), 15–16, 20–1, 47–60.

3 *Novyi mir*, 1985, no. 1, 6–73, and no. 2, 80–155
4 *Druzhba narodov*, 1983, no. 3, 6–111, and no. 4, 8–128
5 *Znamia*, 1983, no. 7; *Znamia* 1983, no. 1; *Nash sovremennik*, 1984, nos. 5, 8, 11, and 12; *Znamia*, 1984, no. 12; *Znamia*, 1985, no. 9; *Zvezda*, 1983, no. 5
6 *Novyi mir*, 1983, no. 2, 9–137
7 Ibid, 1982, no. 5, 64–131, and no. 6, 65–153; 1983, no. 11, 101–90, and no. 12, 8–101
8 For a discussion of such works, see Oleg Smirnov, 'Groznye chetyre goda. Obreteniia i neudachi sovremennoi "voennoi prozy,"' *Literaturnaia gazeta*, 11 June 1986, 4.
9 *Oktiabr'*, 1984, no. 2, 22–107
10 Ibid, 1985, no. 10, 3–87
11 *Druzhba narodov*, 1979, no. 2, 5–88
12 Ibid, 1985, no. 1, 31–67
13 Ibid, 1986, no. 1, 146–60
14 *Voprosy literatury*, 1985, no. 5, 47
15 See K. Simonov's letters to V.I. Kondrat'ev, *Voprosy literatury*, 1985, no. 5, 216–17.
16 *Druzhba narodov*, 1979, no. 2, 23
17 Ibid, 29
18 Vladimir Tendriakov, 'Pravdivee, chem sam fakt,' *Literaturnaia gazeta*, 8 Aug 1984, 7
19 *Druzhba narodov*, 1985, no. 1, 55
20 Ibid, 53
21 *Oktiabr'*, 1979, no. 5, 3–106
22 See the speech of Vladimir Karpov at the Eighth Congress of Soviet Writers, *Literaturnaia gazeta*, 2 July 1986, 10.
23 *Novyi mir*, 1984, no. 1, 6–55
24 Daniil Granin, *Eshche zameten sled. Povesti i rasskazy* (Leningrad 1985), 335
25 *Nash sovremennik*, 1980, no. 10, 14–125, and no. 11, 17–108
26 F. Chapchakhov, 'Tsena vybora,' *Literaturnaia gazeta*, 1 Jan 1981, 5
27 Iurii Idashkin, *Grani talanta. O tvorchestve Iuriia Bondareva* (Moscow 1983), 224
28 A. Ovcharenko, 'Zrelost' realizma,' *Voprosy literatury*, 1981, no. 9, 9
29 *Novyi mir*, 1966, no. 1, 3–66, and no. 2, 7–64
30 See, for example, N. Ivanova, 'Rasshiriaiushchaiasia sovremennost',' *Voprosy literatury*, 1981, no. 9, 37–42.
31 *Nash sovremennik*, 1975, no. 3, 2–87, and no. 4, 47–114
32 Iurii Bondarev, *Igra* (Moscow 1985), 153
33 Ibid, 265
34 Ibid
35 Ibid, 155
36 Klara Skopina and Sergei Guskov, 'To Find a Hero,' *Komsomol'skaia*

pravda, 22 June 1985, quoted in *Current Digest of the Soviet Press*, 37 no. 25, 6

37 *Literaturnaia gazeta*, 18 Dec 1985, 4
38 *Novyi mir*, 1964, no. 2, 3–80
39 Vasil' Bykov, 'Na vysote sovesti,' *Literaturnaia gazeta*, 14 May 1986, 2
40 Igor' Dedkov, 'Pod znakom bedy,' *Novyi mir*, 1983, no. 10, 254
41 *Literaturnaia gazeta*, 23 April 1986, 1
42 I. Kozlov, 'Kharaktera narodnye cherty,' *Literaturnaia gazeta*, 1 June 1983, 4
43 Vasil' Bykov, 'Vystoiat',' *Iunost'*, 1984, no. 1, 55
44 L. Lazarev, 'Veshchii znak,' *Literaturnoe obozrenie*, 1983, no. 8, 50
45 Viktor Koz'ko, *Voprosy literatury*, 1985, no. 1, 52
46 *Druzhba narodov*, 1986, no. 4, 3–85, and no. 5, 68–162
47 *Iunost'*, 1984, no. 1, 55
48 *Novyi mir*, 1972, no. 1, 3–44
49 Ibid, 1974, no. 7, 5–80
50 V. Bykov, 'Kar'er,' *Druzhba narodov*, 1986, no. 4, 55
51 Ibid, 72
52 Vasil' Bykov, 'Na vysote sovesti,' *Literaturnaia gazeta*, 14 May 1986, 2
53 *Novyi mir*, 1970, no. 5, 65–161
54 *Literaturnaia gazeta*, 14 May 1986, 2
55 Vasil' Bykov, 'V tumane,' *Druzhba narodov*, 1987, no. 7, 3–61

Chapter Six: The New Political Novel

1 M. Sinel'nikov, 'Roman i politika,' *Novyi mir*, 1982, no. 11, 260
2 *Znamia*, 1978, no. 10, 3–108, no. 11, 3–69, no. 12, 7–51; 1980, no. 1, 7–52, no. 2, 3–68, no. 3, 3–48; 1981, no. 1, 3–71, no. 2, 6–78, no. 8, 3–71, and no. 9, 71–151
3 Ibid, 1983, no. 9, 3–99; 1984, no. 7, 4–82, and no. 8, 7–66
4 (Moscow 1983)
5 *Druzhba narodov*, 1983, no. 4, 3–74, no. 5, 11–56, and no. 6, 17–53
6 *Literaturnaia gazeta*, 2 July 1986, 7
7 *Moskva*, 1983, no. 7, 12–141, and no. 8, 52–151
8 (Moscow 1986)
9 (Moscow 1979)
10 (Moscow 1983)
11 *Druzhba narodov*, 1984, no. 3, 4–80, no. 4, 50–133, and no. 5, 12–111
12 Ibid, 1985, no. 8, 6–78, and no. 9, 110–82
13 Iulian Semenov, *Litsom k litsu* (Moscow 1983), 446
14 Iulian Semenov, interview with L. Anninskii, *Druzhba narodov*, 1984, no. 1, 264
15 *Oktiabr'*, 1982, no. 1, 3–73, and no. 2, 74–137
16 *Novyi mir*, 1983, no. 5, 33–130
17 *Znamia*, 1984, no. 3, 24–103, and no. 4, 85–154

18 Ibid, 1984, no. 9, 3–78, and no. 10, 3–112
19 In May 1986 Babrak Karmal was replaced in this post by Mohammad Najibullah.
20 *Znamia*, no. 2, 107
21 Ibid, 79
22 Aleksandr Prokhanov, *V ostrovakh okhotnik* (Moscow 1983), 328
23 Ibid, 383
24 Ibid, 386
25 Aleksandr Prokhanov, *Goriashchie sady* (Moscow 1984), 388
26 *Znamia*, 1984, no. 10, 22
27 Ibid, 37
28 Ibid, 23
29 See Georgii Viren, 'Imia dlia vremeni,' *Literaturnaia gazeta*, 24 Dec 1984, 4.
30 A. Prokhanov, 'Formuly, gipotezy,' ibid, 6 Nov 1985, 6
31 *Goriashchie sady*, 579
32 *Literaturnaia gazeta*, 6 Nov 1985, 6
33 Ibid, 2 July 1986, 9
34 Igor' Dedkov, 'Ch'i zhe eto golosa?' ibid, 31 July 1985, 3
35 V. Oskotskii, 'Politicheskii roman, 80-e ...,' *Literaturnoe obozrenie*, 1985, no. 3, 5–6
36 L. Fink, 'Esli sudit' po vysshemu schetu,' *Literaturnaia gazeta*, 10 Sept 1986, 7
37 See ibid, 2 July 1986, 2.
38 See ibid, 9 April 1986, 6. Prokhanov did not receive the prize. The 1986 prize for khudozhestvennaia publitsistika was awarded to Genrikh Borovik, for his narrative *Prolog* (Prologue), about the United States in the late 1960s.
39 *Znamia*, 1984, no. 9, 19
40 Aleksandr Prokhanov, 'Sedoi soldat,' a chapter from a future novel in novellas, *Znamia*, 1985, no. 2, 116–56
41 Ibid, 1985, no. 2, 130
42 *Risunki batalista*, *Moskva*, 1986, no. 9, 33–155, and no. 10, 11–106. Another story by Prokhanov, entitled 'Svetlei lazuri' (Brighter than Sky Blue), was published in *Oktiabr'*, 1986, no. 9, 3–55.
43 According to recent official reports, 13,310 Soviet soldiers and officers were killed, 35,478 wounded, and 311 lost without trace in the war in Afghanistan. See *Izvestiia*, 26 May 1988, 8.

Chapter Seven: The Poet's Prose

1 Originally published in *Tarusskie stranitsy* (Pages from Tarusa; 1961), edited by K. Paustovskii
2 *Bednyi Avrosimov* (The Poor Avrosimov), *Druzhba narodov*, 1969, no. 4, 107–41, no. 5, 133–98, and no. 6, 103–68; republished in book form as

Glotok svobody. Povest' o Pavle Pestele (A Taste of Freedom: A Story about Pavel Pestel') (Moscow 1971). *Mersi, ili pokhozhdeniia Shipova. Starinnyi vodevil'. Istinnoe proisshestvie, Druzhba narodov,* 1971, no. 12, 88–199; in translation: *The Extraordinary Adventures of Secret Agent Shipov in Pursuit of Count Leo Tolstoy in the Year 1862,* translated by Heather Maisner (London 1973). *Puteshestvie diletantov. Iz zapisok otstavnogo poruchika Amirama Amilakhvari* (The Journey of Dilettantes: From the Notes of Retired Lieutenant Amiram Amilakhvari), *Druzhba narodov,* 1976, no. 8, 98–157, no. 9, 31–162, and 1978, no. 9, 69–164, no. 10, 66–120.

For a discussion of Okudzhava's early prose, see Edward J. Brown, *Russian Literature since the Revolution,* revised and enlarged edition (Cambridge, Mass, 1982), 325–9, and Deming B. Brown, *Soviet Russian Literature since Stalin* (Cambridge 1979), 263–4 and 276–7

3 *Druzhba narodov,* 1983, no. 7, 95–142, no. 8, 94–128, and no. 9, 96–153
4 In Iu. Bondarev's novel *Bereg* (The Shore; 1975), the Soviet officer Kniazhko sacrifices his life in order to save a few German youngsters, but even Soviet critics admit that Kniazhko is an idealized hero. For a discussion of *Bereg* see N.N. Shneidman, *Soviet Literature in the 1970s: Artistic Diversity and Ideological Conformity* (Toronto 1979), 57–9.
5 Evgenii Evtushenko, *Tochka opory* (A Foothold) (Moscow 1981), 3
6 See, among others, Evgenii Evtushenko, *Talant est' chudo nesluchainoe. Kniga statei* (Talent Is No Chance Miracle: A Book of Articles) (Moscow 1980), and *Voina – eto antikul'tura. Po tu storonu* (A War Is Anti-Culture: On the Other Side) (Moscow 1983).
7 Evgenii Evtushenko, 'Ardabiola,' in *Tochka opory,* 109–83; in English translation: *Ardabiola: A Fantasy by Yevgeny Yevtushenko,* translated by Armorer Wason (London 1984)
8 *Tochka opory,* 110
9 Ibid
10 Anthony Austin, 'Soviet writer, beaten year ago, still can't work,' *New York Times,* 3 May 1981, 13
11 *Moskva,* 1981, no. 10, 3–123, and no. 11, 52–111; in English translation: Yevgeny Yevtushenko, *Wild Berries,* translated by Antonina W. Bouis (New York 1984)
12 Evgenii Evtushenko, *Iagodnye mesta* (Moscow 1982), 189. The above passages, as well as some others, are omitted from the English translation of the novel.
13 'Proza poeta,' *Literaturnaia gazeta,* 1 Jan 1982, 4
14 Ibid
15 '"Iagodnye mesta": vokrug da okolo,' *Nash sovremennik,* 1983, no. 12, 172
16 Ibid
17 V. Kardin, 'O pol'ze i vrede arifmetiki,' *Voprosy literatury,* 1983, no. 10, 71

18 Ibid, 83
19 'Mera vzyskatel'nosti,' *Literaturnaia gazeta*, 21 Dec 1983, 2
20 John Updike, 'Books: Back in the ussr.,' *New Yorker*, 15 April 1985, 118
21 Ibid, 117. Some Western critics express admiration for Evtushenko's novel, but they are a small minority. See, for example, D. Heith Mano, 'Fairest Socialism,' *National Review*, 14 Dec 1984, 47.
22 *Iagodnye mesta*, 25
23 Evgenii Evtushenko, 'Uroki russkoi klassiki,' in *Talant est' chudo ne sluchainoe. Kniga statei*, 20
24 *Wild Berries*, 195
25 Andrei Voznesenskii, *Sobranie sochinenii v trekh tomakh*, ii (Moscow 1984), 463–6
26 Ibid, 464
27 *Novyi mir*, 1982, no. 11, 111–61
28 Ibid, 113
29 Ibid, 158
30 Ibid
31 Ibid, 143
32 Ibid, 156
33 Andrei Voznesenskii, *Sobranie sochinenii*, ii, 466

Chapter Eight: Women Writers and Women's Problems

1 For a detailed discussion of Tat'iana Tolstaia's prose see Helena Goscilo, 'Tat'iana Tolstaia's "Dome of Many-Coloured Glass": The World Refracted through Multiple Perspectives,' *Slavic Review*, 47 no. 2 (summer 1988), 280–90.
2 'Noch',' *Oktiabr'*, 1987, no. 4, 95–9
3 'Peters,' *Novyi mir*, 1986, no. 1, 123–31
4 See 'Milaia Shura' (Darling Shura), *Oktiabr'*, 1985, no. 12, 113–17.
5 'Okhota na mamonta,' *Oktiabr'*, 1985, no. 12, 117–21
6 'Poet i muza,' *Novyi mir*, 1986, no. 12, 113–33
7 'Krug,' *Oktiabr'*, 1987, no. 4, 99–104
8 'Za prokhodnoi,' *Novyi mir*, 1962, no. 7, 110–31
9 'Damskii master,' ibid, 1963, no. 11, 89–120
10 'Letom v gorode,' ibid, 1965, no. 4, 84–101
11 'Pod fonarem,' *Zvezda*, 1965, no. 12, 43–54
12 'Na ispytaniiakh,' *Novyi mir*, 1967, no. 7, 14–109
13 'Malen'kii Garusov,' *Zvezda*, 1970, no. 9, 119–56
14 'Khoziaika gostinitsy,' ibid, 1976, no. 9, 7–123
15 'Kafedra,' *Novyi mir*, 1978, no. 9, 10–168
16 'Vdovii parokhod,' ibid, 1981, no. 5, 66–147
17 *Porogi, Oktiabr'*, 1984, no. 10, 3–51, and no. 11, 80–181
18 'Fazan,' ibid, 1985, no. 9, 6–58
19 'Bez ulybok,' ibid, 1986, no. 11, 162–79

20 'Perelom,' ibid, 1987, no. 8, 72–149
21 For a discussion of I. Grekova's early stories see Deming B. Brown, *Soviet Russian Literature since Stalin* (Cambridge 1979), 163–7; Edward J. Brown, *Russian Literature since the Revolution*, revised and enlarged edition (Cambridge, Mass, 1982), 321–2; Maurice Friedberg, 'Introduction,' to I. Grekova, *Russian Women: Two Stories – Ladies' Hairdresser. The Hotel Manager*, translated by Michel Petrov, introduction by Maurice Friedberg (New York 1983), vii–xiv.
22 *Novyi mir*, 1981, no. 5, 111
23 *Zvezda*, 1976, no. 9, 28–9
24 Gail Warshofsky Lapidus, *Women in Soviet Society* (Berkeley 1978) 299
25 Ibid
26 Bernice Madison, 'Social Services for Women: Problems and Priorities,' in Dorothy Atkinson, Alexander Dallin, and Gail Warshofsky Lapidus, eds, *Women in Russia* (Stanford, Calif, 1977), 319
27 *Novyi mir*, 1981, no. 5, 135. The truthfulness of the scene described by Grekova is corroborated by Al'bert Likhanov: 'Deti bez roditelei,' *Literaturnaia gazeta*, 27 Feb 1985, 12. According to Bernice Madison: 'Prospective parents must find a child to adopt on their own, and even then, where an abandoned child looks to be a likely candidate, they would be blocked in their plans if the mother cannot be found to relinquish her claim to the child.' See Atkinson et al, eds, *Women in Russia*, 318.
28 *Zvezda*, 1976, no. 9, 118
29 *Russian Literature Triquarterly*, 1973, no. 5, 257
30 G. Brovman, 'Grazhdanskoe chuvstvo i kharakter sovremennika,' *Moskva*, 1966, no. 4, 202
31 Sergei Borovnikov, 'My tol'ko znakomy,' *Nash sovremennik*, 1979, no. 12, 174
32 Ibid, 177
33 Aleksandr Rusov, 'I. Grekovoi (E.S. Venttsel') – 75 let,' *Literaturnaia gazeta*, 14 April 1982, 6
34 'Pervye ispytaniia,' *Novyi mir*, 1954, no. 4, 3–76, and no. 5, 82–157
35 M. Ganina, 'Moi dorogi,' *Izbrannoe. Rasskazy. Povesti* (Moscow 1983), 3
36 'Uslysh' svoi chas,' *Novyi mir*, 1976, no. 3, 11–66. Ganina's other publications include 'Tiapkin i Lesha,' *Znamia*, 1971, no. 12, 61–108; 'Sozvezdie bliznetsov,' *Oktiabr'*, 1974, no. 10, 3–43; 'Den'' pervyi i vse ostal'nye,' *Oktiabr'*, 1980, no. 7, 82–147; *Esli budem zhivy ...*, *Oktiabr'*, 1983, no. 6, 18–132; 'Khronika zhizni Aleksandry Stepanovny,' in M. Ganina, *Sto zhiznei moikh* (Moscow 1983), 208–415; *Poka zhivu nadeius'*, *Oktiabr'*, 1986, no. 10, 3–148, and 1987, no. 11, 13–117.
37 Maiia Ganina, *Sto zhiznei moikh* (Moscow 1983), 3–207
38 Ibid, 45
39 Maiia Ganina, 'Strasti po Shekspiru,' *Literaturnaia gazeta*, 14 Aug 1985, 11

40 Ibid
41 'Kvartira s vidom na more' (abbreviated form), *Neva*, 1969, no. 10, 71–122
42 'Sem' let ne v schet,' *Novyi mir*, 1976, no. 4, 34–107, and no. 5, 130–60
43 *Nesygrannaia rol'* (Moscow 1982). A note at the end of the novel indicates that is was completed in 1978.
44 D. Tevekelian, 'Sotri sluchainye cherty,' *Novyi mir*, 1982, no. 6, 224
45 *Narodnoe khoziaistvo SSSR v 1983 g.* (Moscow 1984), 6
46 *Narodnoe khoziaistvo SSSR za 60 let* (Moscow 1977), 517

Chapter Nine: Innovation and Experiment

1 Sergei Zalygin, 'Vremia bol'shikh zabot,' *Voprosy literatury*, 1986, no. 5, 7. Marquez does not accept the notion of 'magic realism' and considers himself a 'pure' realist. See *Literaturnaia gazeta*, 13 May 1987, 15.
2 *Novyi mir*, 1980, no. 2, 14–84, no. 3, 49–179, and no. 4, 126–63
3 (Moscow 1984)
4 Anatolii Kim, *Belka. Roman-skazka* (Moscow 1984), 269
5 Valentin Kataev, who had the opportunity to read *Belka* not long before his death, observed, not without pride, that he noticed some of his own influence on the work of Kim. See Valentin Kataev, 'Beskonechnost' proshlogo, beskonechnost' nastoiashchego,' *Literaturnaia gazeta*, 7 Nov 1984, 4.
6 For a discussion of the relative merits of *Belka* see, among others, A. Nemzer, 'O chem zhe pela belka,' and L. Anninskii, 'Prevrashcheniia i prevratnosti,' *Literaturnoe obozrenie*, 1985, no. 8, 29–36; Vl. Novikov, 'Pod sousom vechnosti?'; Vs. Surganov, 'Energiia dobra,' *Literaturnaia gazeta*, 13 Feb 1985, 4; and G. Belaia, *Literatura v zerkale kritiki* (Moscow 1986), 97–100.
7 *Literaturnaia gazeta*, 25 June 1986, 3
8 *Novyi mir*, 1982, no. 2, 6–86
9 Vl. Voronov, *Chingiz Aitmatov. Ocherk tvorchestva* (Moscow 1976), 15
10 Nikolai Khokhlov, 'Nachalo dnei nashikh – Oktiabr','' *Literaturnaia gazeta*, 11 Aug 1983, 5
11 For a discussion of Aitmatov's early prose see N.N. Shneidman, *Soviet Literature in the 1970s: Artistic Diversity and Ideological Conformity* (Toronto 1979), 32–46; also N.N. Shneidman, 'Soviet Literature at the Crossroads: The Controversial Prose of Chingiz Aitmatov,' *Russian Literature Triquarterly*, 1979, no. 16, 244–63 and 340–1.
12 Nikolai Khokhlov
13 N.N. Shneidman, 'Interview with Chingiz Aitmatov,' *Russian Literature Triquarterly*, 1979, no. 16, 265
14 *Znamia*, 1977, no. 4, 4–55
15 *Novyi mir*, 1980, no. 11, 3–185; in book form the title is *Burannyi polustanok* (The Burannyi Siding).

16 *Novyi mir*, 1986, no. 6, 7–69, no. 8, 90–148, and no. 9, 6–64
17 For a discussion of the above see Katerina Clark, 'The Mutability of the Canon: Socialist Realism and Chingiz Aitmatov's *I dol'she veka dlitsia den*',' *Slavic Review*, 43 no. 4 (winter 1984), 573–87.
18 Katerina Clark has 'come to a tentative conclusion that the Ana-Beiit legend is not based directly on any Central Asian epic ... for the form of torture which is so crucial to the legend ... seems closer to American Indian than Central Asian lore' ('Mutability,' 578). In an article on the influence of Russian village prose on Kazakh literature, particularly on the author of *Khatyngol'skaia ballada*, Abish Kekil'baev, Vladimir Bondarenko suggests that the mankurt motif has been taken by Aitmatov from Kekil'baev's povest' 'Ballada zabytykh let' (1975), in which an old Turkman avenges the death of his younger brother by subjecting Kazakh prisoners to torture and agony identical to those described by Aitmatov in *I dol'she veka dlitsia den'*. See Vladimir Bondarenko, 'Obnovlenie,' *Nash sovremennik*, 1984, no. 11, 171–2.
19 *Novyi mir*, 1980, no. 11, 182
20 Ibid, 168
21 Chingiz Aitmatov, 'Vse kasaetsia vsekh,' *Voprosy literatury*, 1980, no. 12, 14
22 Chingiz Aitmatov, 'Tochka prisoedineniia,' ibid, 1976, no. 8, 150
23 *Slavic Review*, 43 no. 4, 581
24 'Utopii v kosmicheskii vek,' *Sintaksis* (Paris), 1982, no. 10, 188
25 See, for example, N. Potapov, 'Mir chelovela i chelovek mira,' *Pravda*, 16 Feb 1981.
26 *Novyi mir*, 1980, no. 11, 3
27 Ibid, 4
28 *Voprosy literatury*, 1980, no. 12, 11
29 *Novyi mir*, 1986, no. 6, 48
30 Ibid, 52
31 *Novyi mir*, 1986, no. 8, 121
32 For a discussion of the problem of narcotics in the Soviet Union, see *Literaturnaia gazeta*, 20 Aug 1986, 11.
33 *Novyi mir*, 1986, no. 6, 29
34 Chingiz Aitmatov, 'Tsena – zhizn',' *Literaturnaia gazeta*, 13 Aug 1986, 4
35 *Novyi mir*, 1986, no. 6, 68
36 F. Dostoyevsky, *The Brothers Karamazov* (Harmondsworth 1958), 278
37 *Literaturnaia gazeta*, 13 Aug 1986, 4
38 See, for example, Ales' Adamovich, 'Protiv pravil? ...,' ibid, 1 Jan 1987, 4.
39 V. Kozhinov, 'Paradoksy romana ili paradoksy vospriiatiia?' ibid, 15 Oct 1986, 4
40 Ibid, 15 Oct 1986, 4
41 Chingiz Aitmatov, 'Kak slovo nashe otozvetsia,' *Druzhba narodov*, 1987, no. 2, 235–6
42 *Russian Literature Triquarterly*, 1979, no. 16, 267

Selected Bibliography

This bibliography is far from exhaustive. It is intended to provide the necessary background for the appreciation of contemporary Soviet prose and a guide for further investigation of the current literary scene in the Soviet Union.

The list of suggested background reading is limited to several Soviet and Western histories of literature and a number of books and articles in which different aspects of the theory and practice of Soviet literature are discussed. The list of Soviet prose includes works of leading Soviet authors, officially published in the Soviet Union between 1978 and 1988, representing different thematic and artistic trends. The list of Soviet prose in English translation also includes works originally published before 1978 but just recently translated into English.

Background reading

Anastas'ev, N. 'Dialog.' *Voprosy literatury*, 1983, no. 3, 62–104
Andreev, Iurii. 'Metod zhivoi, razvivaiushchiisia,' *Russkaia literatura*, 1982, no. 1, 124–34
– 'Dlia chego literatura.' *Voprosy literatury*, 1983, no. 9, 28–62
Apukhtina, V.A. *Sovremennaia sovetskaia proza.* Moscow, 1984
Belaia, G. *Khudozhestvennyi mir sovremennoi prozy.* Moscow, 1983
– *Literatura v zerkale kritiki.* Moscow, 1986
Bogdanov, Iu. 'Opyt teorii – opyt razvitiia literatury.' *Voprosy literatury*, 1984, no. 1, 3–30
Borshchukov, V.I., ed. *Sovremennaia sovetskaia literatura v dukhovnoi zhizni obshchestva razvitogo sotsializma.* Moscow, 1980
Brown, Deming B. *Soviet Russian Literature since Stalin.* Cambridge, 1977–9
Brown, Edward J. *Russian Literature since the Revolution.* Revised and enlarged edition. Cambridge, Mass, 1982
Clark, Katerina. 'The Mutability of the Canon: Socialist Realism and Chingiz Aitmatov's "I dol'she veka dlitsia den'."' *Slavic Review*, 43 no. 4 (winter 1984), 573–87

- *The Soviet Novel: History as Ritual*. Second edition. Chicago, 1985
Dedkov, I. *Vasil's Bykov*. Moscow, 1980
- *Sergei Zalygin*. Moscow, 1985
Dement'ev, A.G., ed. *Istoriia russkoi sovetskoi literatury v 4-kh tomakh. 1917–1965*. Moscow, 1967–71
Dunham, Vera. *In Stalin's Time: Middleclass Values in Soviet Fiction*. Cambridge, 1976
Ermolaev, Herman. *Soviet Literary Theories 1917–1934: The Genesis of Socialist Realism*. Berkeley, 1963
Friedberg, Maurice. *Russian Culture in the 1980s*. Washington, DC, 1985
Gachev, G. *Chingiz Aitmatov i mirovaia literatura*. Frunze, 1982
Gibian, G. *Interval of Freedom: Soviet Literature during the Thaw. 1954–1957*. Minneapolis, 1960
Gillespie, D.C. *Valentin Rasputin and Soviet Russian Village Prose*. London, 1985
Hayward, Max, and Edward L. Crowley, eds. *Soviet Literature in the Sixties: An International Symposium*. New York, 1964
Hayward, Max, and Leopold Labedz. *Literature and Revolution in Soviet Russia, 1917–1962*. London, 1963
Hosking, Geoffrey. 'The Russian Peasant Rediscovered: "Village Prose" of the 1960s.' *Slavic Review*, 32 no. 4 (Dec. 1973), 705–24
- *Beyond Socialist Realism: Soviet Fiction since Ivan Denisovich*. London, 1980
Idashkin, Iurii. *Grani tvorchestva. O tvorchestve Iuriia Bondareva*. Moscow, 1983
Ivanova, Natal'ia. *Proza Iuriia Trifonova*. Moscow, 1984
Johnson, Priscilla. *Khrushchev and the Arts: The Politics of Soviet Culture, 1962–1964*. Cambridge, Mass, 1965
Kardin, V. *Tochka peresecheniia*. Moscow, 1984
Khrapchenko, M. *The Writer's Creative Individuality and the Development of Literature*. Moscow, 1977
Korobov, V.I. *Iurii Bondarev*. Moscow, 1984
Kovskii, V. *Literaturnyi protsess 60–70x godov*. Moscow, 1983
Kuz'menko, Iu. *Soviet Literature Yesterday, Today and Tomorrow*. Moscow, 1983
Levchenko, Viktor. *Chingiz Aitmatov*. Moscow, 1983
Lowe, David. *Russian Writing since 1953: A Critical Survey*. New York, 1987
Maguire, Robert A. *Red Virgin Soil: Soviet Literature in the 1920s*. Princeton, 1968
Markov, D. *Problemy teorii sotsialisticheskogo realizma*. Moscow, 1975
- 'Sistemnoe edinstvo sotsialisticheskogo realizma. Problemy poetiki.' *Voprosy literatury*, 1983, no. 1 4–32
- 'O nekotorykh voprosakh teorii sotsialisticheskogo realizma.' *Voprosy literatury*, 1988, no. 3, 3–22
Markov, Dmitrii F. *Socialist Literatures: Problems of Development*. Moscow, 1984

Mathewson, Rufus W. *The Positive Hero in Russian Literature.* Second edition. Stanford, 1975

Metchenko, A.I. and S.M. Petrov, eds. *Istoriia russkoi sovetskoi literatury. 40–80e gody.* Moscow, 1983

Ovcharenko, Aleksandr. *Bol'shaia literatura.* Three volumes. Moscow, 1985

Patera, T. *Obzor tvorchestva i analiz moskovskikh povestei Iuriia Trifonova.* Ann Arbor, Mich, 1983

Petrov, S.M. 'Vse o nem, vse o realizme ...' *Russkaia literatura,* 1984, no. 2, 138–47

Russell, Robert. *Valentin Kataev.* Boston, 1981

Shneidman, N.N. *Soviet Literature in the 1970s; Artistic Diversity and Ideological Conformity.* Toronto, 1979

Slonim, Marc. *Soviet Russian Literature: Writers and Problems, 1917–1977.* Second edition. New York, 1977

Struve, Gleb. *Russian Literature under Lenin and Stalin, 1917–1953.* Norman, Oklahoma, 1971

Surovtsev, Iurii. *V 70e i segodnia.* Moscow, 1985

Svirski, Grigori. *A History of Post-War Soviet Writing: The Literature of Moral Opposition.* Ann Arbor, Mich, 1981

Terakopian, L. *Paralleli i peresecheniia. Sovremennaia proza: geroi, problemy, konflikty.* Moscow, 1984

Vail', Petr, and Aleksandr Genis. *Sovremennaia russkaia proza.* Ann Arbor, Mich, 1982

Žekulin, Gleb. "The Contemporary Countryside in Soviet Literature: A Search for New Values" in James R. Millar, ed., *The Soviet Rural Community.* Urbana, 1971

Russian Soviet Prose Fiction 1978–88

Abramov, Fedor. *Dom* (1978) (The House)
– 'Mamonikha' (1980) (Mamonikha)

Aitmatov, Chingiz. *I dol'she veka dlitsia den'* (1980) (The Day Lasts More than a Hundred Years)
– *Plakha.* (1986) (The Execution Block)

Alekseev, Mikhail. *Drachuny* (1982) (Pugnacious Fellows)

Anan'ev, Anatolii. *Gody bez voiny* (1975–84) (Years without War)

Astaf'ev, Viktor. 'Mesto deistviia. Rasskazy' (1986) (Place of Action: Stories)
– 'Slepoi rybak' (1986) (The Blind Fisherman)
– *Pechal'nyi detektiv* (1986) (The Sad Detective Story)

Baklanov, Grigorii. 'Naveki – deviatnadtsiletnie' (1979) (Forever Nineteen Years Old)

Bazhenov, Georgii. *Vozvrashchenie liubvi.* Povesti (1982) (The Return of Love: Stories)

Bek, Aleksandr. *Novoe naznachenie* (1986; West, 1971) (New Appointment)

Beliaeva, Liliia. *Nesygrannaia rol'* (1982) (The Unfulfilled Role)

- *Skandalistka* (1986) (The Scandalmonger)
Belov, Vasilii. *Vospitanie po doktoru Spoku* (1978) (Education According to Dr Spock)
- *Lad. Ocherki o narodnoi estetike* (1979–81) (Harmony: Sketches on People's Aesthetics)
- *Vse vperedi* (1986) (Everything Lies Ahead)
- *Kanuny. Khronika kontsa 20-kh godov* (parts I and II, 1976; part III, 1987) (On the Eve: A Chronicle of the Late 1920s)
Bitov, Andrei. 'Chelovek v peizazhe' (1987) (Man in the Landscape)
- *Pushkinskii dom* (1987; USA, 1978) (Pushkin House)
Bondarev, Iurii. *Vybor* (1980) (The Choice)
- *Igra* (1985) (The Game)
Bykov, Vasil'. 'Znak bedy' (1983) (The Token of Calamity)
- 'Kar'er' (1986) (The Quarry)
- 'V tumane' (1987) (In the Fog)
Chakovskii, Aleksandr. *Pobeda* (1978–81) (Victory)
- *Neokonchennyi portret* (1983–4) (The Unfinished Portrait)
- *Niurnbergskie prizraki* (1987) (The Nurmberg Phantoms)
Chivilikhin, Vladimir. *Pamiat'. Roman-esse* (1978–85) (Memory: A Novel-Essay)
Dangulov, Savva. *Gosudareva pochta* (1983) (His Majesty's Mail)
- *Zautrenia v Rapallo* (1983) (Matins in Rapallo)
Dudintsev, Vladimir. *Belye odezhdy* (1987) (Robed in White)
Evtushenko, Evgenii. *Iagodnye mesta* (1981–2) (Wild Berries)
Ganina, Maiia. *Esli budem zhivy ...* (1983) (If We Stay Alive)
- *Sto zhiznei moikh* (1983) (My Hundred Lives)
- *Poka zhivu – nadeius'* (1986, 1987) (I Hope as Long as I Live)
Granin, Daniil. *Kartina* (1980) (Picture)
- 'Eshche zameten sled' (1984) (The Track Is Still Visible)
- 'Zubr' (1987) (Bison)
Grekova, I. 'Kafedra' (1978) (The Faculty)
- 'Vdovii parokhod' (1981) (The Ship of Widows)
- *Porogi* (1984) (Thresholds)
- 'Fazan' (1985) (Fazan)
- 'Bez ulybok' (1986) (Without Smiles)
- 'Perelom' (1987) (The Fracture)
Grossman, Vasilii. *Zhizn' i sud'ba* (1988; West, 1980) (Life and Fate)
Kaledin, Sergei. 'Smirennoe kladbishche' (1987) (Humble Graveyard)
Kataev, Valentin. *Almaznyi moi venets* (1978) (My Diamond Crown)
- 'Uzhe napisan Verter' (1980) (Werther Has Already Been Written)
- *Iunosheskii roman moego starogo druga Sashi Pchelkina rasskazannyi im samim* (1982) (The Youthful Novel of My Old Friend Sasha Pchelkin, Told by Himself)
- 'Spiashchii' (1985) (The Sleeping Man)
- 'Sukhoi liman' (1986) (The Dry Estuary)

Kaverin, Veniamin. 'Verlioka' (1982) (Verlioka)
– *Nauka rasstavaniia* (1983) (The Science of Parting)
Kim, Anatolii. 'Nefritovyi poias' (1981) (The Nephrite Belt)
– *Belka. Roman-skazka* (1984) (Squirrel: A Novel-Tale)
Kireev, Ruslan. *Podgotovitel'naia tetrad'* (1981) (The Rough Notebook)
Kondrat'ev, Viacheslav. 'Sashka' (1979) (Sashka)
Kron, Aleksandr. 'Kapitan dal'nego plavaniia' (1983) (The Captain of the
    Merchant Fleet)
Krupin, Vladimir. 'Zhivaia voda' (1980) (Living Waters)
– 'Sorokovoi den'' (1981) (The Fortieth Day)
– 'Prosti – proshchai' (1986) (Forgive and Goodbye)
Krutilin, Sergei. *Grekhi nashi tiazhkie* (1982) (Our Heavy Sins)
Lipatov, Vil' 'Povest' bez nazvaniia, siuzheta i kontsa ... ' (1978) (A Tale without
    a Title, Plot or Ending ...)
– 'Zhitie Vaniushki Murzina ili liubov' v Staro-Korotkine' (1978) (The Life of
    Vaniuska Murzin or Love in Staro-Korotkino)
Makanin, Vladimir. 'Gde skhodilos' nebo s kholmami' (1984) (Where the Sky
    Met the Hills)
Mozhaev, Boris. 'Poltora kvadratnykh metra' (1982) (One and a Half Square
    Metres)
– *Muzhiki i baby* (1987) (Countryfolk)
Nagibin, Iurii. 'Terpenie' (1982) (Patience)
Okudzhava, Bulat. *Svidanie s Bonapartom* (1983) (A Meeting with Bonaparte)
Orlov, Vladimir. *Al'tist Danilov* (1980) (Danilov the Violist)
– *Aptekar* (1988) (The Druggist)
Pasternak, Boris. *Doktor Zhivago* (1988; West 1958) (Dr Zhivago)
Pikul', Valentin. *U poslednei cherty. Roman-khronika* (1979) (At the Last Mark:
    A Novel-Chronicle)
– *Favorit. Roman-khronika vremeni Ekateriny II* (1984) (Favourite: Novel-
    Chronicle of the Times of Catherine II)
Platonov, Andrei. 'Kotlovan' (1987; West, 1968) (The Foundation Pit)
Pletnev, Aleksandr. *Shakhta* (1979) (The Mine)
Pristavkin, Anatolii. 'Nochevala tuchka zolotaia' (1987) (The Golden Cloudlet
    Passed the Night)
Prokhanov, Aleksandr. *Derevo v tsentre Kabula* (1982) (A Tree in the Centre of
    Kabul)
– *V ostrovakh okhotnik ... Kampuchiiskaia khronika* (1983) (The Hunter on
    the Island ... The Kampuchean Chronicle)
– *Afrikanist* (1984) (The African)
– *I vot prikhodit veter* (1984) (And Here Comes the Wind)
– *Risunki batalista* (1986) (Drawings of a Battle-Painter)
Rasputin, Valentin. 'Vek zhivi-vek liubi,' 'Chto peredat' vorone?' 'Ne mogu-u,'
    and 'Natasha' (1982) (You Live and Love; What Shall I Tell the Crow?; I
    Can't; and Natasha)
– 'Pozhar' (1985) (The Fire)

Rybakov, Anatolii. *Tiazhelyi pesok* (1978) (Heavy Sand)
– *Deti Arbata* (1987) (Children of the Arbat)
Semenov, Georgii. *Chertogi Liubvi. Rasskazy* (1987) (Chambers of Love: Stories)
– *Um Lisitsy. Rasskazy. Povesti* (1987) (The Mind of a Fox: Stories)
Semenov, Iulian. *TASS upolnomochen zaiavit'* (1979) (TASS Is Authorized to Declare)
– *Litsom k litsu* (1983) (Face to Face)
– *Prikazano vyzhit'* (1983) (An Order to Survive)
– *Press tsentr: Anatomiia politicheskogo prestupleniia* (1984) (Press Centre: The Anatomy of a Political Crime)
– *Auktsion* (1985) (Auction)
– *Ekspansiia* (1986) (Expansion)
Shtemler, Il'ia. *Taksopark* (1980) (Taxi Fleet)
– *Univermag* (1982) (Department Store)
– *Utrenee shosse* (1983) (The Morning Highway)
– *Poezd* (1986) (The Train)
Tendriakov, Vladimir. 'Rasplata' (1979) (Atonement)
– 'Shest'desiat svechei' (1980) (Sixty Candles)
– 'Den' vytesnivskii zhizn'' (1985) (The Day That Dislodged a Life)
– 'Chistye vody Kitezha' (1986) (The Clear Waters of Kitezh)
– 'Den' sed'moi' (1986) (The Seventh Day)
– *Pokushenie na mirazhi* (1987) (The Assault on Illusions)
Tolstaia, Tat'iana. *Na zolotom kryl'tse sideli ... Rasskazy* (1987) (Sitting on the Golden Porch ... Stories)
– 'Somnabula v tumane' (1988) (A Sleepwalker in the Fog)
Trifonov, Iurii, *Vremia i mesto* (1981) (Time and Place)
– *Oprokinutyi dom* (1981) (The Overturned House)
– *Ischeznovenie* (1987) (Disappearance)
Voznesenskii, Andrei. 'O' (1982) (O)
Zalygin, Sergei. *Posle buri* (1980–4) (After the Storm)
Zamiatin, Evgenii. *Povesti, rasskazy* (1986) (Novellas, Stories)
– *My* (1924–1952–1988) (We)

Soviet Writers in English Translation

Abramov, Fyodor. *Two Winters and Three Summers.* Translated by D.B. Powers and Doris C. Powers. Ann Arbor, Mich, 1984
– *Two Winters and Three Summers.* Translated by Jacqueline Edwards and Mitchell Schneider. Introduction by Maurice Friedberg. New York, 1984
– *The Swans Flew By and Other Stories.* Moscow, 1986
Aitmatov Chingiz. *The Day Lasts More than a Hundred years.* Translated by John French. Foreword by Katerina Clark. Bloomington, Ind, 1983
Astaf'ev, Victor. *Queen Fish.* Moscow, 1982

241 Selected bibliography

- 'Six Short Stories.' *Soviet Literature*, 1984, no. 5, 96–114
Belov, Vasilii. *Morning Rendezvous*. Stories. Translated by Eve Manning.
  Foreword by Sergei Zalygin. Moscow, 1983
Bitov, Andrei. *Life in Windy Weather: Short Stories*. Edited by Priscilla Meyer.
  Ann Arbor, Mich, 1986
- *Pushkin House*. Translated by Susan Brownsberger. New York, 1987
Bogomolov, Vladimir. *The Aching in My Heart: Collected Writings*. Moscow,
  1982
Bondarev, Yuri. *The Choice. Soviet Literature*, 1981, no. 7, 3–80, no. 8,
  17–101, and no. 9, 16–117
- *The Choice*. Translated by Monica White. Moscow, 1983
- *The Shore*. Translated by Keith Hammond. Moscow, 1984
Bykov, Vasil. *His Battalion and Live until Dawn*. Translated by Jennifer and
  Robert Woodhouse. St Lucia, Queensland, 1981
Chakovsky, Alexander. *Unfinished Portrait*. Moscow, 1988
Granin, Daniil. 'Thou Art Weighed in the Balances.' *Soviet Literature*, 1984,
  no. 7, 3–24
Grekova, I. 'The Faculty.' *Soviet Literature*, 1979, no. 9, 3–107, and no. 10,
  16–128
- *The Ship of Widows*. Translated and with Introduction by Cathy Porter.
  London, 1985
- *Russian Women: Two Stories – Ladies' Hairdresser. The Hotel Manager*.
  Translated by Michel Petrov. Introduction by Maurice Friedberg. New
  York, 1983
Grossman, Vasily. *Life and Fate*. Translated by Robert Chandler. New York,
  1985
Iskander, Fazil. *Sandro of Chegem*. Translated by Susan Brownsberger. New
  York, 1983
- *The Gospel According to Chegem*. Translated by Susan Brownsberger. New
  York, 1984
Kaverin, Veniamin. 'The Science of Parting.' *Soviet Literature*, 1984, no. 5,
  3–95, and no. 6, 20–78
- 'A Flowing Hand.' *Soviet Literature*, 1985, no. 3, 26–61.
Kozhevnikov, Vadim. *The Special Subunit: Two Novellas*. Moscow, 1983
Lipatov, Vil. *The Stoletov Dossier*. Translated by Alex Miller. Moscow,
  1983
Nagibin, Yuri. *Island of Love*. Moscow, 1982
- *The Peak of Success and Other Stories*. Edited by Helena Goscilo. Ann
  Arbor, Mich, 1986
Okudzhava, Bulat. *A Taste of Liberty (Poor Avrosimov)*. Translated and with
  Introduction by Leo Gruliov. Ann Arbor, Mich, 1986
Orlov, Vladimir. *Danilov the Violist*. Translated by Antonina W. Bouis. New
  York, 1987
Prokhanov, Aleksandr. *A Tree in the Centre of Kabul* (abridged version).
  Soviet Literature, 1983, no. 7, 3–129

Rasputin, Valentin. *Farewell to Matyora*. Translated by Antonina W. Bouis. New York, 1979
– *Money for Maria and Borrowed Time*. Translated by Kevin Windle and Margaret Wettlin. St Lucia, Queensland, 1981
– *You Live and Love and Other Stories*. Translated by Alan Myers. London, 1985
– 'The Fire.' *Soviet Literature*, 1986, no. 7, 3–55
– 'What Shall I Tell the Crow?' *Soviet Literature*, 1987, no. 2, 30–47
Rybakov, Anatoli. *Heavy Sand*. Translated by Harold Shukman. New York, 1981
– *Children of the Arbat*. Translated by Harold Shukman. New York, 1988
Semenov, G. *Phrygian Cornflowers: Stories*. Moscow, 1984
Semenov, Julian. *TASS Is Authorized to Announce*. New York, 1987
Soloukhin, V. *Short Stories*. Moscow, 1982
Tendriakov, Vladimir. 'A Day That Ousted a Life.' *Soviet Literature*, 1985, no. 9, 3–54
Trifonov, Yuri. *The Long Goodbye: Three Novellas*. Translated by Helen Burlingame and Ellendea Proffer. Ann Arbor, Mich, 1978
– *Another Life: The House on the Embankment*. Translated by Michael Glenny. Foreword by John Updike. New York, 1983
– *One Old Man*. Translated by Jacqueline Edwards and Mitchell Schneider. New York, 1984
Voznesensky, Andrei. *An Arrow in the Wall*. Edited by William Jay Smith and F.D. Reeve. New York, 1986
Yevtushenko, Yevgeny. *Wild Berries*. Translated by Antonina W. Bouis. New York, 1984
– *Ardabiola*. Translated by Armorer Wason. London, 1984
Zalygin, Sergei. *The South American Variant*. Translated by Kevin Windle. St Lucia, Queensland, 1979

Index

LNTX

4123SRC